Writing a Life

TEACHING MEMOIR
to Sharpen Insight,
Shape Meaning—
and Triumph Over Tests

KATHERINE BOMER

HEINEMANN • PORTSMOUTH, NH

HEINEMANN
A division of Reed Elsevier Inc.
361 Hanover Street
Portsmouth, NH 03801–3912
www.heinemann.com

Offices and agents throughout the world

© 2005 BY KATHERINE BOMER

Library of Congress Cataloging-in-Publication Data
Bomer, Katherine.
    Writing a life : teaching memoir to sharpen insight, shape meaning—and triumph over tests / Katherine Bomer.
        p. cm.
    Includes bibliographical references.
    ISBN 0-325-00646-6 (alk. paper)
    1. Autobiography—Study and teaching.   2. Biography as a literary form—Study and teaching.   I. Title.
CT25.B63 2005
809'.93592—dc22   2005012488

EDITOR: *Kate Montgomery*
PRODUCTION: *Vicki Kasabian*
INTERIOR AND COVER DESIGNS: *Jenny Jensen Greenleaf*
AUTHOR PHOTOGRAPH: *Kenneth Hipkins*
TYPESETTER: *Publishers' Design and Production Services, Inc.*
MANUFACTURING: *Jamie Carter*

Printed in the United States of America on acid-free paper
09 08 07 06   RRD   2 3 4 5

This book is dedicated to the children who have bravely written their lives and generously shared them.

Contents

Acknowledgments

This book has a long life story, and like all life stories, its *becoming* depended upon the nurturing acts and intelligent support of many people along the way. But like a good memoirist, I must select only a slice of the whole story of how this book came to be and, in too few words, thank those without whom I can't imagine its existence.

Lucy Calkins, colleague, mentor, and friend, first championed this book in 1990 and granted me countless generous opportunities to make speeches and teach memoir courses at Teachers College, Columbia University, as I developed chapters and curriculum. Lucy's laser-beam intelligence and commitment to children composing their lives and inventing ways of learning taught me how to teach. The community of the Teachers College Reading and Writing Project, with its ever widening family of talented, innovative, devoted literacy educators, was my birthplace as an educator, and it remains a continual source of joy and inspiration. My colleagues at the Project taught me how to learn in and with a community, and our conversations around the library table resound throughout this book. I wish I could name each and every one of them. In particular, I want to thank Dorothy Barnhouse, who introduced me to the contemporary memoir and who guided me to write my own. I am indebted to her for much of the genre knowledge that resides in this book.

To the hundreds of teachers who have filled my memoir courses at Teachers College, I treasure their insights and their willingness to let me grow my ideas about how to teach this genre. They all took great risks to write honestly about their lives, and I will remember and hold those stories close. I offer many thanks to all the teachers and students in New York City and across the country whom I have worked beside for the last fifteen years. They opened their classrooms for me to try out some memoir lessons when they were mere infant ideas, especially Maria Mahr, when she taught at PS 9 in the Bronx; Barbara Clements at Janney Elementary in Washington, DC; and Kay Boruff, Allyson Cockrum, Dorothy Dickman, Diane Glaser, and Glynnis Quick at Hockaday in

Dallas. Thank you to four angel teachers in Austin, Texas, who let me infiltrate their classrooms before the state writing test to try out some ideas for the testing chapter of this book: Michael Griffin, Debbie Vescovo Johnson, Neelam Kulkarni, and Sue Laws.

Thank you to three women I was blessed to have as my principals: Lesley Gordon and then Brenda Steele at PS 11 in Manhattan and Cathy Diersing at Templeton in Bloomington, Indiana. They each encouraged me to be interested in the "openings and unexplored possibilities" in education, as Maxine Greene says, and not just in the measurable and mundane. I could not have developed the moves of teaching memoir writing without their deep trust and support of my teaching.

Thank you to my writing buddies Janet Angelillo, Leah Mermelstein, and Donna Santman, for their smart comments and comforting pep talks. Thank you to Denise Capasso for the bottomless cups of coffee and cheer that fueled my tank! I am grateful to Georgia Heard for her kind support and sisterly advice and for reading the final draft with such a generous heart and spirit. Katie Wood Ray read my initial proposal—and her suggestions reminded me to ground my flights of fancy in practice—then read the final draft noticing exactly what I hoped she would. Kylene Beers graciously read the final draft with the keenest eyes, saving me from several mishaps. Her lovely response to the book kept me company in the eleventh hour.

I want to deeply thank Kate Montgomery, my genius editor at Heinemann, for inviting me early on to write "the book of my dreams" and then helping shape it into exactly that. Her gifts of reading like the wonderful writer that she is, of responding with her heart, and of envisioning wholeness from all the parts made writing a daily privilege. Thank you to Melissa Wood, for keeping all the bits organized. I am indebted to the editorial, design, and production team behind this book, and particularly to Vicki Kasabian, who allowed me to revise up to the last second.

Thank you to my big sister, Pat, my first hero. She bears witness to my life, and for that I am forever grateful. Thank you to my parents, to my dearest "adopted" parents (my in-laws), and to my beautiful niece, nephews, and precious new grandniece for all their demonstrations of love. To my best friends forever, Tracie, Kris, Lynn, and Larry, my gratitude for their unwavering enthusiasm and for allowing me to be away for a while. And also to Maria Marewski—for twenty years we dreamed together how to give children a voice in the world, and finally our dreams have found a place to live in her Children's Media Project in Poughkeepsie, New York, and in this book. To Ingrid Schmidt, thank you for helping me remember and helping me forgive.

Anyone who knows me understands that I always save the best for last—the last bite of cheesecake with blueberries on top, the prettiest package, the favorite poem. So finally, my greatest gratitude goes to Randy Bomer, who is my partner in all things grand. Our daily conversations about writing and teaching live and breathe on every page of this book. Randy is always the reader I have in mind as I write: brilliant and principled. I would not let the draft leave the house until he had read it thoroughly and offered revisions that dramatically improved it. He helped me put the pieces of this and all my puzzles together.

Memories are the days, the minutes your life is made up of.
Remembering requires you to reach into not only the back of your head,
but the back of your life, to recall what that heart is made up of.
The value of memories is, basically, the value of life.

Rachel Brotman, 6th grade

Prologue

The Call to Write Memoir

What calls a person to write his or her life story? Humans seem moved to talk about themselves; that much is clear. People tell stories all day long: "You'll never believe what happened to me!" "Wait till you hear who called last night!" "I remember when. . . . " Yet most people don't commit those stories to paper. So what leads some to search for the heat of a certain memory, just the thought of which makes the heart beat louder and harder? What inspires some to embark on what Robert Coles calls the "existential inquiries," those elemental questions about who we are and what life means? What persuades them to compose their discoveries into texts that others will want to read, to make those stories public?

I think it is this: We want to remember. We want to understand what our lives mean. And we want someone else to witness what life was like for us because it helps us feel real. Writing an autobiography or memoir helps satisfy those longings and brings clarity to the events and relationships that haunt us.

For most people, childhood was a time of intense attention, sensitivity, awe, and sensuality, when our only job was to touch the world and learn about it. When we were young, a summer day stretched into forever. No night was as dark and shadowy and filled with mystery as a childhood night. The precise textures of fabric gave us comfort or misery. Adults fell into four general categories: nice, funny, boring, or mean. We lived for candy. And meeting a best friend felt like falling in love, but we didn't know to call it that when we were little. When we grow up, we sometimes ache for that childhood intensity, even while we are happy to be free of the vulnerabilties of youth.

Writing memoir is one way to recapture some of that sensual mystery and luxuriousness of time spent catching ladybugs and smelling their sharp grassy scent on our hands or lying on the bed, making pictures out of the patterns of cracks on our bedroom ceiling. When young people write memoir, they can hold onto those moments, freeze them right now, before they escape.

I have been helping children and adults write their life stories for at least fifteen years. Each time I study memoir with a group of people, I am convinced again of the genre's power to transform learning and lives. This book is my attempt to share how I have conducted courses of memoir writing and reading with young people, ages eight to sixteen.

Throughout this book, I refer to and excerpt from twenty amazing autobiographical stories written by young adult authors and collected in two volumes called *When I Was Your Age: Original Stories About Growing Up,* edited by Amy Ehrlich (1996, 1999). While I also refer to and recommend dozens more autobiographical stories, essays, picture books, and novel-length memoirs, these two books are must-have companions for teaching a memoir genre study with students in the middle grades. Also threaded throughout the descriptions of how to write a memoir and how to organize a course of study are bits of my own life stories. In a book that claims memoir helps humans observe, describe, and make meaning of experience, short glimpses of my life and my teaching help me do exactly that. I hope that as you read this book, you will feel your own memories rising in you and will seek to find meaning within them.

Why Teach Memoir?

Reasons That Will Change Your Teaching and Your Life

"We never forget." says Dad. "And if we didn't remember. we just made bits up."

Barbara laughs.

"Made bits up! "

"Yes. Truth and memories and dreams and bits made up."

—DAVID ALMOND, *Counting Stars*

The struggle of man against power is the struggle of memory against forgetting.

—MILAN KUNDERA, *The Book of Laughter and Forgetting*

To write one's life is to live it twice . . .

—PATRICIA HAMPL, *I Could Tell You Stories*

Several years ago, my husband, Randy, and I spent three glorious weeks in Italy. This was our dream honeymoon, the one we saved up for, kept postponing for one reason after another, and eventually forced ourselves to take for our seventh anniversary. As we always do to prepare for traveling, we read novels and poems, researched online the charms of villages in Tuscany and Umbria, watched Italian movies, cooked delicious Italian meals—well . . . *Randy* cooked delicious Italian meals; I don't cook—and generally marinated ourselves in the history and culture of Italy.

I was ready for Italy. I knew how to order espresso the way Italians do: drop by the coffee bar in late afternoon, stand at the counter, and chug back the thick liquid like a whiskey shot. I learned that from Frances Mayes' voluptuous memoir, *Under the Tuscan Sun* (1996). I was not surprised to see that Italian people dressed better—fancier—than we did. (I had been warned by the guidebooks not to pack tennis shoes at all, unless I wanted to positively scream out that I was American.) I was even prepared for the wincing sight of Italian women in superspiked heels, hobbling along the cobblestone streets of Florence. No book could have prepared me, however, for the spooky sensation of being in a place that is so ancient, so dripping with history that a building from the 1500s is considered a modern structure.

The streets and the floors of palaces lie on top of Roman and Etruscan walls and tombs, creating layers of history. We slept in the bell tower of a medieval castle. We walked on stone roads in footprints over a thousand years old. I sat in fields of grapevines and olive trees that have been tilled and planted, tilled and planted by generations of farmers. Throughout the trip, I wondered obsessively what people were feeling and thinking so long ago. What did they long for? What was life like for children back then? I placed my palms on the clammy, moss-covered stone walls, wishing I could *read* them, wishing they could talk. I was desperate for human voices telling stories from the past.

For hundreds of years, autobiographical writing has been a popular literary genre because many readers feel the way I do. They have this "deep-rooted yearning to understand the problems of another individual and his time, to see how he coped with them so that they may better understand themselves and their time" (Stull 1985, 19–20). I want to know how ancient peoples felt about their parents. Did they love their spouses? What did they yearn for? The word for history in Italian is *storia,* and that's how I love to learn about the past—through story. They could, like most memoirists, even tell me some inventions, but I want to know the *gist* of what life was like for them. I wish that writers and artists, like Dante and Michelangelo, had written their life stories in tell-all memoirs. Call this, as Bonamy Dobree says, the "love of gossip which is the cement of all societies, primitive or otherwise" (Stull 1985, 19). Poet Ted Kooser said that he thinks autobiographical writing is the "most natural extension of common conversation." I believe that too. It's how we connect with each other, how we find out that other people feel the way we do. It is also how we learn about lives that are vastly different from our own so that our minds and hearts can stretch to understand how life is for others.

Sometimes, I think that memoir may be the most important genre there is, and I claim it can accomplish mighty tasks, not the least of which is this one: reading and writing memoir can help create a better world. So I teach it to young people, year after year. A few students have been reluctant at first to write the true stories of their lives. They explain that the events from their lives aren't worth writing about: they haven't won a gold medal or appeared on television or won a singing contest. They don't live exciting, magical lives like Harry Potter. In short, they haven't done things that would make them famous. For those students, I lean in close, lower my voice in a conspiratorial tone, and ask them if they would like to know a secret that writers know. Their eyes open wider, in spite of themselves. They nod yes. Writers, I say, are magic. They make the ordinary extraordinary. In the writer's world, an ironing board set up in the corner of the room, or a special mash of cauliflower and butter when the tummy feels sick, becomes a symbol of a parent's undying love. In the writer's world, a memory of learning how to swim becomes a metaphor for letting go of fear. Writers know that the smaller the moment, the tinier the detail, the more it resonates with readers and the more it surprises. Henry James said that adventures happen only to those who know how to *tell* them. If that is the case, learning how to write well about one's life, how to take readers by the hand and walk straight into that memory so that they see and feel it, becomes more important than winning contests, enduring major accidents, or finding buried treasure.

Most literary scholars consider St. Augustine's *Confessions*, a personal tale of religious conversion written around 397, the first autobiography. The concept of life writing dates back at least that far, and was called various names, such as *apologies, confessions,* and *essays* (Montaigne in the late 1500s). But it wasn't until 1806 that the genre earned its name from the Greek words that mean a written description (*graphia*) of a life (*bio*) by the self (*auto*), in an era when the personality and worth of the individual rose in prominence in the Western world. Since the nineteenth century, the term *autobiography* has described a genre that records an author's chronological life and also includes self-revelation and self-analysis. Those who have written in this genre have been famous and unknown, rich and poor, but what they all have in common, apparently, is a belief that their life story is worth making public.

Some literary scholars view autobiography as the "prototypical narrative for America" (Smith and Watson 2001, 98), as if pioneers began discovering their inner worlds even as they explored this new external world. Benjamin Franklin's autobiography has influenced entire generations of Americans, most of whom haven't even read it, yet who have instilled in them the possibility of becoming something, despite birth or breeding—the myth of the self-made man, through the hard work, reading, and discipline to which Franklin attributes his success in life. The key word in those earliest

American autobiographies was *man,* and the unspoken word was *Anglo,* for women wrote letters and diaries, and Native American and slave narratives were often presented "as told to" literate recorders (Smith and Watson 2001, 99).

The twentieth century, influenced by the psychoanalytic theories and practices of Freud and others, and the gradual democratization of education, witnessed autobio-graphical writing of an enormous and hearty variety in America. Some literary scholars have broadened the definition of autobiographical writing to include subgenres like au-tobiographical poems, novels, plays, essays, and letters. Sidonie Smith and Julia Watson list fifty-two genres of life narrative (2001), including ethnographies, medical forms, court testimonies, AIDS narratives, and websites. They argue that life narrative has become the dominant form in the West, and if we look at what gets published in magazines and journals, as well as what fills nonfiction book lists, we might agree. A body of critical and theoretical literature about autobiography has also grown, particularly since the 1950s, in conjunction with the ever increasing number of autobiographies and memoirs being published in the last half of the twentieth century. Memoir and autobiography are now an accepted part of the literary canon, with books of critical essays, journal articles, and conference presentations contributing to the study of the genre.

A Definition of *Memoir*

Until the 1980s, the term *memoirs,* a kind of little sister to the typical birth-to-old-age autobiography, still referred to an older literary classification: a retelling of events, usu-ally reserved for persons of some social stature—military men, statesmen, journalists—writing what Russell Baker (1987) calls the "and then I met . . . " books. Memoirs within this old-fashioned tradition celebrate the skill and leadership of great politicians and military leaders, some perhaps setting the record straight or taking "revenge on history" (Gusdorf in Olney 1980, 36).

But in the last quarter of the twentieth century, the genre dropped the final *s* to be-come *memoir* and shrank dramatically to contain a mere slice of ordinary life—a certain time period, a special relationship, a particular theme or angle on a life. Borrowing major elements from its larger relative, the autobiography—honesty, self-analysis, and self-revelation—it opened its doors to ordinary persons and lesser-known writers with stories to tell in interesting, beautifully written ways, and memoir evolved into the hugely popular genre it is today. Since the 1980s, hundreds and hundreds of such glimpses of ordinary lives have been published, and the best examples "shove the novel off the book review pages," as Patricia Hampl (1999, 224) says. It seems clear that readers are hungry to read life stories.

Despite debates among literary critics about precisely how to define (and thus limit) autobiographical writing, many arrive at some version of this famous definition by Philippe Lejeune, in his essay called "The Autobiographical Pact": "Retrospective prose narrative written by a real person concerning his own existence, where the focus is his individual life, in particular the story of his personality" (1989, 4).

The key word in Lejeune's definition is *retrospective.* The writer stands in one place and time and looks back from that vantage point to make meaning of a distant time. *Retrospection* and *reflection* are crucial elements of the memoir genre. The writer gets to do what Georges Gusdorf calls a "second reading of experience," with the benefit of the proverbial twenty-twenty hindsight. Without retrospection or reflection, the writing about oneself might be something closer to a diary or journal, a genealogy chart, or a resume.

Lejeune proposed another definitive element in his essay—that autobiography and memoir should tell the truth, creating an implicit pact or promise of authenticity between the writer and reader. But of course, as soon as we begin to unpack that loaded word *truth,* we run into all sorts of sticky wickets. How does the reader know this is true? Can the author prove it? What kinds of evidence would count as proof? Perhaps the requirement for truth makes more sense using John Morris' definition in *Versions of the Self* (1966), which states that all that is required of the autobiographer is that he write the "truth of his experience." The salient words here are *of his experience*—in other words, the truth may or may not be factual or certifiable, except in the writer's experience of it. I will touch back on the inventions of truth versus authenticity in memoir writing in various places throughout this book, but for now, let us hold onto Morris' requirement for the truth of the writer's experience as we continue to unravel the elements of memoir writing.

A few bookstores now have a special memoir section, but most mix autobiography in with biography or simply lump them in with all the nonfiction selections. These terms can get pretty slippery if we let ourselves get too prescriptive about them. Most contemporary examples of life writing are now called memoir by the publishing world, and that is the term I stick to when I teach this genre. I explain to students that what we are learning how to write comes from the French word *memoire*, which means "memory."

I often begin memoir workshops by talking about what this contemporary memoir *isn't* as a way of coming around to what it maybe *is*. A memoir is not a hideously boring reportage of a life lived. It does not usually begin with a birth date, time, or place, but rather right in the midst of a situation, when the author was eight or twenty-five.

The memoir is not like genealogy, in that it does not rely on documentable facts obtained in civic records. The contemporary memoir does not march through time, naming milestones that the dominant culture or historical era believes relevant, such as military service or ascendancy to power. It does not need to drop names of the famous and well-to-do that the writer has met through the years. And it does not need to stretch from birth all the way to retirement, or near death, like its ancestor, the long-winded autobiography.

Instead, the contemporary memoir is a slice-of-life story. The memoirist takes a slice out of the pie of life and writes about it in a way that makes others care and want to read it. We love reading about Noah Adams learning how to play the piano in *Piano Lessons* and about Robert MacNeil falling in love with words in *Wordstruck* and about Eliza Thomas building a cabin in Vermont in *The Road Home*, not because the topics are inherently interesting, but because these books are movingly, gorgeously written. The authors *make* their topics interesting to read about.

Memoirists determine what is relevant to tell, based on how they wish to represent their lived lives, and it might be the simplest story of learning how to fly-fish, or going to Disney World with some aunts, uncles, and cousins, or it might even reveal situations that the old-fashioned memoirs would have conveniently omitted: a prison sentence, a disability, an alcoholic parent, the painful details of a failed relationship.

Memoirs can be as long as novels or as short as the kinds of essays that appear every month in *The New Yorker, Atlantic Monthly,* and the literary journal *Creative Nonfiction.* I will be dealing primarily with prose examples in this book, but many stunning contemporary autobiographies have been created in such diverse forms as poems, plays, films, and visual presentations. While most memoirs are written in the first person, or as "I" narratives, several, such as Paul Auster's *Invention of Solitude,* have sections written in third person ("He did this"; "He remembers that"), and a few even move in and out of the second person, "you." Perhaps Auster was influenced by Henry Adams, who wrote his entire autobiography, *The Education of Henry Adams,* in third person, as if his life were a novel, happening to some character who coincidentally had the same name as the author.

Many contemporary memoirs devote almost more space to the biography of a relative than to the author's life. Vivian Gornick's *Fierce Attachments* and Tobias Wolff's *This Boy's Life* contain biographies of the authors' mothers. In *Brothers and Keepers,* John Edgar Wideman writes honestly and movingly about his relationship with his brother, who is serving a life sentence in prison. Wideman conducted extensive interviews with his brother, then wrote the notes into a story in his brother's voice, so that it becomes a kind of memoir within a memoir. In each case, the author's life and perspective keep imposing themselves, making it *not* a biography, but some kind of amalgamation. Some memoirs sound almost like a poem: *the winged seed,* by Li-Young Lee. And others, with their inclusion of official documents, read in parts like a police report: *The Duke of Deception,* by Geoffrey Wolff. Some writers find metaphors for the self in myths, legends, and fairy tales. In *Landscape for a Good Woman: A Story of Two Lives,* Carolyn Kay Steedman writes about reading Hans Christian Anderson from start to finish and then back to front when she was seven. She weaves fairy tales in and out of her life story, appropriating characters and stories as metaphors for aspects of her personality and her circumstances. "Kay was my name at home, and I knew that Kay, the boy in 'The Snow Queen,' was me, who had a lump of ice in her heart. I knew that one day I might be asked to walk on the edge of knives, like the little mermaid, and was afraid that I might not be able to bear the pain" (2000, 46).

Many memoirs reveal tragic instances of abuse, poverty, injustice, disability, or illness while others relate content that could certainly be told from a vengeful or victimized perspective but instead are treated with a comic twist. In one of my favorite memoirs, *A Heartbreaking Work of Staggering Genius,* author Dave Eggers plays with every textual and conceptual feature of narrative text that he could think of. The standard parts of any book—preface, table of contents, acknowledgments, even the copyright page— become, in Eggers' hands, a brilliant, laugh-out-loud satire of the real thing. He even gives instructions for how to read the book, suggesting we skip large portions of it! But lest you think this book will only have you rolling on the floor, we learn, when we finally get to the actual story, that his mother died of cancer and left him, at twenty-one, to raise his eight-year-old brother, mostly alone. He writes movingly about her illness and about his deep, incredibly sweet relationship with his little brother. Gigi Anders, a friend of mine from college, recently published her memoir, titled *Jubana! The Awkwardly True and Dazzling Adventures of a Jewish Cubana Goddess*. Gigi writes with brilliant humor and eccentricity about not-so-humorous memories: her family's flight from Castro's Cuba to a suburb of Washington, DC, the ultratraditional expectations of her larger-than-life Latina mami, and the clash of cultures she experienced as a Jewish girl from Cuba growing up in our nation's capital. "It's like gefilte fish crashing into shrimp croquettes," she told me.

Some memoirs keep the focus firmly rooted in the child's voice while others interject frequently with the adult's reflective point of view. And numerous memoirs written in the last two decades contain multiple media images: drawings, charts, tables, documents, and photographs.

What raises this writing—about the relationship with a parent, a troubled adolescence, even just the perceptions of a mind alive and awake to the world—out of private diary writing is the distance, both physical and psychological, afforded by time passing, but also by a thoughtful, concerted effort to set one's life into a larger context. The best memoirs reach past the merely personal to take in something from the world—from cultural and social contexts, from history, anthropology, science, or art—to show that the "I" is living in and affected by the world.

Despite the exciting diversity of contemporary examples, what most memoirs have in common is that they make meaning of the past from the standpoint of the present. Memoir *interprets* experience. Every day, as a person grows, as she gains knowledge and perspective, as she *becomes*, her understandings of and responses to past events will likely alter, thus opening up new interpretations, even on the exact same story. Of course, the longer a person lives, presumably the greater the perspective she can layer onto a memory. But the point in writing a memoir is not to devise fifty ways of looking at a situation, and especially not to worry about having the "right" perspective. The point is only to have something to say about a memory, now that you're sitting here, thinking about it. All life experience becomes immediately, in the very next second, the *past,* and therefore suitable for reflection. For young people, it's true that their immediate past is probably too close to the skin for the analytical perspective taking that memoir invites. But if students are twelve years old, they have eleven years of experience to remember and think about, and that is plenty for a memoir. When a student writes his life story, he both *mirrors* himself, reflects what he sees there, and also, in a sense, *creates* himself. For young people especially, then, the memoir acts as a record of what happened and a forecast of the future. The way kids talk about their memories is a statement about the kind of people they are and who they are becoming.

Everyone has memories, but it takes knowledge of craft to write a wonderful memoir that really draws readers into the writer's life stories. This book describes the elements of that craft. Beyond crafting scenes and finessing dialogue, however, there are two key ingredients that separate powerful memoir writing from weak writing, and they are honesty and reflection.

Honesty

The first secret to strong memoir writing is honesty. When I use the word *honesty*, I mean much more than just not telling lies. Instead, the memoirist makes a commitment to tell the emotional truth as it felt to him. When writing is not coming easily, it is often because the writer is *avoiding* what needs to be written. Russell Baker wrote an entire manuscript, 450 pages, of a thoroughly researched and documented (as a journalist, he knew how to do this) family story. But he was covering the book he needed to write with a slew of facts about his family's genealogy. He had been dishonest about his mother, he realized—accurate in the reporting, but dishonest because of what he had left out. "I had been unwilling to write honestly . . . and that dishonesty left a great hollow in the center of the original" (Zinsser 1987, 44).

Readers of memoir suspend disbelief and presuppose honesty. It is an unwritten contract between the writer and the reader that what unfolds on these pages is primarily the truth of the author's experience. Yet we also create space for this genre that allows the memoirist to profess to be telling the truth while using some literary techniques that fictionalize the story somewhat. If the author makes it clear that she is taking liberties with the truth, perhaps by qualifying with phrases like "I can't remember exactly, but . . . " or "It seemed to me . . . ," we can go along for the ride. It's clear that in *The Woman Warrior: Memoirs of a Girlhood Among Ghosts*, Maxine Hong Kingston (1977) is drawing on her cultural world of myth and storytelling to help tell her own truth. The reader does not think that Kingston's relatives are ghosts, but only that the stories passed down through generations about her family members take on the quality of myth and legend, making the characters seem ghostlike. At the end of Michael Ondaatje's *Running in the Family* (1982), he apologizes for the "fictional air" contained in his memoir, claiming that in Sri Lanka "a well-told lie is worth a thousand facts" (204). But there is a big difference between a fictional air and a lie.

Reflection

The second ingredient of powerful memoir writing is a reflective quality. It looks back on experiences, finds patterns in them and organizes them, and then finds meaning in them. That reflective, analytical move is what makes memoir interesting to read. Let's face it: most of us lead fairly uneventful lives, and if we wrote about them as if we were reporting the weather, no one would bother to read them. Since the memoirist is committed to telling the truth, she is going to be writing about some events and conversations that are not inherently all that interesting. But what she *makes* of them, the intensity of feeling that is behind those moments, if the memoirist will allow it to surface, helps the recalled scene glow with significance. The accumulation of such events and conversations can lead the memoirist to conclude some deeper meaning from them. So, for example, it is not just the facts of that day in high school when I met my best friend, not just her name, what she looked like, the neat vintage yellow sweater with three-quarter sleeves she wore, but how meeting her made me a different human being, set the standard for every friendship after that, how I knew instantly that she was qualitatively the *best* and all the others were now simply *friends*. And that idea might cause me to think for a while about the nature of friendship and why it is so crucial in my life.

Writing about memories without reflecting on them can sound boring and shallow. I think about the tedious kinds of journals that people keep, the kind that compulsively record activities, what someone ate that day or whom he saw at the store. These serve a purpose for the writer, certainly, and when we look at diaries and journals written centuries ago, we can piece together intriguing portraits of what material life was like for our ancestors. But often, we learn nothing of the writers' interior lives. When I read them, I feel like screaming to the author, Who cares! Give me something I can sink my teeth into here!

The reflective aspect of memoir writing may be the difference, if there is one, between memoir and personal narrative. The personal narrative is a school genre, not a term that a published writer would call his writing. This form is supposed to be chronologically structured, with an introduction and a conclusion and transition words between five- to seven-sentence paragraphs and written with "voice." Let's think about the actual words: *Personal*—about oneself? *Narrative*—a story across time. Those words partially describe what a memoir is. But much of the personal narrative writing done in school settings lacks the *reflective* angle of memoir: the theme that ties it together, the thinking about what this memory means to the writer now, as he considers it. I think young people can write personal narratives quite well, if they have a memoir in mind. (See Chapter 9 for ways to craft powerful responses to writing tests that require personal narrative essays.)

Memoir does not have to be a tell-all, in the manner of the those embarrassing television talk shows. Memoir needn't purposely reveal dark secrets, what my family calls dirty laundry, in order to pique the interest of readers. Many of my favorite memoirs have nothing in them about abusive childhoods or tragic events; rather, they relate ordinary events using extraordinary writing. Students should never feel that the writing most valued in their classrooms, or that most pleases their teacher, is writing about abuse and neglect, grief, or humiliation. The craft of memoir involves writing from the inside out, but that inside can be full of light; it can be funny, inquisitive, sweet, cautious.

Also, a student should never feel that a story about winning a football game is somehow not good enough, not reflective enough because the writer can't imagine what the deeper meaning of that game is or how it transformed him. In the course of a memoir genre study, that writer will have spent time remembering many episodes from his childhood, and he will have selected that football game to write about over any other event. The *choice of topic* raises that story to a new level; the meaningfulness of that event is inherent in the decision to write about it. The art of the well-written memoir is like any art: it pays attention to detail, it surprises and delights the viewer with its unique perspective, and it touches us with an honesty that reminds us we are human.

Why Teach Memoir?

There are reasons for teaching any kind of writing—to help students pass tests and progress mechanistically through the grades to college and career—that have to do with schooling and not with education, a distinction Maxine Greene draws. Like Greene, I am interested "in openings, in unexplored possibilities, not in the predictable or the quantifiable." Like her, I want education to mean a "reaching out for meanings, a learning to learn" (2001, 7). I persist because my goal as a teacher is nothing less than to change lives, nothing less than a desire to create a better world. Memoir is one of the tools I use to do that. How can a piece of personal writing accomplish such revolutionary feats? I hope that will become more evident after we journey through this book together. But let's begin with these important reasons to write memoir.

We write memoir to break the silences surrounding who we are

Novelist Edwidge Danticat remembers seeing her first piece of writing published when she began high school in New York City about how her exiled Haitian family celebrated Christmas.

> It was extremely gratifying to see my words in print, to observe my classmates who knew nothing about me or my culture come to understand a very important aspect of my life through something I had written. From that moment on, I decided that I would become a writer, not only for the thrill of recognizing my name in a byline, but to break the silence that surrounded me, to bring to light some parts of the mystery that was my individual soul, to look at my life up close and invite others to do the same. (1997, xii)

Danticat discovered one of the loveliest truths about memoir—that it is the most democratic of all kinds of writing. Everyone has a story to tell. You don't have to be trapped in a lonely or hopeless situation to reap the benefits of asking: Who am I? Where did I come from? What will I do now that I understand all this? What do I want people to know about me?

For the writer, memoir is a way to speak to the world, to say, "This is who I am; this is what life is like for me." Memoir breaks the historical and societal silences surrounding race, gender, and sexual preference. Powerful memoirs of disability, like *Touching the Rock*, by John N. Hull, a memoir of blindness; *Nobody Nowhere*, by Donna Williams, about being autistic; and *The Autobiography of a Face*, by Lucy Grealy, about the disfigurement of a face from cancer, re-create what life is like for persons who are largely invisible in our society. It takes only one memoir of difference to create awareness that everything in our culture is built upon sameness. For readers, learning about someone else's life invites us to consider our own self-perspectives but also broadens our knowledge and understanding of lives that are outside of our narrow experience.

We write memoir to make meaning of our lives and, by doing so, to heal them

In *The Brothers Karamazov*, Dostoevsky's character Alyosha claims, "you must know that there is nothing higher and stronger and more wholesome and good for life in the future than some good memory, especially a memory of childhood, of home. People talk to you a great deal about your education, but some good, sacred memory, preserved from childhood, is perhaps the best education. If one carries many such memories into life, one is safe to the end of one's days, and if one has only one good memory left in one's heart, even that may be the means of saving us" (1991).

Is that true, that one good memory can save and heal us? Viktor E. Frankl, an Austrian psychiatrist, was a Holocaust survivor who was interred at Auschwitz and other camps. Frankl tells us in his extraordinary Holocaust memoir, *Man's Search for Meaning* ([1959] 1992), that the images of his wife's face, who was taken to a separate camp, and whom he never saw again, kept him from committing suicide. In the midst of his own tremendous suffering, and surrounded by the suffering of thousands of human beings, Frankl asked the most profound of all questions: How do people survive extreme hardship and go on with their lives? From what he personally witnessed in concentration camps, he invented *logotherapy*, or "meaning therapy," to attempt to answer that question: when faced with unspeakable horrors, people must try to construct meaning for their suffering, both to help themselves and to help others. In the words of the philosopher Nietzsche, "He who has a *why* to live for can bear with almost any *how*."

Frankl's memoir, which is also part psychological treatise, describes his experience in the camps, surrounded by others' death and illness and suffering himself from freezing temperatures, extreme labor, starvation, beatings, and humiliation. He felt his will to live most threatened with breaking when he felt existence reduced to minutiae, to a decision of whether to trade a cigarette for a bowl of soup, for instance. He realized that in order to survive, he was going to have to create personal meaning, to find *why* he should want to continue living and not give in to death. So he began to compose a story in his mind about how he would give lectures after the war was over about his personal experience in the camp and would help others learn how to find meaning in otherwise hopeless situations. This dream of his important work, outside of his personal circumstances, kept him going.

We can imagine that Holocaust survivors and victims of other horrific atrocities might understandably be unable or unwilling to re-create their experiences. A hallmark of traumatic memory is that the survivor blocks it out entirely or realizes it only in nightmares or horrific images that relate to nothing happening in the present. Frankl wrote about his memories to try to create sense out of the senselessness. He survived and realized his dream, and by sharing his memoir with the world, he has helped countless people find meaning even inside of tragedy.

Writing memoir is a device, and a powerful one, for constructing meaning from one's life. For millions of people, those who have survived personal, social, and political abuses, or AIDS victims, people with disabilities, people with what Smith and Watson (1996, 14) call "culturally unspeakable" lives, writing a memoir gives them the opportunity first to destroy the silence about who they are and what has happened in their life and then to try to make meaning for themselves. A written autobiography may present itself as the only chance some have to be heard. Writing it, we become agents instead of victims, actors instead of acted upon.

I have a picture of twelve-year-old Maria in my study, along with all the other pictures, candles, special stones, and mementos that I keep near me for courage and the inspiration to write. I think Maria was one of the bravest, most intensely compassionate and socially concerned children I ever taught. She always saw many sides of an issue, but the right side, for her, was always against oppression, against greed, against injustice. She was courageous because she used her personal writing to make meaning of her life and to ask for help. In her notebook, she wrote entries about how sad and scared she was at home, where she felt trapped, alone with her father. She was hungry for information and a picture of what life "should" look like. She asked me what "normal" families are like. "How much alcohol does a normal person drink every day? Is it normal for your father to scream and hit you?" She wanted to read her notebook entries to the class. "Are you sure?" I asked. "Your classmates will have questions; there might be consequences for making this public."

She was sure. "I want them to know what my life is like," she said.

When this class wrote memoirs, Maria, normally a fantastic, prolific writer, laid her head on the table and cried. "I have no good memories." Hearing herself say that was too hard to bear, so she changed it to "I have no memories at all." After several conferences, during which I suggested she could confront the painful episodes, ignore them altogether, or sidestep them by writing in the third person instead of the first, she finally decided to write about her life through her father's eyes. She interviewed her father about what *he* remembered about Maria's childhood, and then in her writer's notebook, she listed incidents that proved how smart and responsible Maria had been from an early age.

> My dad said that by 16 months I knew all my ABC's and how to count to 10. He said I was off my bottle at 12 months, and I was running by 20 months. He said by age 3, I knew all the things a kid should know how to do, including how to take care of my dad when he was sick. I knew how to get out the Tylenol and a wet cloth for his headache.

And then Maria remembered something that was prompted by her father's list: "I remember I climbed on the counter to get my father a cup from the cabinet, then climbed up the sink to get him some water for the aspirin. I must have been very young because the cabinet was so high, and the sink was so scary to climb on."

Because people are calmed when things make sense to them, they can gain relief from writing, making meaning about things they have been through, even if those things are horrific. For victims of any kind of trauma, whether it is child abuse, acts of terrorism, or surviving cancer, relief can come from writing about it, according to doctors and psychiatrists, who often prescribe journal writing as one therapeutic tool. Some call this "Testimony Therapy" (Schacter 2002, 178). I love that there is actual research now, "scientific proof" that validates what writing teachers have always known: writing can be a healing tool.

Perhaps Maria's final memoir piece was not her favorite thing that she wrote that year in my fifth-grade class. She struggled through the unit of memoir writing, and watching her, and other students as well, helped me realize that beautiful writing should not be the ultimate goal of teaching and writing memoir. Instead, recognizing each particular child became my goal, and the memoirs were going to help me.

We write memoir to awaken the "I" and come to know who the "I" is

Azar Nafisi says that we write to know the intimate strangers within ourselves. The specific, compelling, subjective stories that each one of us holds inside our memories make us uniquely ourselves and not someone else. We play our roles of student, teacher, husband, mother, barely glancing over our shoulders to question why and how we came to be who we are. But in the process of looking back, remembering, and reflecting, we learn that different past experiences influenced how we feel about ourselves, how we feel about other people, and how we feel about our future prospects. While critics might suspect that the goal of memoirists is to trumpet their own causes or sing their own praises, the truth is that most memoir writers plunge into the stories of their lives in order to figure something out. There is no joy, for the modern memoir writer, in listing awards, significant dates, or achievements in a life; rather, the thrill comes from the process of discovering what she had not realized, had not considered before.

Memoir provides a means to define the "I" the way I want to. The external world will define me in various ways and place me in a clearly labeled box in order to know how to deal with me and what to expect from me—female, married, teacher, white, middle-aged—but I have the opportunity, in my memoir, to awaken new possibilities of self-definition and to complicate some of those cultural labels. I am a poet. I have dreams of being a musician and an artist. I may look middle-aged, but I feel about twenty years old on my good days, and some days I feel like an infant, screaming for food and attention. This unveiling of hidden realities, internal truths, discrepancies between what the world sees and defines the self to be and what, in the memoirist's experience, is actually the case can be profoundly important to make visible and public. When we are made aware of the inner realities of the people we live with, whether it is in our own homes, schools, cities, or across the globe, we knock down preconceptions and prejudices.

For African Americans, autobiographical writing was, in the eighteenth and nineteenth centuries, the only means available for proclaiming the "I" and telling its multiple stories. No one else could have authentically written about what life was like for slaves. The history of slave narratives is also the story of selves becoming articulate, learning to read and write, which was a skill punishable by death. Slaves who became literate could read about other people's lives and other realities, including the possibility of freedom. And slaves who authored their life story let the world know, for the rest of eternity, who they were and what they had experienced.

Memoir is not the only way to develop and define the "I," of course. Art, music, dance, and drama also provide avenues for self-exploration and self-expression. Psychotherapy takes the client or patient on a similar journey through the forest of memory, interested in what the symbols are, what stands out, what recedes, what cannot be touched or talked about. All these activities share in common a process of uncovering and unveiling deep mysteries. The memoirist proceeds as through a cave with a head-lamp. The writer must feel that he is "conducting a search, not traipsing down chronology or corridors of power. We are so used to ourselves that we forget we are a labyrinth" (Pritchett 1977, 6).

For young people, the process of memoir writing can be a way not only to discover who they are but also to learn how to reflect—to learn that one can place an image, a remembered conversation, or an event under a microscope, study it, and have things to notice about it, things to say about it. In the act of scrutinizing, they might also discover that memory is a reconstruction of an event. A memory is not a document, like a birth certificate, that remains the same for all eternity. Instead, memories fade and flower, shift and change shape, depending on the lens of the current self through which they are viewed. An event remembered at age eighty will likely come with different meanings attached than when it gets recalled at age ten. Children may also come to feel that they could write a hundred memoirs and each time remember or reconstruct a new and different self, each time with a different turning point in their life or different revelations about the same turning point. This fluid nature of memory may frustrate the beginning memoirist, but what freedom we have, not to be trapped inside one way of being!

When young people are given the chance to name and identify themselves, to become three-dimensional, it helps teachers and the other students in the classroom create relationships and form a community for learning. Here are some "I" statements written by my fifth-grade students in Texas.

I hate my little brother.

I'm afraid I'm not going to pass the state test, and I'll have to stay behind in fifth grade.

I'm really great at football. It's all I care about actually, and everything we do at school is just boring until it's 3:30 and I can go to football practice.

I feel so sad. Sometimes I wish I could die.

These were the voices that my students allowed into the classroom as we began to build our classroom community. In the past, I had been lucky to be able to teach children for at least two, sometimes three, years in a row. During this year, however, I had to get to know each of my fifth graders as quickly and as well as I could, and then I had to let them go to middle school. The day before school started on August 13, all the teachers spread out into the neighborhood with street maps and went to meet our new students in their homes.

It was 104 degrees, I remember well. Sweat was running down the backs of my legs, my skin felt pricked by pins, and I was nearly blind from the punishing sun. I remember going into Ricky's apartment, where it was dark and felt even hotter than outside. I walked into a living room about ten by twelve feet big, with laminated flooring. Ricky and four of his eight older brothers were parked on the couch in their underwear in front of a small fan and a television, with the volume on high, while music from a CD player blared in the background. Ricky would not identify himself when I shouted out that I was his new teacher, but his brothers shouted right back, "He's the little one!" and pointed to a sullen-looking boy, short and wide, arms across his chest, who would not look at me. For the rest of the school year, whenever I felt like strangling Ricky, I pictured that couch in the noisy, boiling room, with all those big boys teasing him about being short.

Instead of allowing the standards or the state-mandated test to create a world in which certain children would consistently measure up and others never would, my class created that year, through extraordinarily hard work, a world that invited everyone to participate and included all of us. We wrote and told stories about ourselves—the kinds of stories that make you tingle, that change the feeling in the room. We negotiated and revised the way we lived together in that classroom. We had a hundred class meetings, and at the top of the chart where we kept notes from these community meetings was always the challenge *What kind of classroom do you want to create?* We kept constantly in our minds the insights we had gained from sharing our personal stories. We held Maria in our arms when she had had a bad night at home. We asked Marcus how his weekend football game went, knowing that football was his sole passion, his sole reason for living. And we never, not in my earshot certainly, said words that might resemble the kinds of taunts that Ricky received daily in his home and on his block about being short.

When children and teachers share their memories, their personal stories resonate with others in the classroom. We can build a community of persons who know how life is for one another as human beings, not merely as test scores, reading levels, competitors, freaks.

We write memoir to give the gift of personal and family history to loved ones

Inside a closet in the house I grew up in is a shelf that holds a dozen photograph albums. One summer, my mother was possessed by a burst of organizational energy, and she taped boxloads of photographs into albums labeled by year. Unfortunately, she did not have enough stamina left to label the pictures. Whenever I visit, I spend at least one evening poring over those albums, always coming up with new questions for her, new mysteries to solve. And I always come away unsatisfied. Either my mother can't remember who the people in the pictures are or else she's not saying. If I press her for more specific details, she clams up. "That's not open for discussion," she says, or "I don't know why that is so; we just didn't talk about it."

My parents had me late in life, so my immediate family has witnessed an unusual span of history. I am hungry for details of that history. I want to know what my mother thought about and felt when she was fifteen years old, dancing on a stage in a giant Chinese restaurant on Fulton Street in Brooklyn, New York, for fifteen dollars a week. I want to know what my grandfather thought about as he rode the train home every evening from Grand Central Station. What did he say to his family the evening of the stock market crash in 1929? Did he know any of those men who supposedly jumped from office buildings to their death because their fortune had crashed overnight?

My father's parents steered their covered wagon, carrying my infant father, to settle in Oklahoma before it was a state, when it was "Indian territory." This family of eight remained on their tiny farm in Oklahoma during the Great Depression and during the dust bowl years, made famous in John Steinbeck's novel *The Grapes of Wrath*. Did my father's family talk around the table in the evening about going to California, like so many of their neighbors did? And later, what possessed my father to leave home with two dollars in his pocket and hitchhike to Galveston, Texas, when he was seventeen years old? Why must I feel so bereft of details?

For people of my parents' generation, who grew up in the decades before the social and cultural revolutions of the 1960s in America, there were things that were just not talked about. These included sexuality, alcoholism and incest, mental health, and for those who survived the World Wars and the Holocaust, extreme physical and mental trauma. I have tremendous respect for and understanding of the impulse to clam up about difficult issues. But I am from a different, more open era. I believe that holding in secrets can result in stress and even mental illness, and can condemn those who don't know better to repeat the same mistakes.

So one important reason for people to write their life stories is to give them as gifts to loved ones. Someone will be grateful to have the memories and feelings of their ancestors captured on paper. For novelist Toni Morrison, autobiographies are not merely a nostalgic gesture, nor private family matters, but are the origin of African American literary heritage (Zinsser 1987, 103). Well over a hundred autobiographies, recollections, and memoirs, called slave narratives, were published in the nineteenth century, and they provide windows into one of the worst periods in America's short history. Although, for Morrison, the narratives leave out what she calls the "interior lives" of their authors, they still lay bare the factual atrocities of slavery in voices that become, for African Americans, part family and cultural history and part literary history. These memoirs are priceless, as no one else could have told the story of what it meant to be a slave.

We write memoir to record what must never be forgotten

In Venice, Randy and I walked around and around for hours, searching for the "ghetto" made famous in Shakespeare's play *The Merchant of Venice.* In sixteenth-century Italy, Jewish people were forced to live in isolation on a little island called Ghetto Nuovo, which simply means "new foundry." (The word *ghetto* has become, in English, a metaphor for living in impoverished isolation.) Near the entrance of the Jewish Museum there was a Holocaust memorial. Barbed wire topped a wall of twisted metal sculptures of people pouring onto the trains that ferried them to concentration camps. An inscription written by Andre Tronc read:

Men, Women, Children, Masses for the Gas Chambers
Advancing toward horror beneath the whip of the executioner
Your sad Holocaust is engraved in History
And nothing should purge your death from our memories
For our memories are your only grave.

Autobiography allows us to freeze our lives on paper at least so that they will not disappear. Memoirs preserve, re-create, and remind us of what must *never* be forgotten.

Memoirs pass on stories, sometimes as people's "only grave." They provide a map, a guide for how to live and how not to live. For many countries in the world, what must be remembered and never forgotten are the shared histories of genocide, torture, and slavery. There are countries where the very act of writing is political and dangerous and could get a person imprisoned, tortured, or murdered. East European and Latin American memoirists get impatient with Americans' delight in probing the subconscious and the history of individual childhoods. They write memoirs of *nations*—of rapidly changing borders, of class systems, and of dictatorships.

The poet Czeslaw Milosz wrote his memoir called *Native Realm* in order to tell the shattered, brutal history of his native Poland. But even that, Milosz says, must be rooted in the personal memoir. Otherwise, "History will always be more or less an abstraction. Every family archive that perishes, every account book that is burned, every effacement of the past" leaves us only "a kind of popular digest" ([1968] 1981, 20).

So we need the particular, personal stories to help us remember and to guide us toward the right way to live. We need it for our nation, and we need it for our own lives. In *Hungry for the World*, Kim Barnes (2000) tells a harrowing story of her relationship, when she was a young woman, with a man who emotionally and sexually tortured and controlled her. I could imagine many people deciding this is exactly the kind of memoir that has gone overboard, dredged up intensely personal details that should be kept private and secret. Yet Barnes found herself wishing, in the midst of her private hell, that her mother had told her about what can happen between a woman and a man so that she might not have stumbled so ignorantly into this situation. She writes:

> "There are some things better left unsaid," my mother has told me. I wonder what those things are. I wonder if somewhere in those untold stories, I might have found a map of experience I could follow, some way to believe I was not alone in my confusion and misjudgments. We give what directions we can: keep your nose clean, your chin up, your legs together, your mouth shut. Yet so often the truth lies in what we cannot say. Blind cartographers, tongue-tied guides, we send our children off with maps drawn in invisible ink, pointing down the Yellow Brick Road toward Oz, without a word about flying monkeys. (174)

Adults try to protect children from difficult or dangerous realities, and they also try to protect themselves by forgetting or veiling those things in secrecy. Yet forgetfulness and secrecy produce confusion, mistrust, and shame in children, and in communities and cultures, those feelings get magnified tenfold. Perhaps by sharing details that normally are not talked about, Barnes can help prevent other young women from falling prey to an abusive man's power.

We write memoir to bear witness

Memoir transcends the private journal or diary entry because writing one is a public act. It assumes some kind of audience, a reader, an other. The author is the "I"; the reader is "Thou"; and as Martin Buber (1958) wrote, I and Thou are in a relationship. In a writer-reader relationship, the writer says: "There is a reason I am telling you this story from my life. I want you to hear me, see me, understand why I am the way I am. I want you to bear witness to all that I have celebrated and all that I have suffered." Bearing witness to someone else's life is a political act, for the reader now has responsibilities toward the other. In a democracy, language is the medium by which we come to know how life is for each other, as well as the tool we use to make decisions and write laws that protect and benefit everyone, particularly those most vulnerable. In such a culture, listening to someone's life story becomes a privilege and a responsibility. "Failing to ask people to tell their stories is not only rude and uncivil but also a functional failure of a democratic public. If voices of the vulnerable are silent, there is no hope of renewal and justice" (Bomer and Bomer 2001, 2). The reader must respond: "Now that I know your story, I cannot treat you the same way. I cannot look through you, or above you, but must meet you steady-on, deal with you as a human being who feels the same or differently from the way I do. I must ensure that you have all the rights and privileges that I enjoy, and I must ensure that no harm befalls you. Now we have a relationship, and it is up to us to learn from each other's experience so we won't to make the same mistakes again."

Telling and being heard creates a relationship, and that can be healing, claims Margaret Wheatley, author of a book about listening called *Turning to One Another* (2002). Wheatley writes about South Africans whose testimonies during the Truth and Reconciliation Commission about the atrocities they had endured under apartheid had a healing effect on the tellers. One young man, who was blinded by being shot at close range by a policeman, said, "I feel what has been making me sick all the time is the fact that I couldn't tell my story. But now . . . it feels like I've got my sight back by coming here and telling you the story" (89).

Toni Morrison writes that the slave narratives published in the eighteenth and nineteenth centuries were written primarily to bear witness. Their mission, she said, was to prove to the reader, who was probably not black, that the writers were human beings "worthy of God's grace and the immediate abandonment of slavery" (Zinsser 1987, 105). They also proved that despite conclusions by thinkers, including Thomas Jefferson, during the Enlightenment, persons of African descent were capable of intelligence and were not "stupid" (108). One slave narrative writer named Olaudah Equiano recorded his life for one purpose: "to change things" (105). Apparently, there was a great demand by people in the mid-nineteenth century for firsthand accounts of the brutality of slavery. The narratives met with harsh criticism as well as pity and contempt, but they also fed the abolitionist movement and perhaps went a long way toward ending the practice of slavery.

In a classroom, the teacher must create a receptive community—persons who care to hear about what it is like to be Ricky and Marcus and Maria, even what it is like to be the teacher, so that all can live together during their time in that room, and the stories will be maps to guide them. Some individuals feel too vulnerable to share the deepest truths, even in the most empathetic community. There are always things someone can't tell you. Ricky could never write directly about being short, about being bullied and picked on by a house of giant older brothers. Yet I felt this was his deepest pain and it was what motivated much of his difficult behavior. Are there truths not to be expressed except to a priest or therapist? Perhaps. But keeping them in, we know now, causes physical and mental disease. Keeping them in does not allow others to know us, does not allow us to come out with our shame and be forgiven, does not allow others to bear witness and to help make things better.

We write memoir to help us understand broader social and political realities

Reading memoir helps instruct and influence our political imagination. When we read the stories of human beings making decisions, falling in love, having babies, and hurting, just like we do, it makes it harder to drop bombs on them. When we see inside someone else, when we bear witness to her or his stories, we can no longer be enemies because we are in a relationship: I and Thou.

When students tell us what life is like for them, they invite us to understand social and political realities that are different from our own. Some children live under tremendous physical and psychological stress from poverty, hunger, and war. Many children live with racism that confronts them from the instant they leave their homes until they return at night. Until we listen to their voices, there is a silence wrapped around the specific injustices that children endure. In Boston, in response to an essay contest for all sixth-grade students that asked participants to write about a time when they had shown courage, one girl wrote: "I showed courage the time I had to put on my Berka [the veil that Muslim females must wear], on September 12, 2001, and go to school."

Even when memoirs reflect decent, contented life situations, those happy childhoods that we wish for all of our children, the diverse worlds that reside in classrooms all over this country should open our eyes to cultures and customs we know next to nothing about. At Machan Elementary School in Phoenix, Arizona, a school that continues to adhere to its dual language philosophy and practice despite movements against it, Ernestina Aragon and Rebecca Osorio wanted their fifth graders to write the stories of their lives, the lives that are underrepresented and misrepresented in our country. They talked with their students about "how Latinos and kids in bilingual education were being misrepresented by the media, that minorities are often spoken about in the media, but they don't often define themselves" (Edelsky 2003). When Ernestina and Rebecca shared their students' writing with other teachers at a national conference, the circle spread, the ripples went out—we all caught a glimpse of lives that cross borders continually. The fifth graders wrote in Spanish and English. When they translated the stories, they kept Spanish where it belonged—in their grandmothers' voices and in the naming of things dear to them. The kids' stories, about cooking and fishing and going swimming, felt so delightfully familiar, and yet we heard another language, and we learned that some children have to wait a very long time for their fathers and mothers or their sisters and brothers to have the money or the legal papers to be able to leave Mexico to join them. Carole Edelsky points out, "For the kids, this wasn't about learning memoir for the sake of schools; it was about putting their stories out there for the sake of their own families and communities." And for the sake of all of us who were privileged to read them.

The reasons to read and write memoir are as enormous as the world, as ancient as history, as crucial as human life. And they are also as seemingly small as to give one person, reading one story, the hope to keep living. My hope is that you will find the lessons in the next eight chapters both practical and poetic enough to give your students the chance to write their lives so that the world can read them.

Week-by-Week Plans

A Map to Guide You Through a Genre Study in Memoir

W
hen I was little, I remember taking the five-minute drive from our house in Albuquerque, New Mexico, to Aunt Marie and Uncle Earl's house to go "viztin." Dinner was usually part of the event, and afterward, if it was summertime and still light outside, a game of badminton or croquet with my cousins. The Fourth of July always included sparklers and homemade ice cream. It was my job to crank the handle on that old-fashioned freezer and to fill the wooden bucket to the top with ice and rock salt.

But when it finally grew dark, we always ended up in the living room, perched on couches and easy chairs, and commenced to viztin. Viztin meant sitting around for endless hours, telling tales about the "original Bearden brood." It meant that my aunt and uncle would spin out some long, detailed yarn of their youth (they have been married since she was fifteen and he was sixteen) on their farms in Oklahoma. My father usually figured into the story because he was the closest sibling in age to my aunt, and her favorite. Since he never spoke of his childhood, I would be riveted to any details I could extract from his sister.

Their stories reminded my mother of her own stories, even though she grew up as far from a Midwest farm as you can get, in Brooklyn, New York, and off she would go on her own reminiscences. If Nana was there, she would chime in too, and so would any other stray relatives who happened to be over. I remember sitting between my mother and my father, growing steadily sleepier, until the voices of the adults sounded like they came from inside a long tunnel. My head would topple over onto my dad's shoulder as I fought to stay awake. It was delicious, this sleepy time of adults talking quiet and slow, and I never grew tired of hearing the stories.

What remained constant, until I was seventeen years old, eager to go off to make my own life story, was that I never talked about *my* memories. None of the kids did.

Memory weaving was for the old folks. The older they were, the more they wanted to talk about their past, as if afraid of losing it. We rarely violated our roles as children who were to be seen and not heard. I believe I was the only one who enjoyed hearing the adults yammer on about their pasts. The other kids played games in the back bedroom or fell asleep in different parts of the house until their parents carried them to the car to drive home.

Now, as an adult writer and teacher of the genre of memoir to people of all ages from five to ninety-five, I know the value of remembering and retelling life stories for any age. Even the youngest children should be able to let others know what the world has been like for them. Every time we know someone's life story, we become rich with perspectives that we wouldn't have had without this offering. We learn about different places, time periods, and cultures. We find out that we are not alone in our grief, our anger, or our intense feelings of love, and we learn how to see beneath the skin of people who might have felt "other" to us before.

I don't know any young person who doesn't beg to hear stories about his or her early childhood. "Tell me again about the day I was born, about how I fell and broke my arm, about my first words." It's almost as if hearing the stories of their becoming holds a mirror up that says, "This is who you are." It helps situate them in time. And that is exactly what writing a memoir can do. It can help students figure out how they came to be who they are. Because it comes from lived experiences, from data and facts that reside inside their own memories, nothing to look up or reference, memoir is probably the easiest genre for students to write well. They are experts on their own lives, so instruction can focus on how to craft the contents of their lives.

I want to create in my classroom the kind of easy community I felt at my aunt and uncle's house, where my students can go "viztin," where they can remember their lives and make their memories public. But I also want a rigorous learning environment, where my students will spend several weeks reading and learning the craft of writing that freezes their life stories in print so that they can travel to other places and live across time. Whether or not you teach a writing workshop (see Atwell 1987; Bomer 1995; Calkins 1994; Ray 2001), you might devote a portion of your school year to teaching your students to write their memoirs. In Chapters 3 through 8, I will describe the details of teaching within the structures that I sketch briefly in this chapter. For now, let me provide something like a map for how to proceed through a genre study of memoir that should work well in a language arts block in a self-contained elementary setting or in an English class in a middle or high school.

I keep several large parts of the writing process in mind as I plan any course of study that might last no fewer than four weeks. I will outline those segments here, and inside each, I'll direct you to a subsequent chapter that describes in greater detail how to teach the segment. Here, I just want to give a quick overview so that we know the territory. In the latter portion of this chapter, I propose a general time line for a memoir genre study as well.

Immersion

The idea that in order to learn anything, people need to be immersed in the topic, concept, or skill they are learning comes from Brian Cambourne's "Principles of Learning" (1988). Shelley Harwayne used to say we need to "marinate" kids in the genre we want them to write, that we should give students a lot of experience with the kind of text we wish them to make. If they are planning to compose memoirs, then students should be reading examples of the genre, hearing them read aloud by the teacher and by other members of the class, and discussing their features. (See Chapter 3 for a detailed description of how to read and interpret memoir texts.)

The main goals of immersing students in any genre are to introduce its features and to help them fall in love with it. So I choose carefully what book-length or excerpted memoirs I read out loud to a particular group, knowing that I want to entice them into this wonderful genre. As we read together, we begin to explore the memoir genre, noticing what it looks and sounds like, what its properties and conventions are. Students will notice, for instance, that memoir almost always uses the pronoun *I*, and that, of course, is almost always a convention of the genre. They might also find that some memoirs begin in early childhood and proceed chronologically while others begin at the supposed moment of writing, when the author is much older. I write what my students notice about the qualities of memoir on a chart called "The Features of Memoir" or "What Is a Memoir?" and we continue to add to this chart throughout the study.

Naturally, teachers will want to make examples of memoir available to students at the beginning of a study of memoir. But it is also important for the class to remain immersed in model texts *throughout* the study, to revisit the concepts again and again with added insights and new experiences, and then to pull in even closer to the texts as they compose their own memoirs.

Generating

Students need a portion of time to simply brainstorm, or generate ideas for writing. This is a risk-free activity, a luxurious opportunity to think on the page, without being bound by rules, structures, or consequences (such as grades or tests). Writers do this kind of work constantly, all day long, even in their dreams! Many writers keep some type of writer's notebook (see Bomer 1995; Calkins 1994; Fletcher 1996; Hindley 1996) in which they record their brainstorming work, and that is what I ask students to do as well. For a chunk of time, usually at least one week, I invite my students to make lists, snippets of writing, sketches, and brief renderings of as many memories as they can squeeze out. Chapter 4 provides a detailed list of activities for generating childhood memories in the writers notebook. The resulting lists, dialogues, descriptions, and small narrative moments will constitute the junkyard, treasure chest, photo album, or whatever metaphor you use to describe a collection of thought entries from which students will choose ideas to develop in their memoir draft.

Selecting a Topic, Collecting, Layering, and Planning

The generating, or brainstorming, portion of the process helps writers feel rich with memories to select from when they write the first draft of their memoir. Having many entries in the writers notebook creates a feeling of fullness and possibility, like having a field of lovely flowers to choose from in order to pluck just the right small bunch to collect into a bouquet. The final draft of the memoir will not list *all* the memories a writer can think of, but rather a thoughtfully selected *few* memories, organized and focused by a frame, lens, angle, or structure. So at the beginning of this selecting, collecting, and layering phase, students reread all the entries in their writer's notebook, looking for patterns and themes, and then select some way in which to limit and focus the content of the memoir draft.

During this phase of thinking and writing, I provide students with options for looking at their life and memories with interpretive lenses, so that their memories begin to add up to a cohesive whole, a pleasing bouquet of flowers, and are not simply random or isolated bits. As they collect these memories that will fit into the frame or focus, the vase they have devised (in the classroom, I use a variety of metaphors to describe aspects of the writing process, and I encourage my students to invent their own language to help them understand the concept), writers concentrate on answering the deepest question of memoir—so what?—and reflecting on what those events mean to the writer, how those situations shaped who the writer has become. (Chapter 5 provides a detailed discussion of interpretation as well as questions and activities that students might attempt during this collecting phase and well into the drafting phase that follows.)

Once the writer has chosen a theme or focus for the memoir, he will continue to collect in the writer's notebook more memories, connected incidents and images, and reflections about the chosen focus. During this part of the writing process, many students will begin to envision how they want their memoir to go, and that is completely normal. The parts of the writing process overlap and intersect; no part works in isolation, step one, step two, like those prepackaged writing process materials you see at teacher supply stores. People who write for a living go about their day with drafts and ideas for future writing projects swimming in their head. But certainly, as they near the end of this collecting and layering part of the process, students will begin to make informal outlines and plans for a structure for the memoir. (See Chapter 6 for lists of possible forms and structures for memoir.)

Drafting, Revising, and Editing

On separate pieces of blank paper, outside of the writer's notebook, students begin their first draft, having made plans for its basic structure in the previous stage. Drafting must feel liberating to writers, so they will approach revision and editing as gifts, opportunities to renew and redo, and not curses. The draft must feel like a chance to write almost in a skeleton-like way, as if they are building a house, first laying down a foundation, then putting up supporting walls, beams, and cross-beams, later filling in with drywall and molding, and finally, applying several coats of paint.

Throughout this process, students find ways to revise their drafts. To revise means to resee. Every time the writer looks at the draft again, she sees it in a new way. No one can be certain how many drafts it takes to reach a high-quality end product; however, I know that as I teach more strategies for how to revise, for how to make the text sing, students will make more versions of the original draft. (I devote Chapter 8 to revision strategies pertinent to memoir writing.) In the end, when the draft feels as if it is saying all that it can say, in the best way it can say it (or else when the deadline has arrived!), it is time to make the final edits, correcting any remaining spelling and punctuation errors, so that the memoir is ready to go public.

Publishing and Celebrating

For all the reasons I outlined in Chapter 1 and more, publishing students' memoirs to an audience is perhaps the most important part of the whole process. Writers need authentic response to their products more than they need a grade or even teacher approval. Because of the personal nature of the memoir genre, I ask my students to help me think of ways to go public that feel comfortable and special for them. One year, I typed all of the memoirs into an anthology, and I wrote a preface to it. A parent volunteered to make copies for everyone in the class, and with a student-designed cover, it looked like a collection of edited memoir essays that you might find at the bookstore.

Another year, I spread the children's memoirs out on tables in two classrooms (how lucky I was to have an unused science lab across the hall from me). Families roamed through and read each memoir, much as they might wander through a museum, gazing at the artwork and reading the typed descriptions of each piece. I asked that this process occur in silence so that readers could really concentrate on what they were reading. Beside each memoir, I provided a pad of paper and several pens. I asked families to write a letter to the memoirist noticing what the piece made them think about from their own lives and any other "powerful, emotionally evocative, enticing" thing they wanted to comment upon. I think the fact that I angled readers to make connections and to be emotionally affected helped those comments to be the loveliest responses I've ever seen from adults to student writing. It enabled parents to respond authentically to the memoirs of other kids besides their own. One parent wrote to a nine-year-old: "You have made me remember going fishing with my father. I haven't ever thought about that time, but now I remember it as the happiest moments of my life with him."

Another year, I hit upon the following structure and have used this format for celebrations of fiction and nonfiction ever since because I love how it honors the social community of my classroom. This method of going public worked because my students had spent several weeks working together in peer response groups (see more about this later in the chapter). They knew their writing partners' memoir pieces as well as they knew their own and had been actively supporting and nurturing each other's drafts all along. We invited families in for a memoir reading. Students sat with the members of their writing group, four or five in each group. Each student read a memoir, and afterward the other members of the group talked about what their friend's process had been—how he or she had generated memories and then how he or she had selected and structured that particular memoir. I asked families to question each author in the writing group about his or her process. I remember adults responding with respect and admiration about many of the stories my students wrote that year.

Ongoing Activities

I just outlined a chronology of the phases of the writing process for memoir, from generating ideas to publishing. The next few items describe activities that occur throughout the memoir genre study, no matter what phase of writing students are in.

Reading Memoir

Chapter 3 details how to provide rich reading experiences in the memoir genre, but for now, let me mention the importance of providing students with examples of the kind of text they are trying to make so they can read and discuss them. While you may begin the unit of study with reading and discussion about the features of memoir, students should continue reading on their own and choose at least one text as a mentor or model to refer to throughout the composing process.

Minilessons and Conferences

At every stage of the process of memoir writing, the teacher is teaching. Sometimes, teaching comes in the form of short lessons to the whole class about some aspect of composing a memoir. (All the chapters in this book provide content for lessons in the craft of memoir writing.) Other times, the teacher will sit beside a writer in a conference and ask about his particular intentions for the writing of the memoir and then teach how to realize those intentions. (Chapter 7 is devoted to particular kinds of questions and comments you might have in conferences with students as they write their memoirs.)

Peer Response

Throughout the memoir genre study, I give my students opportunities, at least three times each week, to hold conversations with other writers in the class about their progress and to get and give advice on various aspects of the process. I ask students to meet at the end of writing time with someone who is an ongoing writing partner during this study, or I have students choose three or four other students to meet with in a writing group. How well these social interactions go depends on how seriously students take their writing process, how much they have internalized methods of talking about writing from your minilessons and conferences, and how often they have practiced working with other students in respectful, productive ways.

The first few times students meet with each other to confer, they provide less than stellar writing responses for each other. I think the reasons for this are twofold. First, students may not have been given many opportunities to talk to each other in class. Talk is the least valued means of learning in schools, and in fact, in many classrooms and school buildings, students may be punished for talking to each other. So of course, anything that is not practiced again and again, or which in fact is usually expressly forbidden, cannot go well at first.

Secondly, young people may not yet know how to read like writers; that is, they do not have ways of looking at text the way producers of text do. Most students are used to talking about texts solely as consumers; they are accustomed to mining texts for the answers to comprehension questions or test questions but not used to looking at the specific elements of an author's writing style in order to imitate that style. Throughout the school year, I teach in minilessons both how to read like writers and how to work together productively. When I confer with individual students about their writing, I am modeling ways to talk about writing. When students work in response groups, I confer with the whole group, observing their discussion for a few minutes and giving feedback about how well they are listening to and supporting each other. I might even give someone in the group the words to say or the question to ask as a way to demonstrate a quality response to writing. For instance, I might suggest to one student: "Ask him what his plan is for how he is going to structure these four different memories into one draft," or "Ask her what part of her draft she needs our help with right now."

For a course in memoir writing, students can help each other generate initial ideas and memories; once a child tells a story, eight other children might have that "me too" feeling. Students can provide a sounding board, an active ear to hear how their partners' drafts are shaping up. They can learn to respond honestly and helpfully when they are unable to envision a scene or when they are confused about what is happening because of gaps in logic or an underdeveloped point. Most importantly, they can generously laugh when the story is funny and empathize when the story is difficult or frightening. They provide a real audience to their peers' life stories.

A Time Frame for a Memoir Genre Study

Most units of study in the writing workshop (see Angelillo 2002, 2005; Bomer 1995; Bomer and Bomer 2002; Calkins et al. 2004; Nia 1999; Ray 2001) last from two to eight weeks. I have never been able to teach a memoir genre study with students in grades four and up in less than four weeks. Usually, I carve out a six-week chunk from my year-long plan in writing, and then during the actual study, I watch for parts of the process that might call for more or less time. I aim for a kind of tension between a relaxed season of contemplation, remembering, reliving, and reflecting on experiences and feelings, and a more rigorous, deadline-driven period for shaping those remembrances and reflections into a final draft.

Decisions about the length of time to devote to one genre depend upon the interests and demands of your own classroom, school, district, and state. Many teachers feel that the requirements of state tests and district assessments determine their schedule and curriculum. In Texas, for instance, the fourth grade must take a high-stakes writing test, which features a personal narrative task, in February. Some teachers decide, therefore, to teach memoir first and then a unit on test practice, helping students write essays that build on the memoir work and rise above the formulaic quality of most test writing. I talk about preparing for standardized tests in Chapter 9.

A Time Line for a Possible Six-Week Unit in Memoir Writing

The following schedule is not meant to prescribe, but to offer a template for teachers to try out, if they so choose. I assume people will adjust for their students and curricular schedule.

WEEK ONE: IMMERSION IN THE MEMOIR GENRE

- Students read as many memoir picture books and excerpts from book-length memoirs as possible.
- Teacher reads aloud from book-length memoirs, excerpts, and picture books.

WEEK TWO: GENERATING

- Students generate as many entries in their writer's notebook as possible, including lists, sketches, bits of remembered dialogue, events, episodes, and images.

WEEK THREE: SELECTING, COLLECTING, AND LAYERING IN THE WRITER'S NOTEBOOK

- Students choose a lens, frame, angle, or theme as a focus for their memoir draft (one or two days). After they know what their memoir will mostly be about, they collect more information and layer additional text about this lens, frame, angle, or theme (at least three days).

WEEK FOUR: PLANNING AND DRAFTING

- Students spend some time in the writer's notebook making informal outlines, time lines, storyboards, or diagrams for how their draft might be organized. These should be seen as temporary guides only; organization of the draft will likely change during the revision process.
- Students begin a first draft, outside of their writer's notebook, using their outlines and the material they have collected during week three.

WEEK FIVE: DRAFTING AND REVISING

- Students continue to draft their memoirs, applying several revision strategies to rework the structure, develop characters or scenes as appropriate, cutting and pasting to create new versions of a draft. They share their changing versions with classmates and the teacher, getting feedback on what works and what still needs fine-tuning.

WEEK SIX: EDITING, PUBLISHING, AND CELEBRATING

- Students reread their final draft, adding, changing, and fixing the surface features of punctuation and grammar. They can exchange with several peer editors and allow the teacher to serve as chief editor. A final, corrected copy might by typed or handwritten, illustrated or bound.
- Students read their published memoir to an audience, pass it along in printed form, or in some way make their story public.

(For a four-week version of this schedule, simply shorten each segment by a day or two.)

How a Memoir Unit Fits into a Yearlong Writing Curriculum

Many teachers plan a unit of study in personal narratives or short memoir pieces at the beginning of the school year to build community. Teachers and students get to know each other through their personal stories, and I support that impulse. Also, Donald Graves (1983) claims that children write best what they know most about, so it makes sense to begin the year helping students feel successful. Before they study fiction, poetry, or nonfiction, students might take up memoir as the first unit of study in a yearlong writing curriculum, during which teachers can learn their students' writing strengths and processes.

I want to argue, however, for holding off on a longer, more genre-specific study of memoir writing until near the end of the school year. Students will trust the community more and so perhaps write more honestly, closer to the heart of their thoughts and feelings. If they have been in writing partnerships and peer response groups all year, they will have deeper trust in each other's comments as well as more sophisticated ways to respond to each other's memoir drafts. Later in the year, they will be comfortable with the entire process of generating ideas in the notebook, selecting a topic, collecting more information about that topic, drafting, and revising. Students can bring all that they have learned about writing from other genre studies studied throughout the year (see sequence chart on p. 37) to bear on this one so that the quality of their writing will be superlative. Imagery, voice, dramatic tension—all of the lessons from poetry and fiction (see Bomer 1995; Calkins 1994; Fletcher and Portalupi 1998; Heard 1995; Flynn and McPhillips 2000; Ray 1999) will make their memoir text that much stronger.

Many teachers compose their year in writing instruction similarly to the way I do. I begin in August by laying out a dream year, a wish list of what I might teach across the year. Three things help me determine what the focus of major units of study will be:

1. What the students studied in writing the year before. When I taught in a school where most teachers provided intensive writing instruction, we met as a faculty to discuss a plan for what genres each grade would be sure to include. This type of collaboration across grades ensures that students receive some experience in writing a variety of genres in the time they spend in one school. On the other hand, we did not expect any one teacher to give up his or her particular passions or successful units simply because children had done that one the year before. We simply found ways to complicate and

raise the level of sophistication of those genres. For instance, if the second-grade teachers had taught their students how to focus on one event, stretching it out with details and dialogue, the fifth-grade teachers might want to help students learn how to play with time or create dramatic action in longer narratives.

2. What my students need help with. In the beginning of each school year, I spend several weeks assessing students' writing capabilities in writing conferences and by reading their writer's notebooks, recording their strengths and areas in which they need more support (Anderson 2005). My yearlong dream curriculum has preplanned space in it for one-, two-, and three-week-long "writing intensives." Topics for those mini-inquiries have been things like how to write with meaning, and improving the writing we do for homework. Donna Santman describes mini-inquiries in reading, with topics such as finding the issues hiding in books in *Shades of Meaning* (2005). Janet Angelillo describes intensive units of study in punctuation and revision in two wonderful books (2002, 2005).

A Typical Sequence of Genre Studies in a Yearlong Writing Curriculum in My Classroom

SEPTEMBER:	Writer's Notebooks (and routines and structures of the writing workshop)
OCTOBER:	Genre of Choice
NOVEMBER:	Nonfiction Writing (feature articles, editorials)
DECEMBER:	Poetry
JANUARY:	Fiction
FEBRUARY:	Test Preparation
MARCH–APRIL:	Writing for Social Action
MAY–JUNE:	Memoir

3. **What my students want to study.** I compromise my dream curriculum because it is, conspicuously, *my* dream. My students also have dreams and wish lists, and so I always include at least one genre study that they have requested. (The most popular choice, hands down, is fiction.) In addition to the genre study by popular demand, I plan a few one-week stints of just plain notebook writing to punctuate a year of intensive periods of studying genres. My students relish this break when they don't have to think about writing to satisfy my curriculum requirements, don't have to think about structures and genre elements. My only requirements for these notebook breaks are the same ones that apply all year long in the notebooks: continue to write in them every night for fifteen minutes (in addition to the thirty to forty minutes of writing workshop time); date every entry; write about what matters; write a lot; and write thoughtfully.

When I drive anywhere, I usually take directions that I have printed out from the MapQuest website. They sit beside me on the car seat, unread. I tend to strike out in the general direction of my destination, and I don't consult the map until I get closer, after I am physically in the area where I'm headed. I understand better what the map means when I can check it against the actual neighborhood. Perhaps this chapter will serve that purpose for you. As we turn our attention to the details of how to teach each segment of the process, perhaps this chapter will be the map you check when you are in the neighborhood.

Reading to Write

Discussion Questions and Projects That Probe Published Memoirs for Craft Lessons

I had once tried to write, had once reveled in feeling, had let my crude imagination roam, but the impulse to dream had been slowly beaten out of me by experience. Now it surged up again and I hungered for books, new ways of looking and seeing. It was not a matter of believing or disbelieving what I read, but of feeling something new, of being affected by something that made the look of the world different.

—RICHARD WRIGHT, IN *The Open Door: When Writers First Learned to Read*

As a graduate student at Teachers College, Columbia University, in the 1980s, I took a writing course on memoir taught by writer Dorothy Barnhouse, who was a colleague of mine at the Teachers College Reading and Writing Project. Dorothy introduced to me the world of contemporary memoir.

True, as a little girl, I drank the gorgeous writing and fascinating story of learning in Helen Keller's memoirs as if they were milk sating my empty tummy. When I was thirteen years old, Nicky Cruz's memoir, *Run, Baby, Run* (1971), about his conversion from violent street-gang member to born-again Christian, inspired me to join a national Lutheran youth group for about six months. And I pored over Joyce Maynard's memoir, *Looking Back: A Chronicle of Growing Up Old in the Sixties* (1973), when I was a senior in high school. I was obsessed with Maynard's book and wished to emulate her life story, especially the part about publishing a book at the age of eighteen! I remember her picture on the cover of that book vividly—I thought she was the most beautiful woman I had ever seen, and I thought that if I stared at her long enough, I could make myself look like her too.

I read quite a few autobiographies while pursuing undergraduate and master's degrees in English literature. St. Augustine's *Confessions* ([397] 1991) gave a rare glimpse of a tormented internal life amidst the impersonal literature of the Middle Ages. Montaigne's autobiographical *Essays* ([1595] 1958) taught me how to write essays as journeys of thought. *Memoirs of a Dutiful Daughter*, by Simone de Beauvoir ([1958] 1974) rocked my world as it introduced me to the idea of the oppression of women. I loved Virgina Woolf's *Moments of Being* (1976) and still consider it my authority on how to write about memory. But in ten years of literature study, I had not taken a single course that focused on autobiography as a genre, and I didn't hear the term *memoir* used as I do in this book before 1985. Although I had taken numerous creative writing classes to study poetry and fiction, I had not received a minute of writing instruction specific to autobiography.

Dorothy's class changed all that. Her reading list was one of the best I had ever encountered. Her choices successfully expanded her students' notions of what autobiographical writing can look and sound like. Since that class, I have devoured scores of memoirs written for adults and children. These published texts helped me write my own memoir pieces, and Dorothy's lessons about looking at the past through the lens of the present, and the internal and external selves, have helped me teach children and adults how to write their memoirs for the past fifteen years.

Reading books in the genre one wishes to write in is crucial practice for a writer. Most writers will admit that they learned to write from reading. "Read like a wolf," Gary Paulsen advises young people, and I agree. I want my students to become hungry to make literature, hungry to hear the lilt of language that inspires them to write their own texts. When students read a genre with an eye toward making something like that genre, they read with a particularly analytical mind. They notice how the text is structured and what's possible in terms of point of view, use of time, even topic choice.

Young or unpracticed writers often feel that they are copying when they use a published work as their writing mentor. But unless they are lifting whole sentences word for word from published texts, they are merely echoing, or doing in the manner of an expert—a practice all writers use. Mostly what happens when we read other texts with an eye toward making ones like them is we learn how to write. In museums all over the world, you can watch artists with their easels poised before a painting by El Greco or Monet or da Vinci, learning how to paint by imitating the masters.

Children's illustrator Anita Lobel, in her extraordinary Holocaust memoir called *No Pretty Pictures*, writes that when she went to an art museum in Sweden as a teenager, she was not just looking at the paintings to admire them, but to learn from them how to paint: "I became the hungry wanderer and intruder into the outlines of lace on a wrist, into eyes and noses and hair, a traveler among trees and mountains against cloudy skies, a chiseler of shapes of flower petals and of the human body. I was a conspirator and a thief. I was an artist" (1998, 176).

I love that Lobel calls herself a conspirator and a thief. I can name exact lessons I learned from reading adult memoirs as I was writing my own memoir, and yes, at times, I felt like a thief. In *The Woman Warrior*, Maxine Hong Kingston (1977) weaves a lengthy myth in which she plays the role of the little girl training to become a warrior. I "stole" the idea of beginning my memoir with a legend from a movie I saw in New Mexico when I was a little girl. The movie was based on a Native American legend about a little boy who raised an orphaned eaglet, and when he had to set it free, he turned into an eagle himself to escape the taunts of some bullying children. This story establishes the metaphorical frame for my whole memoir, which contains numerous stories of my escape from difficult relationships inside my house to the haunting landscape of New Mexico and my close kinship with plants, animals, and insects as a child. It also illustrates my *simpatico* feelings of empathy for a culture that resonated with me more than my own. I learned from Kingston that memoir does not have to read like a genealogist's report on family lineage; instead, the self can speak through metaphor and myth.

From Paul Auster's *Invention of Solitude* (1982), I learned that I could write a biography of my mother inside my own memoir. More than half of Auster's memoir details his father's life. Geoffrey Wolff does the same thing in *The Duke of Deception* (1979), where he researches archival documents about his father in order to discern what is true about his father and what his father made up about himself, which is almost everything. A number of memoirs contain biographies of parents and grandparents within them. It makes sense that if a writer is making meaning of her life, she might need to explore the lives of the people who created and shaped that life.

It feels every bit as crucial for young people to learn how to write from reading published memoirs as it has been for my own writing. Exposure to a variety of autobiographical texts provides models for everything from topics and time frames to structure and tone. Every time I use Sandra Cisneros' autobiographical novel, *The House on Mango*

Street (1989), for instance, students are overjoyed to learn that their own memoir could be similarly structured as a collection of poetically titled vignettes, contained within a limited time period. *Bad Boy: A Memoir,* by Walter Dean Myers (2001), has given several of my students the courage to write about living in extended or unconventional families and to help the rest of us see the powerful love, devotion, and commitment shared by the people in those nontraditional arrangements. Jamie Lee Curtis' picture book, *Tell Me Again About the Day I Was Born* (1996), although not a memoir, has given many kids the idea to ask their parents the story of when they were born and to incorporate that into their memoir. *The Circuit: Stories from the Life of a Migrant Child,* by Francisco Jimenez (1997), gave one of my fifth graders the courage to write about crossing the border of Mexico to come to Texas when he was seven years old, hiding behind bushes and walking only at night with his mother and siblings. He told the class that he had not remembered doing that until I read *The Circuit* out loud to the class, and then the memories came flooding back.

Purposes for Teaching Model Texts in Memoir

In some ways, if everyone used literary texts to study how to read and how to write, literacy educators would be out of business. Everything a writer needs to know about how to write can be found in the texts that exemplify the genre. In *The Open Door: When Writers First Learned to Read* (1989), famous authors from Benjamin Franklin to Frederick Douglass, Gertrude Stein to Stephen King, write about the act of learning how to read (frequently a laborious, insidious task), and the experience of ecstasy when literature cracked the world open for them. I read excerpts from these little autobiographies to my class at the beginning of the school year and then ask students to write their own reading memoir. This is just one way to combine reading and writing in a special project during a study of memoir (see a list of additional reading projects at the end of this chapter). Here is the beginning of Sinnae's reading memoir, called "The Journey Through Time (and Space, if You Like)":

> My very first book was *The Little Engine That Could.* I still have my copy, hidden among piles and boxes of books—old picture books, mostly. I think I started reading in pre-kindergarten. One of the teachers there told my mother about my

abilities and of course, nobody believed I could really read at first. Then that day, my mom was doing the dishes, and suddenly I take up the book whose pictures I had been admiring. I stumble over a couple of new words, and the overall going is very slow—but rejoice! I had read my book through, from cover to cover.

My mom helped me learn to read by reading to me in bed, and encouraging me, but never pushing. I think if you push kids to do things, they get scared of it and they don't want to do it. You have to help them to some point, but don't go further than that.

Fortunately, students *do* need us; they need us to introduce literature and to guide them in how to read the texts as instruction manuals in the art of writing. The list of autobiographies written for young people is not a long one. What many teachers do in response to this dearth is use picture books that have a first-person narrator and that contain experiences of childhood that resonate with young writers (see Recommended Literature at the end of the book for a list of my favorite memoirs and memoirlike picture books to use with children of different age groups). The collection of model texts grows exponentially when we introduce picture books into the mix, and their brevity makes them easy to use in minilessons about the craft of memoir. Also, the short length of most picture books more nearly resembles what students in the middle grades will actually produce, so they make a better match for imitation of overall structure than a book-length autobiography. Still, I believe it's important to select one or two novel-length texts to read aloud to your students and to provide other long selections (see Recommended Literature) for them to read independently or in book clubs so that the whole class can discuss the ways in which memoir looks different, sounds different, and means differently from other genres.

From exemplary texts, you can teach children how to

generate memories and areas of focus

structure the content

play with time

write with detail, image, and voice

write fantastic beginnings and endings

revise and edit

Ways of Reading Memoir

We read autobiographical writing understanding that it can be only a subjective inter-pretation of the past; it cannot claim to represent reality. The writer takes liberties with time, dialogue, and detail to create a sense of how things felt to him. The writer makes choices of what to put in and especially of what to leave out—lying, technically, by omis-sion. The writer is, in effect, "telling stories," the words my relatives used when they ac-cused my sister and me of lying when we were children.

On the other hand, readers of autobiography desire, even demand, that the author tell the truth (remember Lejeune's "autobiographical pact"?). But since the truth can sometimes be boring, we want it embellished and embedded in an interesting narrative. So we read memoir with both requirements simultaneously. Lively discussions ensue when we probe text to see if it fulfills either our need for the truth or our desire for a great story. With our students, we can read memoir texts while pointing our radar to-ward what the memoirist could possibly know and not know (and therefore has con-sciously constructed). For instance, let's consider this tiny passage from *Growing Up Inside the Sanctuary of My Imagination* to try to discern what Nicholasa Mohr remembers and what she likely constructed. In this scene, Mohr writes about her earliest memories, lying in a stroller on a busy, noisy street in New York City, sucking on her bottle and contemplating the clouds.

> Up there, I point . . . I want to be up there, where there is space, where I can breathe, and where it is quiet so I can think and dream.
> I try to explain to my mother, but I can't really form words yet or communicate with speech. I babble forcefully. She stops the stroller and warns me to sit still or I'll get a smack. My mother is afraid I'll fall out and hurt myself. And so I settle back again, suck for more orange juice, cup my hand so that the bright sun does not smart my eyes, and gaze upward, trying to search as far as I can into the vast sky. I continue searching for space, for quiet, for a chance to think and a chance to imagine.
> That was when I first learned that although I could not shut the noise out of my ears I could somehow, like magic, erase the noise from my mind. (1994, 2)

Mohr may certainly remember gazing at clouds from her stroller and feeling trans-fixed by their shifting shapes. But in *retrospect*, she decides that this was the moment she discovered the capacity to tune out unpleasantness with her imagination. The way she describes her baby self, pointing, trying to communicate—surely this is the adult writer re-creating the scene and attributing actions and speech to herself. Also, for a moment, Mohr enters her mother's consciousness, fearing an accident, threatening a smack. True, Mohr might remember a gesture toward slapping, or that may have been her mother's frequent response to her daughter's restlessness. But here, the "I" pretends to be an omniscient narrator, for she could not have known what her mother intended or felt.

I put that bit of text on an overhead projector and asked my students to discuss what they thought Mohr could have remembered or where she was "telling stories." Not surprisingly, they had lots of ideas. Sherrisa wondered how Mohr could be having such "grown-up" thoughts about clouds. "I mean, when I was a baby, I was probably going, like, 'goo-goo-ga-ga'!" The class laughed about that.

But then Marcos disagreed: "No, it could happen! I remember being a baby and thinking that my dog was talking to me and I talked back to him. I mean *now* I know that I didn't know how to say words yet, and I guess dogs can't really talk . . . but I thought we were really saying things back and forth!" In the end, we all agreed that Mohr certainly made this moment fun to read, even if her memory was pretty implausible.

The glory of discussion, if we open up ways of reading to our students that allow for divergent thinking and multiple interpretations, is that we come to new insights that benefit both reading and writing. I begin all reading discussions with an open-ended invitation for students to describe what they notice or what they are thinking about the text they just read. The discussions become dialogues, and my main purpose as facilitator is to help students move around inside the ideas and responses of others and aim for complexity of interpretation rather than simple, pat answers to my questions. The only limits are time and civility as we jostle, argue, ask for evidence, circle back, and pose questions.

Though discussions begin by casting about for ideas, they don't end there. I also bring to class discussions and individual conferences a kind of tool kit of genre knowledge that I wish to teach my students about any genre we study. What follows is a list of large themes related to memoir, with specific questions that get to the heart of autobiographical texts. I use these tools to provoke discussion and open up important genre concepts as I facilitate whole-class conversations or confer with individual readers about their independent texts. Not all these categories and questions pertain to all memoir texts, so I don't treat this as a comprehension checklist to march through, but rather as background information to help me complicate or lift the level of student conversations.

I borrow heavily here from a list in *Reading Autobiography: A Guide for Interpreting Life Narratives*, by Sidonie Smith and Julia Watson (2001). Their audience for that text is college-level English and composition courses, but I love their work and have learned a great deal from all their books about autobiographical writing. Their questions helped inform my *reading* discussions, but I also find their text gave me even more ideas for *writing* memoir. I recommend reading their more extensive, more theoretical list of categories and questions for memoir, especially if you teach high school or adult students or if you wish to stimulate ideas for your own reading and writing of memoir.

Identity, Voice, and Relationship

- What kind of person does the "I" seem to be: competent, shy, aggressive, compliant?
- What roles does the "I" play in this story as it relates to gender, race, class, occupation, status in society?
- How does the "I" who is writing the memoir (older, changed) view him- or herself as a child, or a younger "I"?
- Is the issue of voice or not having a voice a theme of this memoir?
- Is there more than one voice in this memoir? For instance, does the author include other people's perspectives on an event?
- Is this memoir about the influence of an important person or persons? How does the author interpret that influence on his or her life?

Truth

- Do you believe the stories and memories this author is telling you? What helps you believe the author? What makes you doubt the author?
- What kinds of evidence does this author give you to help you believe the memories?
- Are there things the author is clearly not writing about? Why not, do you think?
- Are there people obviously missing from this story? Why do you think so? Do you think they might have witnessed this story differently from the author?

Memory

- What does this author use to help remember his or her life—objects, history, places, photographs, childhood stories, interviews with family members?
- Does this author claim there are things he or she cannot remember?
- Does this author use the concept of memory itself as a theme of the story?

Time

- How does the author organize time in this story? Does this memoir tell a chronological story, or does it skip around in time?
- What effect do the gaps in time have?
- About what age do you think the author was when he or she wrote this story? Does this author tell you inside the story?
- Does the author write the memoir from different periods in his or her life? What effect do the different time periods have?

Structure

- What type of structure does this memoirist use—chronological narrative; confessional; inciting moment; the self set in historical, social, or political context?
- Where does the story begin and end? What effect do those choices have on the story?
- What artifacts are used—documents, letters, photographs, drawings? What effect do these artifacts have on the story?
- Does the text use other kinds of structure or genre, such as poems, plays, myths, or journalism? What does the use of other genres do to the memoir?

Purpose

- What does this author come to know about him- or herself and about the world? What about school, religion or spirituality, relationships with others, dreams, life experience?
- What can the person reading this story learn? Can this memoir change the world?

Besides drawing from the previous list of questions to stimulate discussions about memoir texts, I also present ideas for reading projects that students can attempt independently or in small groups we like to call memoir clubs. Some students decide to use an idea from this list while others invent their own exciting ways to explore and make meaning of the memoirs they are reading. Again, the line between reading and writing blurs when these inquiries into published texts actually give students ideas for things to write about in their own memoirs.

I hope that several memoirs from my suggested reading list at the back of the book, as well as any that I have failed to mention, will make good companions for your

Reading Project Ideas (for independent reading or memoir reading clubs)

- As you read a memoir, prepare a mock interview of the author. What questions do you want to ask this writer? What else do you wish you knew about this story?

- Gather five autobiographical pieces of writing about a favorite subject of yours, such as cats, sports, family, or ethnic stories. Notice the different ways each author has structured his or her story. What has each author included and what has he or she left out? Notice differences in terms of gender, race, class, or place.

- Take an incident from a memoir and try writing it from the point of view of a different person in the story. What does this say about the author's perspective?

- List five people whose life story you have read. For each person, write something that you learned from him or her about a place, time period, culture, race, or gender that you didn't know before.

- Read a short story. Think about whether it is a memoir or not. What makes it a memoir or not a memoir?

- Imagine the notebook entries that may have led to a memoir you have read.

- As you read different published memoirs, what parts or aspects do you find attract you or hold your interest the most?

- Sketch what a scene or place looked like from the narrator's perspective. Sketch the narrator from a different character's perspective.

- Act out a scene from a memoir. Write a reflection about what it felt like to be in that scene. Begin the next day's discussion with evidence that might support that idea.

(A few of these prompts are based on ideas in *Reading Autobiography*, by Sidonie Smith and Julia Watson [2001].)

students as they write. Reading memoir teaches how to write memoir. Without the help of published memoir texts to study and talk about, my writing lessons feel naked and ugly. I need the sounds and shapes of others' words to help me find my own. With books cracked open in the classroom, I feel the comfort of kindred souls beside me as I teach my students how to write about their lives.

Rafting Down Rivers of Memory

Getting Ideas Going in the Memoirist's Notebook

"Floods" is the word they use, but in fact it is not flooding: it is remembering . . . All water has a perfect memory and is forever trying to get back to where it was . . . Writers are like that: remembering where we were, what valley we ran through, what the banks were like, the light that was there and the route back to our original place. It is emotional memory—what the nerves and the skin remember as well as how it appeared. And a rush of imagination is our "flooding."

—TONI MORRISON, "The Site of Memory," *Inventing the Truth*

All water has a perfect memory . . . forever trying to get back to where it was." If only our minds had perfect memory, like water! Toni Morrison believes we *are* like water when we allow our emotional memory to flow. Everyone has experienced suddenly remembering a moment as if it were happening again: the texture and scent of the air that day, the shirt we were wearing, even someone's exact words come washing over us. We also know the feeling of confusion, of total blankness, when we try to reconstruct other times in our lives. Why can we remember some things so clearly and others not at all? My hope is that the ideas and exercises described in this chapter will let loose the floodgates of memory and will help students go to the places where the nerves and skin remember everything. We can get there by reading, thinking, talking, and writing about our lives. Memory begets memory, and all we need to do is follow along behind with our pens and notebooks.

Teachers of writing encourage students to live like a writer, to live wide-awake lives. Like all artists, writers have their radar fine-tuned at all times, noticing the specific colors of things, the particular ways that people speak, and the gestures they make.

Writers notice the touch of breeze on skin and the scent of freshly sawed wood. Nuanced detail feeds the writer's consciousness because that's what she will use to create the world of her story, poem, or play. Readers respond to those tiny details whether they are aware of it or not—they are feelings and situations that the reader can almost hear, see, or smell, and they help the reader more easily enter into the world the writer creates.

When we teach students how to write various genres, we help them think and observe so that their writer's notebooks reflect the habits of mind specific to that genre. So, for instance, a nonfiction writer might have a notebook full of facts, references to other books and articles, observations of the physical world, even sketches of things. A poet's notebook might contain flights of language, visual imagery, and metaphor. A memoir invites different kinds of thinking: it asks the writer to immerse himself in memory and to manipulate it. Unlike other types of nonfiction, the memoirist works with largely unverifiable material that by definition belongs solely to the writer.

One way to begin the memoir genre study is to ask students what they think might go into a memoirist's notebook. I make a chart of students' ideas, which are often quite sophisticated because they have written memoirs, or personal narratives, in former years. I always bring the notebooks I kept while writing my own memoir to show how they contain entries about many of the subjects listed in this chapter. Of course, there are not definitive distinctions between how poets and memoirists think, but I think it helps kids to turn their attention toward this new angle on their observations and their notebook collecting. I find it helpful to mark this new place in the notebook with a colorful sticky note. Younger students might benefit from making brand-new notebooks specific to each genre they study. I have accomplished this casually, by folding ten to twenty pieces of lined or unlined paper in half and stapling them into construction paper covers. I've also bought my students special little notebooks for a dollar apiece at discount stores.

For the remainder of this chapter, I will describe the activity of the second week of the memoir study, the generating phase, through the process of keeping a memoirist's notebook and writing dozens of entries, some of which will evolve into the memoir draft. The work here is to remember, list, make connections, burst forth on the page—not to craft an organized, cohesive draft (that comes later in the process). The notebook allows the writing to be just that—notes toward a larger prose piece.

Activities to Get Ready for Memoir Writing

I call this part of the process *invoking memories*. When I present the goals of the memoir genre study to students, I want and expect them to create curriculum with me. I know that when we get going on this together, my students will invent ways to invoke memories that I have never thought of before. But to help get them going on this project, I teach from bundles of ideas for getting memories flowing that I've been adding to for years. Some of these activities relate directly to stimulating memories while others provide windows into developing a concept of identity. Both will become necessary in the writing of the memoir draft.

Often, I introduce a study of memoir by asking students to imagine why anyone would want to write down memories. Kids suggest that people might write things down so as not to forget them. Or when someone is dying, she might want to be sure her children will know what she did in life. Or when someone moves to another state, he might leave behind his story for his friends and neighbors to remember him by. Sometimes, students have ventured to guess that if something really exciting happened to you, like getting on television, or something terrible happened, "like if you got beat up by a burgler," you would want people to know about that. And once, a young girl imagined that she would want to write down her memories so that she could remember her childhood when she got old.

"All these reasons, and many more, are why people write down their memories," I tell my students. Then I say, "And people also write so that they can know what they think and feel about their lives, and that is what I want to teach you how to do in these next few weeks."

The next four subsections describe some activities I have used especially when working with students who seemed reluctant to write or who didn't know each other well. These get at the writing a bit more indirectly than the activities described later in the chapter, but I ask students to make notes in their writer's notebooks following these activities so the memories that arise won't get lost.

Storytelling

Many teachers begin memoir studies by having their students tell stories about things that have happened in their lives. Teachers might begin with an evocative story of their own: getting their first puppy from the pound; their first day of school (can we really remember that far back!); a time they got hurt on the playground. The effect is contagious; instantly, students raise hands or call out their own "me too" experiences. To keep some semblance of order, I often provide a structure for the storytelling; I've passed around a story rock or a story stick that signals whose turn it is to talk. I've also drawn names from a hat, or tried a Quaker share, in which you speak when the spirit moves you, when you feel that your story adds to or connects with the story that has just been told. Some teachers devote several days to storytelling. They might take notes for their students to help them hold to their stories until writing time. Other teachers invite different kids to tell stories during the minilesson each day or have them talk in pairs or in small groups and then go immediately to write down those memories in their writer's notebooks.

Creating Art

Reflecting on Self-Portraits

The following activities, though not directly related to writing, help many students think about how they literally see themselves as well as generate images from the past. I always follow up art sessions by asking students to reflect on their creations in their writer's notebooks.

The practice of self-portraiture in art is ancient, perhaps as old as cave paintings. I take some time with my class to study how artists portray themselves visually. I collect books and postcard reproductions from museums I visit, and I've also checked out slides of art from libraries. One year, my fifth graders studied some self-portraits by Rembrandt, van Gogh, and Frida Kahlo. We talked about how each artist's self-perception changed dramatically over time. With Rembrandt in particular, we noticed a growing sense of humility, perhaps a touch of sadness behind the eyes, as he got older.

I like to have students produce self-portraits at least two or three times across a school year, and not just as a getting-to-know-you activity at the beginning of the year. I provided a variety of media for my students to use. Some preferred to use watercolor, others used charcoal or Cray-Pas, and still others sculpted their heads out of clay. I provided small mirrors so that they could study themselves—notice the particular shape of their eyes, the fine lines, the expression around the mouth.

Besides straight self-portraits, I have also had students paint metaphors of themselves. For instance, I asked each to think of a visual metaphor to describe him- or herself as a learner and then to write about what that image said about him or her. Rachel painted herself as an open book, wanting to learn from books and also to be seen as someone who had a lot to give. Misha painted himself as a rocket at liftoff. He wrote that he was not "in space" yet, but he was beginning to take off as a learner. Sinnae created multiple panels to reflect the multiple aspects of herself. One part of her was private and dark, like the night; another part was full of question marks; another part had the certainty of a math equation.

Reflecting on Sketches of Memories

Another way students use art as a precursor to memoir writing is to paint a memory. At first they might imagine they need to draw every action of an episode, like a comic book. But paintings can capture aspects of memory in a single image, and that image can feed pages of words in the writer's notebook. The image should be a powerful, meaningful one: a house, an animal, a landscape. I have attempted countless sketches of my beloved Sandia Mountains, part of the Rocky Mountain range that hugs the entire eastern border of Albuquerque, New Mexico. The specific shape of them is etched in my eyes and heart forever, and I can draw them entirely from memory. *Sandia* means "watermelon" in Spanish, so named for the gorgeous shade of crimson they turn at sunset. I bring one of these little watercolor studies to show my students, and then I demonstrate how I let the painting lead me to memories of my childhood by either writing in front of my students or just talking about what I would write about in my notebook.

In Glynnis Quick's class, her seventh graders wrote for a while in their notebooks about a memory, and then they sketched the memory right beside the words. Myrna's sketch of being lost in the Seattle Market (Figure 4–1) gave her a brand-new insight on an old, familiar memory.

She realized, after re-creating this moment visually, that the market stalls loomed so tall above her four-year-old self that it made her feel completely alone and abandoned. "Even though there were lots of people around," she wrote, "I felt alone, abandoned. 'Seattle's Finest Food' seemed to smirk at me as I walked by."

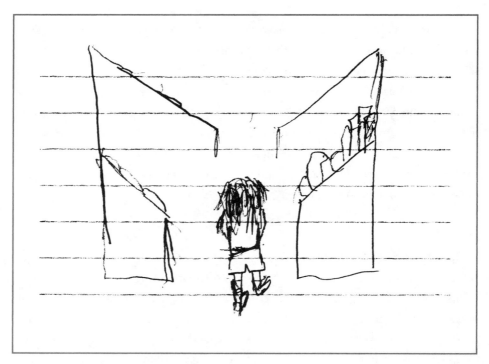

Figure 4–1 *Myrna's Sketch of Being Lost*

Writing from Literature

Responding to Published Memoir

At times, I ask my students to respond in writing to the memoir texts I read aloud as well as the ones they read independently and in small groups. I pose the question, "What does this memoir remind you of from your own life?" or "What does this memoir make you feel, and what from your own life informs that feeling?"

I don't make this a formal, analytical essay assignment. My purpose here is to introduce another way to help my students generate memories in their writer's notebook. If I didn't have time to devote to reading discussions, as mentioned in Chapter 3, I would definitely provide this opportunity to respond to texts.

Responding to Selected Words from Literature

Sometimes memory can be the most obstinate thing. We sit in front of our writer's notebook and command ourselves to remember . . . remember . . . and we draw a blank. That's because memory doesn't operate like a gumball machine, where you put your penny in (I guess now you would need a quarter) and out comes a big blue gumball. Memories come to people most often while they are doing something else: washing the dishes, driving to work, listening to music, walking the dog. Memory comes in split-second images; it hides in the cracks of daily activity, and to find it, sometimes we have to sneak up behind it, pretend we're doing something else, like scrubbing the bathtub, and be ready to write when memory shyly shows its face.

To pretend to scrub the bathtub is not practical in a classroom during writing work-shop, so instead, we can use writing to lure and to coax memory, to come up behind it instead of merely standing there, demanding that it come out from behind the tree. I'm going to describe one of my favorite writing exercises, variations of which I have used for almost thirty years with myself, with adults, and with kids. I use this exercise during a memoir genre study, certainly, but I also use it at the beginning of the year to get students going in their writer's notebooks. Many students find it so successful as a generating type of activity that they use this exercise whenever they feel stuck for things to write about.

1. I read two or three short, evocative poems. I almost always use poems from the magnificent anthologies edited by Paul Janeczko (1990) or any book of poems written or edited by Naomi Shihab Nye (e.g., 1999; 2002).

2. I ask students to write at the top of a blank page in their writer's notebook one or two words or a phrase that "rang out like a bell" from the poems that I just read out loud.

3. I ask students to look at that word or phrase as if it were brand-new to them. What does it make them think about? What memories do they have that connect to that word or phrase? What does that word or phrase mean in their life? (I vary these questions depending on my purpose for the exercise.)

4. I ask students to write for about ten or fifteen minutes, just about that word or phrase and what it means to them.

Notice that this exercise does not require students to analyze or explain the poems I read out loud. I know from experience that several things will happen from this exercise: the poems will evoke strong emotions and memories for almost anyone who hears them. The exercise capitalizes on those aroused emotions. It's almost as if magic words have filled the air from the poems, like little Tinker Bell fairies, and they call to everyone's memories, "Come out, come out, wherever you are!" Sometimes the memory will directly link to the topic or theme of the poem that stimulated it, but often the word or phrase leads the listener down her own, private path of memory, to her personal associations.

Cleo, in Glynnis Quick's seventh-grade class, wrote an entry in response to one of my favorite poems, called "Speech Class," by Jim Daniels (in *The Place My Words Are Looking For*, edited by Paul Janeczko [1990]). The words from the poem, "I . . . wanted you to have my voice," evoked a powerful memory for Cleo of wanting to help her friend who had difficulty saying the letter *r*.

> I remember going to speech class with a friend I've known forever, when I was about six. I remember seeing her mouth trying to make that distinct "Rrr" sound. I could sense the irritation flowing from the specialist, to Irene, to me, circling around and around. Mouthing the words with her, I wanted to put the words in her mouth . . . "birrrd," "chairrr," "rrring." I yearned for that "rrr" to rush into her mouth.

When I conduct this exercise with teachers in workshops, some ask if it would have been better if I had told them *before* I read the poems that they should be listening for words to write about. But I don't want kids trying hard to grab a single word as the poem goes by. The exercise should ease writers into the stream of memory. I tell students to let the words wash over them, "like a warm shower." They should not be already tensed up, working hard to be moved by a word. "Let your mind go where it will today as I read this poem," I say. Tomorrow, a different word might call their memory out to play.

Freewriting

There is nothing like simply opening the vein and putting words down on paper however they come in a freewriting session. Set a timer for no less than ten minutes, no more than twenty. Write whatever comes into your mind about yourself. Don't stop. Don't think. Don't get up. Those are the rules of freewriting.

My friend Michelle Dionne and I gave each other a freewriting assignment over the telephone. "Talk to me about the 1960s," I begged her. (We are the same age.) "Just say words about the 1960s. What was your favorite TV show?" And with that, we were off, laughing hysterically and screaming out names of things—toys (Barbie, Ken, and Skipper, whose long iron-straight mane will always be my ultimate ideal for hair), songs ("Why don't you fill me up, fill me up, buttercup baby . . . "), and TV shows (*Bonanza, Star Trek, The Ed Sullivan Show*). Are some of you getting a "me too" feeling yet?

At first, we just made lists of words; then we took turns choosing one thing on the list to say more about. We suddenly felt rich with possibilities for stories, so we agreed to go write for six hours without getting up and then call each other again. I planted myself in my study, in front of my old IBM Selectric typewriter. I typed without stopping, paying little attention to spelling, grammar, or punctuation.

I began by typing *Bonanza* at the top of the page, but I couldn't tell about watching that show, faithfully, every Sunday night without telling about watching it sitting near my father, which I couldn't write about without telling about how my mother always interrupted our precious time together. As soon as I typed the word *interruption,* I went into a kind of six-hour trance. I just let it all out, kind of like vomiting, honestly, and I ended up having to go to bed and pull the covers over my head for the rest of the weekend. But I had enough material from those twelve single-spaced, typewritten pages to make a memoir and several short stories. I still have those pages, and I consider them one of my turning points as a writer and as an adult.

Freewriting to Connect the Present to the Past

When we begin to live like memoirists in our writer's notebook, all of life can become fuel for the fire of memory. You might ask your students, "What is happening right this minute, right in front of you, that can connect with memory or with an emerging theme or angle of your memoir?" For instance, one day Gracie, the wonderful young woman who helps me cling to my youth by cutting and highlighting my hair, was demonstrating how I could twirl a few pieces of my wet, gel-laden hair around my finger so they would dry into spiral curls. (She's so sweet; if she knew the miniscule amount of attention I give my hair, she would have saved her time.) Watching in the mirror as Gracie wound a strand around her finger, I had an immediate, visceral image of my beloved Nana doing that exact same thing when I was three or four years old. I wrote this in my notebook while I waited under the hair drier:

> I see myself on a bench or maybe the cedar chest, Nana beside me holding a brush and a tall plastic cup of water to wet my hair with. I can smell her breath, sour with smoke from the unfiltered PallMall cigarettes she smoked constantly. I can feel my twitchy impatience with this activity—I had to sit still for as long as it took to create shoulder-length ringlets, a la Shirley Temple, all around my head. Nana pulled a lock of hair straight out from my head, brushed it through with water, twisted it around her tobacco-stained index finger, held it there for a moment, then let go. It dried into a corkscrew curl and remained that way all day, without gel! Did she do this every day? I don't remember. Was this image coming from one single episode, or a collection of times, of sitting exactly like that, day after day? Did we talk? Certainly, if I said anything, Nana listened and laughed. Or listened and expressed her sympathy or her agreement or her amazement. Oh, Nana, what I would give to have your fingers in my hair one more time.

This event happening in real time, right in front of me, could give me enough memory data, reflective questions, quotes, and imagined dialogue to write a whole memoir.

Freewriting from Literature Prompts

I use a small section from Paul Auster's *Invention of Solitude* (1982), a memoir for adults, for this exercise. For a few pages, Auster writes in the third person, beginning each sentence with "He remembers," creating seemingly random memories from when he was a very young boy. I don't know what Auster's writing process for this section was. Maybe he set a timer and said, "For the next hour, I'm just going to write down whatever comes into my consciousness." It's clear that ultimately he crafted this little section, for there is an arc to it—a beginning, a middle, and a definite, powerful ending—but as he wrote it, did he say to himself, "Here, for a couple of pages, I'm just going to repeat these words over and over, like an incantatory chant, to get my memory flowing?" For that is the result, a chantlike song of memory. Here is a sample bit of text:

The Book of Memory. Book Thirteen.

He remembers that he gave himself a new name, John, because all cowboys were named John, and that each time his mother addressed him by his real name he would refuse to answer her . . . He remembers sitting in the bathtub and pretend-

ing that his knees were mountains and that the white soap was the ocean liner
. . . He remembers the day his father gave him a plum and told him to go outside
and ride his tricycle. He remembers that he did not like the taste of the plum and
that he threw it into the gutter and was overcome by a feeling of guilt. . . . He remembers taking apart the family radio one afternoon with a hammer and screw-
driver and explaining to his mother that he had done it as a scientific experiment.
He remembers these were the words he used and that his mother spanked him.
. . . (166–67)

I ask my students to imitate Auster's writing as a freewriting exercise. It's liberating, just writing what seem like random memories, linked only by the repeated phrase, without regard to plot, character, time, structure. The memories often connect quite compellingly, but don't worry if they don't. The point of this exercise is just to jog the memory.

When I read Auster's writing to Diane Glaser's eighth-grade students, their pens scratched wildly against their notebook pages. Some of the students used the words *I remember*, but many did not or decided to drop them after a few items in their list. Here is what Beatrice wrote in response to this exercise:

She remembers her grandfather slowly approaching her, a sweet smile on his face
. . . she remembers his hand turning white because of clutching the cane with so
much force in order to keep himself from collapsing . . . she remembers him slowly
bending his fragile knees, to sit on the old bed, the only furniture in the room . . .
she remembers the old man, now a stranger, gradually become the grandfather
she had seen two years before . . . she remembers seeing his smile never fading
away although his dark face seemed worn out, sullen . . . she remembers her
grandfather hugging his child, her dad . . . she remembers their deep conversations
on how their lives have changed and progressed as they lived half a country away
from each other . . .

As I mentioned earlier, I often ask students to freewrite in response to literature, and Auster's is just one of dozens of authors I read out loud to stimulate memories. In a sense, all notebook writing is freewriting, but most kids benefit from lists of possible topics such as the ones listed in the rest of this chapter to jump-start their memories. The key to keeping this work meaningful and personal for students is to offer the topics as *possibilities* only—as open-ended thinking prompts, not as a list of assigned topics or story starters.

Topics for Invoking Memoir Writing

On the first day of the generating week, and for homework, I usually have students begin a running memory list in their writer's notebook. This is a whirlwind activity, as they brainstorm memories, snatches of conversation, fleeting images at the corners of the eye. Their list might look something like eighth grader Haley's (see Figure 4–2).

After a day of brainstorming their own memory topics, students select items from their list to write entries about in their notebook. The length of entries varies. Some topics run into dead ends while others inspire pages of writing. I don't assign content to write about during workshop time or for homework; rather, I prescribe the amount of time, usually twenty to thirty minutes, that they will write. Or I might assign a number of pages to be filled: for younger students, I ask for one to two pages, and for middle school students, I require around three to four pages each day.

For the remainder of this first week (or longer), I submit items from the following lists as memory prompts for notebook entries. Similar to the word association exercise from psychoanalysis, the point is not to define precisely these original words; instead, the writer associates freely, going wherever her mind takes her, perhaps to a place unrelated to the initial idea. These are not exhaustive nor authoritative lists.

Usually, I select a handful of memory prods from these lists to focus each day's mini-lesson. We keep a running "Memory Topics" chart, to which students contribute also. At any point, students can choose an idea from the chart to write more about in their writer's notebook. They can also continue to add to lists they keep in their notebook throughout the study. Again, it is crucial that these lists be viewed as memory joggers, not assigned topics. Autobiographical writing, by its very nature, is a personal pursuit: a topic that gets memory flowing for one person may not do the same for anyone else.

Impressionistic Memories

The Nature of Memory

All memory is impressionistic; that is, we have a sense, an impression, of how it went, what it felt, looked, and sounded like. But with the exercises in this section, I try to evoke those memories that exist only as shards of an image, snatches of sound, dots of color, as in a Seurat painting. These elusive memories frustrate beginning memoirists because they can't recapture with any precision what happened. But we learn through reading

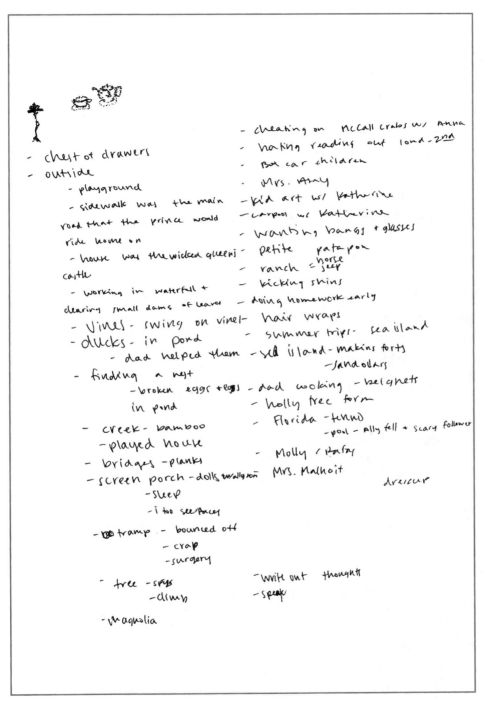

Figure 4–2 *Hattie's Memory Topics List*

memoir that we can make meaning of even the briefest, most transluscent image if we ask when and where it occurred, under what conditions, and especially, why it haunts us.

So many contemporary memoirists write about the nature of memory itself that I include this option on the list of impressionistic memories. Writers wonder on the page about memory's conundrums: Why do some events slip away or get erased completely, though we might even have evidence of their occurrence? And why do other events haunt us, appear in our dreams or nightmares? Why do some memories play like a movie in our minds and others consist only of a word we heard or a fragment in time?

At the very least, contemporary memoirsts indicate their awareness of memory's tricks with language like "I think, but I'm not sure . . . "; "Maybe what she said was . . . "; and "As far as I can remember. . . ." When writers use this equivocating and qualifying language, we trust them later when they claim to remember something very well.

When I put an excerpt of a book-length memoir on the overhead projector, I ask students to mark places they see where the writer talks about memory. Then I invite them to play with this kind of language in their notebook entries and later in their memoir drafts. Here, fifth grader Sinnae writes about a very early moment, using language to navigate what is clear in memory and what feels murky. I underline the places she uses language to reveal memory's lapses and inadequacies.

one wind

I can still smell the wind and I can taste it. It tastes like death, but the sweet death of Autumn. <u>Not that I'm sure</u> it was Autumn, but there is a special taste to Autumn wind that very often hints itself in other seasons, perhaps to let you know that he's coming. I can see the chickenwire fence in front of me. It's silver and cold with the wind. On the grey playground floor there's a tile. <u>I think I found it then</u>. And then my private little film here ends, and time runs different now. Fast. And it stings.

I travel back again, and I'm outside, and the wind is whipping through my hair and my ears. The sun is going down, <u>I think</u>. <u>I'm not sure</u> what time it is. <u>I can't tell</u> how old I was. <u>It's so hard to remember</u>, but now <u>I'm almost sure</u> the sun was not very high, almost down. And darkness tinged the sky, <u>surely, if it was</u> near dusk.

Preverbal Memories

Before you even had the language to describe them, what images can you conjure up? If we relax, get very quiet, and go deep inside our earliest memories, we can find an amazing web of possibilities. These can be some of our most profound memories, yet we rarely give them credit because we haven't yet pillowed them in meaning or imagined the story around them.

I tell my students about memories I have from when I was a baby or a toddler, before I could talk and before I understood what was happening to me. I show them how I can, in a sense, invent a story about the memories that holds the kernel of truth inside it, even if the surrounding details are not true.

Another option for writing about these nebulous images—colors, sounds, body memories (whether painful or pleasurable), a sense of warmth, light or darkness—is simply to list them, almost as a poem, and to question what the story was, based on some likely answers:

> A color—was it the sky? No, we hardly ever left the house before I was old enough to walk. Was it my bedroom wall? A sound—my own crying maybe? The washing machine? A cat's purr? Mom told me the cat slept with me in my crib.

The First Memory

Freud claimed that a person's first memory is an extremely important one simply because we remember it. Out of the millions of seconds we lived, when everything was unknown and being discovered by our young mind and body, this memory rises above it all to lodge in our consciousness. So there must be some important meaning hiding there, and uncovering it can fill pages in the notebook. Don't worry, this is not a test! No one can refute that this is officially the first memory. It is the best we can remember, right now, during this exercise. Five years from now, thirty years from now, we may uncover an entirely different first memory.

In one of her memoirs, "A Sketch of the Past," Virginia Woolf writes for several pages about what she feels must be her first memory, when she was tiny:

> This was of red and purple flowers on a black ground—my mother's dress; and she was sitting either in a train or in an omnibus, and I was on her lap. I therefore saw the flowers she was wearing very close; and can still see purple and red and blue, I think, against the black; they must have been anemones, I suppose. (1976, 64)

Woolf amends this with another "first" memory:

> It is of hearing the waves breaking, one, two, one, two, and sending a splash of water over the beach; and then breaking one, two, one, two, behind a yellow blind. (1976, 64)

Notice that both memories are sensual, merely flashes of color and sound. She goes on in this essay to say that these "moments of being" left her "feeling the purest ecstasy"—perhaps shaping her artistic genius.

I ask questions to help students recall their first memory:

- What is your first memory of being in public? Where were you? How did you respond to it?
- What is your first memory of being completely alone, in private? Where were you? How did you respond to that?

Landmark Memories

First Moment of Conscious Awareness

The Yup'ik people of southwestern Alaska call the moment when a person becomes aware of him- or herself existing on the earth *ellangellemni*—when memories take shape and the world begins to make an impression. This is a sacred moment, I believe, for to realize that one has a self apart and separate from anyone or anything else marks the birth of choice, responsibility, will, and compassion.

When I introduce this idea to students, I also read this quote by Annie Dillard, talking about a large theme of her memoir, *An American Childhood:*

> It's about waking up. A child wakes up over and over again, and notices that she's living. She dreams along, loving the exhuberant life of the senses, in love with beauty and power, oblivious of herself—and then suddenly, bingo, she wakes up and feels herself alive. She notices her own awareness. And she notices that she is set down here, mysteriously, in a going world. (Zinsser 1987, 56)

Here, fifth grader Sinnae writes about becoming aware of a separate physical and conscious self:

I remember sand. It was at Coney Island, under our feet as we sat on the beach. It was my first sand. I think I was sitting by the fence, or on it. I felt sand under my feet and it was warm. Those were things outside of me and not in me.

I tend to remember myself in third person. In many of my memories, I am looking at a girl named Sinnae. I wonder, should I analyze myself that way too? Not as "myself" but as another fellow human being? And how would I change her?

Stand-Out Moments

The smallest moments in life are often what live on as memory. For some people, the moments of feeling happy may be so few and far between that they are remarkable, like small green islands in oceans of blue. For others, thankfully, the opposite is true, and so the sad moments or instances of feeling genuine fear stand out amid an otherwise contented life. These stand-out moments can become one way of organizing the story we tell about ourselves. We might ask students, in this initial generating stage, to answer a question raised by Robert Coles: What are the moments in your life that you remember as important, as happy or sad? (1989, 11)

It's also powerful to name one certain day, one certain event as the *inciting moment,* when the exact confluence of persons, times, and events combined and combusted into a moment that changed everything. The moment may be literally that—a space of time from seconds to minutes to an hour. But it may also be one notch on a long time line of events. The time it occupied might be weeks or even months, but from the long view looking back, it appears to be a moment in time.

In "Everything Will Be Okay," James Howe (1996) ends the memoir as if the events he's written about led to one moment that made him sit down and decide what kind of man he was going to be: "I feel alone and frightened. And then all of a sudden I don't feel any of those things. All of a sudden it's as if Paul has already left and I am on my own and I know some things so clearly that I will never have to ask an older brother to help me figure them out" (48). Howe probably didn't think these exact thoughts when this event actually took place, at age ten, but only in looking back through his adult lens as he crafted the story. He writes about that process in the comments section: "In time, I came to understand that the reason for writing this story had less to do with the kitten and more to do with my brothers and myself" (49).

In a person's life, the moment that seems to define a before and an after might be a serious illness, the birth or death of a loved one, a major move to a new place, discovering a talent or an occupation, changing careers, or starting or ending a relationship. In the short span of our students' lives, almost any experience can seem to define a shift in how life feels, since everything is full of discovery. Defining moments for students might include some of the following:

- birth of a sibling
- getting a pet
- learning how to do something
- discovering something you do well
- winning or losing a contest
- moving to a new country, neighborhood, or school
- meeting a best friend
- falling in love; a first kiss
- a special birthday, holiday, or vacation
- doing something that took a lot of courage
- a major illness or accident
- being lost
- developing physically in adolescence
- divorce
- death of a loved one

The key to helping students construct meaningful notebook entries that then lead to meaningful memoir drafts is to allow them to choose their own landmark moments. Adults can easily imagine that escaping an oppressive regime to come to the United States, or experiencing divorce, changed everything for a child from then on. But for a memoirist, the point is to make his own meaning of a life. There is not a right answer to what stands apart from the daily flotsam and jetsam of life as pertinent and full of meaning; in most cases, defining moments are simply what the writer construes them to be at the time of writing. We might look back from where we stand right now and say, "I knew when he said good-bye that I would never find another love like that one." Well, most certainly we were *not* thinking that at the time; it just seems now, as years have passed, that it was true. We usually aren't even aware, as we are living inside events, as they unfold before us, that they are defining moments. It is the act of reflecting on a life, with the passing of time and the wisdom and maturity gained from experience, that makes a moment appear life-changing.

We can help students search for stand-out moments by asking questions that will frame their investigation: Can you point to a time in your life that your worldview shifted?

Andrea Lowenkopf, a friend and former colleague of mine at Teachers College Reading and Writing Project, used to ask that question at parties and at happy hour gatherings over margaritas. She said it was a sure conversation starter, a way to get people to tell the juiciest, most interesting stories of their lives. She coached us to respond with the first thing that came to mind, not to belabor the question, and said there could be different answers on different occasions of reflection.

When she asked me, I immediately thought about my freshman year in college, when I took a women's study course. The year was 1976, and courses devoted to the history and issues of women and minorities were just beginning to hit campuses across the nation. The reading we did in that class opened windows into a world I did not know existed. We read Mary Daly's *Beyond God the Father* (1973), in which she analyzes the Bible and the Christian Church critically, from a feminist point of view. I had just come from eighteen years of living in a family whose practices and values reflected strict adherance to the teachings of the Lutheran Church, and here, finally, I found critical explanations for why certain doctrines had felt unfair and repressive to me, ever since I was six years old. Still, my weekly activities and my identity were wrapped up in the routines of the church, and I wasn't sure who I was or how to act outside of my home and church.

We had to keep a journal during the women's studies course, and when I look at that little notebook now, it's like looking at a mind on a collision course with madness. My handwriting, once so round and flowing, the writing of a carefree high school girl, got smaller, more cramped, and eventually turned into an indecipherable chicken scratch. My worldview—where the answers were contained in one book of absolute truth—was suddenly up for interpretation. This course marked the beginning of my intellectual life.

It might seem odd to ask a twelve-year-old when his worldview shifted, but asking kids to think about a moment that changed their life can foster a habit of interpreting. Students have written thoughtfully in response to Andrea's question when I've phrased it in the following ways:

- Can you point to a time in your life that you figured out something that you didn't know before? A feeling of some truth being revealed?

- Can you point to a time in your life when you thought a certain way and then something or someone changed your thinking?

Here's what Ilana, a fifth grader, wrote:

I remember when I was a small girl. I used to sit on my grandmother's knee and she would bounce me up and down like a horsey. But I always had to be careful not to sit on the butterfly knee. I would be about to sit and she would warn, "Ah, ah, ah! Don't sit on the pretty butterfly, you'll squish her." And I would beg to see her butterfly until she finally gave in. She would roll up her skirt to just below the knee and there it was. She would show it off like a tattoo or a prize or maybe I was the one who turned into those things. It didn't really look like a butterfly, but I assume she called it that so as not to scare me. I then used what she told me and my little girl imagination together to create a living, breathing creature that lived below her knee.

It was not until much later that I realized our Butterfly was a mass of veins, arteries, and blood vessels. I realized it wasn't the butterfly she had been protecting but her fragile leg that could easily be damaged. But to me it will always be her butterfly.

People and Groups

Family Stories About You

"You were such a happy baby, always smiling and saying 'hi-lo' to complete strangers."

"You used to ask to be lifted up by saying 'lift you, lift you' instead of 'lift *me*.' You always said things in the cutest ways. You made us all laugh."

"One day, when you were only three and a half, you decided you were old enough to go to school like your brothers, and you just walked out the door behind them! No one even noticed you were gone until you were two blocks away!"

Much of our self-identity is formed by the language and stories that our most intimate relations use to describe us. Often, it's hard to separate our personal memories from stories we've been told about ourselves. I ask students to interview family members to get their memories and impressions of them. In the memoir, they can choose to tell these stories as if they actually remember them, or they can say something like, "My mother always told me I said 'hi-lo' to strangers. Maybe she's right. I have no memory of doing that at all."

Another alternative to writing family stories about individual students is writing about community and cultural stories. When I was growing up in New Mexico, a traditional tale from Mexico affected me deeply and still haunts me today. Called "*La Llorona*" (weeping woman), it is the story of a woman who drowned her children (several versions ascribe different reasons for committing this horrible crime) and has been haunting the Rio Grande as a ghost, calling out for her lost children ever since. This was not a story that my Anglo family repeated, but Latino culture was thick in my school and in the whole city, so I must have heard it outside my home. I incorporated this tale into my memoir, remembering how moved I was when I was little by the woman's grief over losing her children, and how I used to make myself morose and hysterical wondering if my own mother would be sad if I died.

When I was telling my fifth graders in Texas about this story, many of them gasped and said, "I know that story, I know that story!" Turns out *La Llorona* haunts Austin's rivers and creeks as well! We spent the next two days telling various versions of "*La Llorona*" and our memories of hearing it, and being scared out of our pants about it, when we were little.

Selected People

Countless contemporary memoirs revolve around the author's relationship with, usually, a parent or guardian, but also grandparents, siblings, friends, teachers, lovers and spouses, even beloved pets. In these memoirs, the relationship *is* the story; that is, the memoir documents the history of the interactions between the two people and how those interactions affected and influenced the memoirist.

In *Bourgeois Blues*, Jake Lamar explores this kind of self-identity, inseparable from his father's: "These were the times when I felt abstracted from myself, when the past became present and I imagined I could hear my father's voice inside my head; when I wondered how his mind had shaped my mind, where my father's way of thinking ended and my own way began" (1991, 12).

Young people are especially prone to write about special relationships in their lives because this is the center of their world. Hardly anything exists outside of home, family, and neighbors, except school, which hardly seems to figure at all in comparison.

Thankfully, for most, the stories about family are happy, safe, and full of fun. We love to read those memoirs, the ones that make us feel that all is right with the world. Unfortunately, for others, family does not feel safe and happy, and writing about that can sometimes pose problems for students and teachers.

When I propose to students that they can write about an important person in their life as one way to generate memoir entries, I tread carefully. On one hand, I want to be honest with children, to let them know that relationships are complicated, and some are not what we expect or desire them to be. On the other hand, I think we must respect students' desires to protect their families or themselves by not looking to find difficulty. Most children have no need to explore any dark sides of their relationships to their parents. Others clearly abandon that prospect as too emotionally draining. Still, there are kids who have felt liberated by exploring complicated social interactions, possibly as a result of writing about that topic openly and honestly and getting the support of their teacher and peers in the process. Even if students decide they do not want to unveil difficult relationships directly, they learn that they can purposely craft the writing to *hint* at something, mysteriously *allude* to something, and thereby create interesting tensions that ring true to most readers, much more so than writing that sounds like the empty sentiments in greeting cards.

That last point becomes even more crucial when students write about *good* and *strong* intimate relationships. When children write that they love their dad and mom, the reader passes right over those statements as he might rush past descriptions of the weather; they hold no meaning for the reader because the *character* of the mom or dad has not been drawn. The words are empty without the voice of the parents, the most precise details that make one dad different from another dad. I teach children how to do this by telling them about how actors sometimes prepare for their characters by inventing little physical tics—a habit of clearing their throat when they have something difficult to say or a tendency to wear their glasses pushed up on their head—to bring the character alive. In the same way, writers can watch and listen closely to the tiniest gestures and movements or to the oft-repeated phrases, the special family language that they share ("*Quien es mijo favorito?*"; "Please pass the salt and please pass the peas. Please pass the butter knife and don't kick my knees!"; "You're my plum pudding, my sweet pumpkin pie . . . ") to fill out a portrait of the person they are writing about.

In the generating stage, kids often write about persons as strict biography or character portraits. So in minilessons and conferences, I ask kids, "Why this person?" much as I would ask, "Why this memory?" (See Figure 4–5 at the end of this chapter for a reproducible worksheet that asks students to think deeply about a person who is important to them. At times, I have given this sheet as a homework assignment in the generating phase of a memoir genre study. I have also substituted the words *object* and *place* for person, and adjusted the three questions accordingly.) The point of writing in depth about another person in one's autobiography is to explore what influence, positive or otherwise, that person had on one's life (see Figure 4–3). I might present a list of questions to help students think and write about a person in powerfully intimate ways:

- How does this person move through life—in a frenzy of activity? Hesitantly? Walking almost on his toes? Sitting straight upright as if there is a wall right behind her?
- What are some words or phrases that this person repeats over and over? Why do you think he or she says those particular things often?
- If you could characterize this person's way of dressing, what would you call it: all business; whatever T-shirt was next in the pile of clean clothes; a flair for the dramatic; homemade hippie clothes; always pale pastels?
- Write a scene or two in which you and this person talk about something. Try to capture the rhythms of his or her speech, the words he or she would most likely say in that type of discussion.
- If you live with this person, spy on him or her with your notebook in hand. Notice little details such as how your dad always crosses his legs at the knee, not with an ankle up on his thigh like other guys seem to, or how your mom chews the very ends of her hair when she's reading the newspaper at night. You remember when she hugged you before bed, you could feel a bit of wetness on your cheek that must have come from those strands of hair.
- Write about your very first memory of this person, even if it's simply a feeling or a splash of color.
- Write about what this person means to your life. How do you think you have been shaped by this person? How are you similar to this person and how are you different?

Estimada MaMa,
Yo me requerdo cuando yo era bebé
y tu te ibas ha la cocina. Yo empesaba
a llorar porque yo no te quise dejar.
Yo tambien me requerdo cuando yo estaba
parado en la silleta, y me calli en
el suelo y usted se epanto y me llevaste
afuera.
Tambien me requerdo cuando yo estaba
llorando, mucho y luego usted se enaio
y me dejo en el sofa y yo lloré más y
más hasta que me viniste a lebantar.
Ahora que ya soy un niño grande,
deseo que yo todavia sea un bebé.

TRANSLATION:

Dear Mama,

I remember when I was a baby, and you were going to the kitchen. I started to cry because I didn't want to let you. I also remember when I was standing on the highchair and I fell and you got scared and you took me outside.

   I also remember when I was crying a lot and later you got angry and left me on the sofa and I cried more and more until you came to pick me up.

   Now that I'm big, I wish that I were still a baby.

Figure 4–3 *Francisco's Writing About an Important Person*

Religion

Two of the ten stories in the first volume of *When I Was Your Age* (Ehrlich 1996) take place at the church, a testament to its power (with both positive and negative effects) in many people's lives. In "Taking a Dare," Nicholasa Mohr writes about daring to take her first Holy Communion after eating breakfast (supposedly a no-no) and without having gone to confession first to "tell the priest all the bad things you done."

Walter Dean Myers writes in "Reverend Abbott and Those Bloodshot Eyes" about being in a group of teenagers that played a mean trick on a visiting minister who had tried to put an end to their dance parties. Both Mohr and Myers relate in their comments afterward that religion was a strong, positive presence in their lives, but their stories record recognizable rebellious feelings against the strict rules of the church.

Ethnicity and Culture

For many memoirists, their family's ethnicity and culture are sources of great pride as well as sites of rich stories. Nicholasa Mohr devotes a whole chapter of her memoir to a detailed portrait of Christmas in her home in New York City, which was celebrated in the "traditional Puerto Rican manner." She believes that those holidays established her cultural pride and also exposed her to poetry and storytelling in experiences that instilled a love of the "beauty and power of language" (1994, 45).

Other memoirists write about feeling disconnected from their ethnic origins or about being treated cruelly or unfairly because of their ethnicity. In *The Lost Garden*, Laurence Yep names both of those issues and honestly reveals the difficulty he had accepting the "Chinese-ness" of his grandmother. "At a time when so many children are now proud of their ethnic heritages, I'm ashamed to say that when I was a child, I didn't want to be Chinese. It took me years to realize that I was Chinese whether I wanted to be or not. . . . It's something that is a part of me from the deepest levels of my soul to my most common, everyday actions. For one thing, my wife, Joanne, tells me that my family and I speak to one another in a different rhythm than what we use outside the home, our voices rising and falling though we are speaking English" (1991, 43).

The idea of culture can mean something larger than ethnicity, since people from many different ethnic groups participate in the same mass culture. Culture includes ways of talking, interacting, and dressing. It encompasses the tastes, mores, and values held by people who share common space, common goals, or some reason to be living together. In other words, prisons, churches, temples and mosques, neighborhoods, clubs and societies, even schools have a culture, and it can be described best by the people living inside of it.

One surefire way of nailing a particular time and place in history is to describe its cultural artifacts, including TV shows, childhood games (marbles, kick the can, hide and seek, war, hopscotch), movies, ads, fashion and diet trends, toys, video games, and song titles. Doing this, we can name a different set of categories than Chinese or African American or Anglo. Our stories can become related to the ideas of twenty-first century, middle class, the television generation, and so on.

Politics, Parties, Elections, Candidates

Whom my parents voted for was always kept secret. "That's why we vote in a booth," my mother said, "to keep it a secret." So for years, I thought politics was one of those taboo, and therefore immensely intriguing, subjects, like sex. When I became a teacher, I discovered that many of my students actually accompanied their parents to the voting booths, and their parents talked about whom they were voting for, how, and why! Either way—a taboo subject or a topic for dinner table conversations—politics might provide a link to some students' memories.

Places

Landscapes

I grew up in New Mexico, where the landscape of mountains and desert, sand and rock, the clean smell of pine trees, and the crystal quality of the light all formed my writer's soul. Other people have forests in their soul, or ocean shores, or gentle streams. Still others have skylines and buses and streetlamps. The landscape outside us when we were little lives inside us too, like a map of the heart, and we can return to it in our writing to find memories and comfort. Young people may not notice while living inside it that the landscape is forming their life's map. Ask them to take some time to look, listen, feel the place they live in—to see if they can name some of its pleasures.

Students who have moved to the United States from other countries might find gold mines when writing about their homelands. In *The Land I Lost*, Huynh Quang Nhuong (1982) describes the lush landscape and creatures of his Vietnam boyhood with such a keen sense of wild danger, and delight, that he brings that country alive for adults and children alike. A number of memoirs explore topics related to emigrating, from grieving over the lost country and feeling lonely in the new one (*New Kids in Town: Oral Histories of Immigrant Teens,* by Janet Bode [1989]); to feeling split between countries and cultures, belonging wholly to neither one (*Homesick,* by Jean Fritz [1985]); to struggling to learn a new language and new customs; to finding safe harbor in the United States. I keep a file of passages excerpted from adult memoirs on these topics to give more ideas and inspiration to students who want to write about their native country. Here, for example, is a paragraph from *My Invented Country,* Isabel Allende's gorgeous memoir of her homeland, Chile, which resonates with many students who have recently immigrated:

> I often ask myself what exactly *nostalgia* is. In my case, it's not so much wanting to live in Chile as it is the desire to recapture the certainty I feel there. That's my home ground. Each country has its customs, it manias, it complexes. I know the idiosyncrasies of mine like the palm of my hand; nothing surprises me, I can anticipate others' reactions, I understand what gestures mean, silences, formulas of courtesy, ambiguous responses. Only there do I feel comfortable socially—despite the fact I rarely behave as I'm expected to—because there I know how to behave and my good manners rarely fail me. (2004, 132)

If the category of landscape feels too huge or vague to students, they might focus on smaller terrains, such as a neighborhood or block, even a certain house. A former student of mine, named "September," wrote a memoir in eighth grade, which she later published in the community newsletter, about the large New York City apartment building she had lived in her entire life. She brings this world of hers alive with the details she remembers, and she ends:

> Manhattan Plaza is more than a home to me. Manhattan Plaza is a place where I can be myself. A place I will never forget, and hopefully never leave. A place where I know almost everyone and almost everyone knows me! Where "everybody knows your name," because, as we all know, we see each other in the elevator so often! A place I like to call "my forever home." And when I come home after a tiring day of school, I'm still smiling because I know that at the end of the day I'll be living in a place that I love, a place that loves me. Thanks, Manhattan Plaza.

Secret or Private Places

I almost always invite my students to write about this topic at some point in their writer's notebook (sometimes at the beginning of the school year, when we are just getting to know each other and filling our notebooks with things that matter in our lives). Every kid has a place he or she goes to be alone. Even in New York City, where some of my students lived in the tiniest apartments and shared bedrooms with several family members, there would be some perceived secret hiding place that my students wrote about. For some, it was the fire escape attached to the back of their building; for one, it was her bathtub!

In *Writing Toward Home*, Georgia Heard (1995) calls the place where one feels safe, powerfully at home, *Querencia*. From the Spanish verb *querer* (to want), querencia describes a "wanting" place. For some kids this might be their kitchen table or a tree in the backyard. It might be a type of geography that resonates—the ocean, a crowded city street, the banks of a river.

In "Bus Problems," Howard Norman (1999) calls the bookmobile where he worked as an assistant when he was a little boy a "secure and peaceful place." It was an old school bus, lined with books and a card catalog, where he could indulge his passion for reading about the Arctic. In "Pegasus for a Summer," Michael Rosen (1999) tells us that he finds this safe feeling on the back of a horse named Sparky. "I'd climb in the saddle, and instantly, other riders, other horses in the ring, whatever it was I didn't want to do after camp or beginning in September at junior high—it all ceased to exist, along with the rest of my life on the ground" (111).

For other writers, it might be more of a metaphorical place, like the places a book can take them or the feeling they get from running. Georgia Heard talks about writing itself being her querencia and says that when she falls away from writing, she feels "cranky" and less at home with herself.

The Material World

Certain Photographs

I ask students to bring to school a picture or two of themselves when they were younger. I make a big production about the pictures being candid photographs, not posed school or studio portraits. The photographs can have other people in them too, but they should be relatives or close friends that are part of the story of the picture. I ask them to bring a picture that has rich stories behind it or that evokes strong feelings when they look at it. Lois Lowry shaped her entire memoir, *Looking Back: A Book of Memories* (1998), around remarkably beautiful photographs of herself and her family. Her writing demonstrates how to look behind the image to tell stories, and it makes a great model for students who might want to make a whole book about photographs.

I have also shown kids how to write about a photograph using a picture of myself and then thinking and writing about it right in front of them. I think kids love seeing pictures of their teachers and hearing about what we were thinking and feeling when we were their age (see Figure 4–4).

> Sigrid was the daughter of my parents' Czechoslovakian friends. Her older sister, Hege, and my big sister, Pat, used to tease me. I was the little four-year-old runt of the bunch. Sigrid was nice to me, so I loved her. Sigrid's father took this picture of her helping me get a drink. It was a day we went to Big Sur, both families, for a picnic on the beach. Later that day, I have a memory of my sister and the other

Figure 4–4 *Picture of Author (r), Age Four*

two girls carrying me into a dark, underwater cave inside a giant rock outcropping that jutted out from the shore. I remember screaming and crying, believing I was going to drown right there. I remember the icy salt water burning my nose and throat and stinging my eyes. But that happened later. In this picture, I was still safe. Still in love with the feeling of cold water rushing down my throat.

If students are having difficulty writing about their photographs, I might propose the following questions to get them thinking in reflective and generative ways. These questions will not apply to all students, so they should feel free to revise and improvise.

- Describe the place where this photograph was taken.
- Describe the other people in the photograph and their relationship to you.
- What happened right before this picture was taken?
- What happened right after this picture was taken?
- Describe how this photograph fits into some pattern in your life, or how this photograph is a shocking departure from some pattern in your life.
- What surprises you about this picture, now that you really look at it?
- Who is missing from this picture? What can't we see in the picture?
- If that little person who is you in the picture could talk, what would he or she be saying?

Here is another activity to try with photographs. Students might want to bring in five or six photographs that seem to characterize their family fairly well. They can lay the photos out on the table in front of them and then, in their writer's notebook, write an entry about the story that those photographs tell. For example, a student might bring in a picture of his extended family around the kitchen table, where his aunts, cousins, and grandfather often gather to talk. And then perhaps he has four pictures of each of the children when they were babies to show that his family loves babies. Then he might also have two or three pictures of picnics, parties, and holidays. He might write that his family photo gallery shows a large, loving, and celebratory family, just as he thinks of them.

Certain Objects

Everyone has objects at home that hold stories inside them. Collections of rocks, shells, and sand from different beaches we've been to. Hard-earned medals and trophies. Jewelry that belonged to a beloved grandmother or great-aunt. Works of art that we are proud of making. Even things we no longer own, like our first car or bicycle, can evoke rich memories. There is the story of where the object came from and the story of what it means to us. Beyond that, there are stories of who owned them before we did and what they meant to those original owners as well. Christopher Bollas calls these "pregnant objects" (1992, 56), ripe with meaning, and he says these objects are like ghosts living within us, beside us, conjured by a name.

Randy has a precious object, a little bust carved out of wood by his beloved grandfather, Papa. It sits in a place of honor on our shelf. He wrote about it:

> Papa dropped out of school in the ninth grade and became a man who made things. My earliest memory of something he made is a small pine bust of himself he brought home from work one day when I was about three, a bust he carved during breaks at the shop where he was a welder. I still have it, and I'm looking at it now. I remember him striding into the house and presenting it to Mammaw, and both of them laughing. To me, it does look like him, maybe only because this object helped form my image of him. I remember being amazed that someone could *make* something that *looked like himself*. It's an important piece from my life's museum because it says so much about one of the central issues of my life: the making of things from the chaos of experience, a sense of craft, making something that looks like myself. These are the reasons I write. (1995, 159)

Randy's writing perfectly illustrates how memoirists take the material of memory and write to discover meaning in it. In this seemingly small item, Randy finds the birthplace of his life's work: the reasons he writes.

When I teach a memoir unit of study, I ask students to bring a special object or two to school, ones that, as in the photographs exercise, they know they can write a lot about. If the object is too large to carry, I ask them to take a photograph or draw a picture of it. Occasionally, students have even written about objects they lost, and again, drawing a picture of it helped. I also bring an object of my own to class, along with the writing I have done about it. Or I might use examples from former students to demonstrate, such as this notebook entry about a favorite stuffed animal. Written by ten-year-old Ivan, this honest piece about an object almost every person feels sentimental about opens the door for adolescent kids to write about it without embarrassment.

> I have had my little brown bear for years, ever since I was born. I like him because of his wise orange eyes. And the little red ribbon around his neck. I also like him because he was my father's toy when he was a child.

I remember the fun naps we had together. And I remember the day my dog ripped him apart, I cried. I begged my mom to sew him back together. I couldn't stand the thought of him being lost in such a stupid way. My mom sewed him back together, but his eyes were a little screwed up.

I also like him because he was so small and I could bring him everywhere. He was my favorite toy for a long time. I hope I can pass him on to my children. So they will have as much fun as I did.

In *Looking Back,* Lois Lowry writes about a photograph of herself as a little girl, standing in a man's plaid hunting shirt. I use this piece to show children how to write not only about the object itself but about what it *means* to them. Lowry accomplishes that by setting her story inside an historical context, the poignancy of war and how it interrupts (and often severs) relationships and families.

1946

I was nine years old. It was a man's woolen hunting shirt. I had seen it in a store window, its rainbow colors so appealing that I went again and again to stand looking through the large windowpane.

The war had recently ended, and my father, home on leave before he had to return to occupied Japan, probably saw the purchase as a way of endearing himself to a daughter who was a virtual stranger to him.

If so, it worked. I remember still the overwhelming surge of love I felt for my father when he took me by the hand, entered Kronenburg's Men's Store, and watched smiling while I tried the shirt on. Even the smallest size hung below my knees.

I wore it for years. I loved that shirt. I loved my father for buying it for me. I loved the entire world for being the kind of world where such a shirt, and such a father, existed. (1998, 81)

Again, if students have difficulty generating memories and stories from objects on their own, I propose a set of questions to get them reflecting on what an object means to them.

- Describe the object precisely. What is it made of? What does it feel like? How is it the same or different from other objects like it?
- Describe who gave this object to you and what your relationship was or is.
- Tell the story of the moment you acquired this object.

- What was your life like before you had the object?
- How did your life change after getting this object?
- What would happen if you ever lost this object?
- What does this object say about you? I am the kind of person who . . . (loves anything blue; likes things that are imperfect; values homemade gifts over storebought ones; wants the latest video game or technological gadget).

Certain Smells

Smells have the power to transport us instantly, almost violently, back in time. Babies and young children live inside scent; besides touch, it's their closest connection to the material world. Some fragrances recall our loveliest memories, and we connect them to happy times and people we loved in childhood. The smells of different foods can conjure up those warm, safe feelings, or else memories of illness or powerful disgust.

Students can list some memory-laden smells and then choose one at a time to write about for several minutes. Some scents that I could write meaningfully about are hot milk; Shalimar perfume (what my Nana always wore—I hated the scent but loved her unconditionally); mountain pine trees; the warm, fresh scent of cat fur; amonia and bleach.

Certain Melodies or Song Lyrics

Like scents, song lyrics that bring their melody quickly to mind can rocket us to the past faster than the speed of light. When you get the lyric and tune inside your head, you suddenly remember where you were, whom you were with, that it was a sultry summer night or a bleak, rainy November day. You can hear your mother calling you in, but you didn't want to come; you were having too much fun dancing with your best friend to the song "Crimson and Clover." You took turns shining a flashlight, like a spotlight, on each other, practicing grinding your hips just so.

Students have written powerful memoir entries about lullabies sung by parents and grandparents; songs and nursery rhymes they learned as toddlers, like "Old MacDonald Had a Farm" and "Las Mañanitas"; songs from TV shows and movies; songs from church or temple; and songs in their first language that conjure up emotional memoires of family and homeland.

When my fourth-grade class joined with a kindergarten class to perform a concert for each other one year, Isabella let the music and the experience take her on a journey in her memory:

> Today when we sang to the kindergarden I felt something inside me like a little butterfly. I felt shy when I sang. Then when the little kids sang to me it made me remember being their age. I remember we sang songs in Spanish and English. I think it was Silent Night, Noche de Paz. I was shy back then too. Even more because the other kids were so big and old! But the beautiful sounds of music always make me feel so good inside. Like a love poem inside or like I might start crying.

When a Student Says, "I Can't Remember Anything"

Finally, I know that most teachers wonder what they might do for a student who says she has no memories or can't remember the details of what she is attempting to write about. I have several ideas for how to address this issue:

1. *Trust in the process.* If we fill our classrooms with model texts, with conversations and storytelling, and with at least one week of generating activities such as the ones I've described in this chapter, most, if not all, students will have something to write about. The power of a safe, stimulating writing community is usually enough to open up even the most recalcitrant writers.

2. *Confer.* In writing conferences, we will be able to talk more personally with individual students to find out what their particular barriers are to writing. For some, the blocks might be emotional; they may be avoiding writing about intense feelings of inferiority or fearful of disclosing difficult home issues. For these students, a gentle reminder that they need not write about anything that feels unsafe will be enough to get them started. I find that kids who feel blocked are often relieved to know they might write about something that happened in school, or about their weekly excursions to the mall with friends, as long as they put themselves—what they were thinking about, what felt important, and how it reflects what kind of person they are—into the story.

   In Chapter 7, I write about things you might say in conferences to help writers remember more as well as what to say about other issues and writing strategies peculiar to the memoir genre.

3. *Accept what these writers are able to do for now.* Truthfully, I have had to accept from some students the most meager of memoirs. There have been a few kids over the years who could not or would not put their inner life on the page. Instead, they wrote about their new bike or their video games or their dog, in a flat or impersonal style. There is no final publication or grade or promotion worth causing some students to feel terrified about writing, and we should never force them to go to places inside themselves that they are not ready to meet.

The activities of this chapter provide students with opportunities to explore their lives through language in order to name what has happened to them. This work would be valuable even if students never published memoirs for audiences, but I hope they will publish. Questioning, interpreting, and shaping experience to bring it to the public, to say, "This is who I am," will be the subject of the next few chapters.

Name: _____ Date: _____

WRITING ABOUT A PERSON

1. Study a person who means a lot to you, whom you can't get out of your mind. Describe how he or she looks, talks, walks, moves, dresses in tiny, tiny details. How has he or she changed physically since you've known him or her?

2. Fill the space below with lots of writing about what you think and how you feel about this person. You can feel a certain way sometimes and then a different way other times about the same person.

3. Write a memory of a time that would demonstrate some of those thoughts and feelings about that person.

YOU CAN USE THE BACK!!!!

Figure 4–5 *Writing About a Person*

Making Meaning of Memories

Selecting, Collecting, and Layering

We all return to memories and dreams like this, again and again; the story we tell of our own life is reshaped around them. But the point doesn't lie there, back in the past, back in the lost time at which they happened; the only point lies in interpretation.

—CAROLYN KAY STEEDMAN, *Landscape for a Good Woman: A Story of Two Lives*

Word by word I have created the person I am and the invented country in which I live.

—ISABEL ALLENDE, *My Invented Country*

Now we come to the heart of the heart of what it means to write memoir: interpretation. What is a life after all, except what someone declares it to be? There are the material facts of blood, bones, body. There are the dates and times and momentous occasions: birth, school, marriage, career, children. There are the characters: the "I," parents and guardians, siblings, friends, spouses, grandparents. But all those facts, persons, dates, and times float like dust particles in space. They hold no shape or substance, no intrinsic meaning save for what the person telling the story *says* they mean.

More than anything else, writing the memoir is an act of discovering the self, creating on the page almost an "imitation of the self" (Olney 1980, 19). Like an anthropologist, the memoirist traipses the landscape of childhood, traveling in the country of the self, observing, gathering insights, saying, What an interesting, mysterious thing is this *self!* The memoirist does not settle for the surface images, no matter how vivid, but questions the self that lives inside memory, asking, *What kind of person would do that thing, say that?* Rather than merely list historical facts, the memoirist constructs ideas about those facts that lift them off the page and breathe life into them.

A life story makes a "text," like any poem, novel, or essay, and like any other text, it is open to interpretation. The ideas we construct don't have to be the right ones, and that makes interpretation fun: we can have one idea about ourselves this year and ten years from now, having learned and experienced more, see ourselves in a whole new light. Writing autobiography is "a way of construing experience—and of reconstruing and re-construing it until our breath or our pen fails us" (Bruner 1993, 38). Complicating this act even further is the impossibility of interpreting our past without being subject to the language, culture, and conventions alive at the moment of telling. How I would write about my childhood today, in the twenty-first century, is so vastly different from how I would have written (I might not have been literate!) about myself in 1860. Childhood meant something entirely different in the nineteenth century and in different cultures. And that's just one of hundreds of ways that my social and historical situation affects my construction of self.

Understandably, looking at their memories in order to question and interpret their meanings might feel difficult for some young people. One writer might look over all her notebook entries, trying to figure out if they have anything in common, if they say any-thing big about who she is. Another writer might have a draft of his memoir, all polished up, ready to go, but then notices that although he has gotten all the facts right—places he's been, people he knows, video games he owns—there is no point, no angle on it, again, nothing big to say who this person is.

To help students through this part of the process, I offer in this chapter not one, but several ways to think about how to lead students through exercises in order to layer their memories with interpretive ideas.

Interpreting Written Text

In the second half of this chapter, I discuss how to help students turn interpretive moves toward their memoir entries and provide a list of possible questions and prompts that your students can apply to their concepts of self and memory in order to compose rich, complex memoirs. But first let me describe what we do when we interpret as readers of written text.

Interpretation describes an act of imagination. In reading, it requires moving beyond the black squiggles on the white pages and into the realm of meaning making and world proposing that each reader brings to the text. Azar Nafisi, author of the bestselling *Reading Lolita in Tehran: A Memoir in Books* (2003), says that the act of reading great art should be about going to the text prepared to face "question marks," not answers. To interpret means to have big ideas about the text that open up multiple viewpoints, and not just what color the character's hat was in chapter 3.

The primary move of interpretation is toward abstract thought. It is similar to what readers do when they *infer* from text, in that they must extrapolate ideas about what is going on and what it all might mean from a variety of clues, only some of which are directly embedded in the words of the text. But interpretation goes even farther away from the printed text and applies surprising twists and turns of meaning to it that are not apparent at first. Let me give an example of inferring something that's not actually in the words of the following bit of text, and then I will demonstrate some ways to interpret this same text.

> She arrived five minutes late to yoga class, tiptoed over to the last available spot on the floor and unrolled her purple mat. Her hair was plastered to her head, and she whipped it into a pony tail while rushing to get into the cross-legged meditative position that everyone else in class already held. She had brought a towel this time, fortunately, and she used it to mop her forehead and the back of her neck. If she could only get settled and begin to breathe deeply, consciously, she knew her heart would stop racing and that peaceful calm could begin to descend over her.

With very few clues, we can *infer* from this passage that this woman feels hot. The words *she was hot* do not appear, but we can infer it from the image of the plastered hair and the action of mopping her face and neck. To infer that, we had to stay close to the bone of the printed words.

Interpretation, while it also builds on ideas that are not directly stated in the actual text, moves even farther away from the words than inference does. Interpretation moves toward some abstract concepts, invokes similar incidents from the reader's own life or from other characters in different texts that might help the reader recognize this current situation and compose some meaning from it. As we read, we dialogue with the text, making interpretive moves, reaching out to new meanings and understandings of what we read.

Interpretive work might begin in questions:

Is the woman hot because it's hot outside?

Is she sweaty because she's late to class, and she's nervous about that?

Interpretive work might begin in pronounced statements:

She's nervous about being late to class, and that made her all hot and sweaty. Maybe she really hates being late to things.

She is just plain nervous all the time. It seems like she often feels that frantic feeling because it says she knows that if she will just get quiet and settled, it will go away.

Interpretive work might begin with personal connections to what the reader knows from his or her own life experiences:

I feel just like her when I'm late to things. I used to get in trouble all the time about being late when I was little, so now I'm just a wreck if I'm not on time.

I can't stand being hot either, just like her. I get little sweat beads on my upper lip that drive me crazy! I always carry a handkerchief in my pocket to wipe them off.

Interpretive work might begin in connections to other texts that remind the reader of this one, or whose story can provide a marked contrast to this one:

The main character in this other novel I'm reading is always late. He makes his friends wait; he is consistently late to important meetings; his life is always crashing around him because people are furious with him. But he won't change! What makes a person be either one type or another? It's got to be something buried deep within their psyche—some kind of personal reward they get from being on time or from being late.

We could imagine that all the previous insights came from different readers. When readers bring their interpretations to a discussion, they discover rather quickly that there are other ways to think about the text besides their own. The thrilling and important work of book clubs and literature circles, when they function well, has the effect of opening texts to endless possibilities, as many as there are readers. When participants listen actively and remain open, they can also change their mind when someone proposes another way to read the text and substantiates it with evidence from the text, and then that new way makes a lot of sense.

Interpretation lays down a larger abstraction on the printed words of the text. Interpretation goes beyond simple retelling of plot to a concept the text does not state directly. Interpretation brings something to a story that almost seems to have been taken out of it. In the previous sample, the text doesn't say one word about the woman feeling nervous or insecure about being late, yet once someone interprets it that way, it becomes entirely possible to argue that. Nervousness and insecurity are concepts laid, like a screen mesh, over the words of the text. We can look through the screen to see if those words fit. This interpretation of her inner state might be further substantiated if there were a lot more text about her and if she acted nervous and intimidated in more than one situation in the story.

Interpreting Life Stories

Now, we can bring those same interpretive moves to our life stories. Just as we look for clues in a novel or short story for how to make meaning of the text, we can also look for patterns and clues in our memories to compose meaning about them. We can question what we formerly accepted as truth. We can connect to other memoir texts that remind us of our own experience. And we can layer our memories with abstract concepts, finding new meaning in the old stories. Our job, as memoirists, is to look at our lives with open, questioning minds. We should believe that there are mysteries to solve, unknowns to discover. In fact, we should believe that these unexplained places are the treasure sites of memoir writing and go after them as we might pursue pots of gold.

There are a number of ways to help students go about this interpretive work. Some of the work they will do alone, in their writer's notebook, in response to your prompting and questioning. Some they will do in conversation with you in writing conferences, and some can become the work for writing partners or response groups, since having more minds think about a text can result in multiple ideas for writers to play with.

Two backbones of autobiographical writing offer sites for rich interpretation: the self and memory. I want to discuss these concepts briefly here, simply to provide some background information that helps me when I confer with students who are writing about themselves.

Self

Let's face it—as we go about our day, reading the newspaper on the subway, shopping for groceries, bathing the kids, or unwinding in front of the television, most of us just don't give a lot of thought to what our self is all about. We leave that to the philosophers and psychologists and religious figures—people who have spent centuries debating and defining what constitutes the self.

The concept of self has changed dramatically over the course of human history, from the boxy roles of servant, wife, king, and so on of the Middle Ages, to Descartes' mind–body split in the seventeenth century, to the idealized, romanticized individual of the nineteenth century, to the fragmented and unfinished self of the twentieth century. Those changing definitions liberate us, it seems to me, to literally author our lives, to choose among numerous possibilities for how to think and write about ourselves, and not to trap us into what others might proclaim us to be.

Let me describe quickly and broadly four contemporary views of the self that I draw upon in my work with students. I have thought and written about these concepts in my own autobiographical writing, so I know how to angle the information in ways that help students. This is not necessarily information to package into minilessons (although I have sometimes), but I definitely turn to these notions frequently in conferences as my students search for ways to think and write about themselves with an interpretive lens.

Self Is Fluid

We change constantly. Some changes take place minute by minute while others take decades. John Dewey believed the self is "something in continuous formation through choice of action" ([1916] 1944, 351). Perhaps it happens through action, but also we change our minds, our tastes and passions, and our opinions. If we could not change ourselves, many people would not be able to move past their addictions, their anger and grief, toward health, love, and forgiveness.

For young memoir writers, one way to make meaning of a life is to notice how they have changed over time. For instance, Tony wrote this in his notebook: "I've always hated reading because I wanted to be outside, racing or fighting or just riding around and around on my bike. But then my teacher read this book to the class called *Joey Pigza*

Swallowed the Key, by Mr. Jack Gantos, and then I read it by myself, and then I read the other Joey Pigza books, and now how much I read is equal to how much I run." The next writing step for Tony might be to interpret why his feelings about reading changed when he read the Joey Pigza books.

Questions to ask yourself: How have your tastes, opinions, looks, knowledge, desires changed over time? Write a brief a description of your self at age thirteen, and at your current age. What aspects seem fluid and which seem more fixed?

Self Is Fractured

We are not one, solid, unswerving "I" operating exactly the same way no matter the situation. In fact, it's possible to experience contradictory or competing thoughts and feelings at the same time. Most people, speaking of themselves in the twentieth century, say things like, *"Part of me* wants to retire and just garden and read books, but *another part of me* feels like looking for a whole new career. I mean, I'm only fifty—I've got a lot of good years left!"

Most of us know, whether we admit it or not, that we have multiple, divergent desires and attitudes. That we can feel simultaneously attracted to and repulsed by something, like the sight of a car accident, for example. Or that we can act demure and dignified in one situation and let our wild beast out in a different context. Talking about our inner child has become part of our popular culture. We can feel confused or even frightened when we are at cross-purposes with ourselves, but most of us learn to control ourselves, to act appropriately for any given situation. We learn to cope with our multiplicity, and even indulge it, say, by decorating our living room in a sleek, clean, ultramodern look and our bedroom in flowers and lace.

Young people are quite aware of their rapidly changing physical, mental, and emotional selves, and the adults around them can help them know that this is part of growing up and part of being human. But noticing that they have feelings and desires that clash or put them at odds with themselves can cause young people to feel alienated and depressed. Writing about it can help because it gets anxious thoughts out of the continuous loop of the mind and onto the page. Others can read it and respond, "I know what you mean; I feel that way too." Many teachers are familiar with the short story called "Eleven," by Sandra Cisneros (1992), in which the character talks about feeling all her younger ages inside, even though she is supposed to be eleven years old. I use this story when I teach memoir writing because it so beautifully illustrates the idea of the fractured self.

Questions to ask yourself: What areas of your life or of the world around you give rise to conflicting desires or opinions within you? Which aspects of yourself have you given power and voice to? Which aspects do you suppress?

Self Is Language

What we call the self at any point in history is merely *language* for the self. The self is simply what we say it is, making it, in essence, what Jacques Derrida calls "A fiction that resides in discourse, in the space of storytelling." And language is framed by the culture in which it emerges. So, for instance, following the work of Sigmund Freud, Carl Jung, and others in the early twentieth century, people began to speak comfortably in the discourse of modern (Western) psychology, saying that someone had a big *ego,* or someone was an *archetypal* mother, or saying something like, "I *unconsciously* locked my car keys in the car."

Language is a superbly powerful medium. We use it to think, dream, get what we want and need, and communicate our most intimate feelings. We also use it to label, judge, and condemn others. Language has the power to create both positive and negative feelings of self; it can both expand and limit the possibilities for who we think we are, so some of the work of composing a life involves finding new language with which to define ourselves.

Young memoirists can explore the language that others use to talk about them and realize its effects on their self-perception. Has someone called him a sissy, or a geek, for instance? What effect did that have? What words does the writer normally use to describe herself? Where did those words come from? Memoirists can choose the words to call themselves; in essence, they can name themselves. Our ever evolving language, situated in the culture of the United States in the twenty-first century, continues to provide us with new language to describe ourselves. For instance, we are beginning to refer to our brains as being hardwired or programmed, borrowing from the discourse of computer technology. Who knows what new ways we will have to describe ourselves in the near future, as more of us connect with the global language of the Internet.

Questions to ask yourself: How does language describe you? What is limiting about the language you choose to describe yourself with? What kind of language expands your sense of who you are?

Self Is Relational

No man is an island, as the saying goes. We are not isolated, individuated selves, but rather we are selves in affiliation with groups. Most people are or have been at one time members of a group called family. So we define ourselves as mother, or oldest child, or little brother. The family may be one of the few groups to which we do not choose to belong. Race and sexual orientation may be others. But beyond those, we can choose by our affiliations and our actions, as Dewey said, to belong to groups in which we feel comfortable and happy. Most often, those groups overlap, and that is what creates a dynamic and healthy society. We can belong to groups called female and Native American, but at the same time belong to race car drivers and liberals and biologists. We can call ourselves male and African American, but also dart players and teachers and Methodists.

When young people think about the meaning that their life holds, they can look to their affections for and affiliations with others as important mirrors on who they have been and who they are becoming. If we teach our students that these affiliations are open and fluid, that they needn't be fixed by external realities of race, class, and gender, we give them possibilities for becoming as big as they can be.

Questions to ask yourself: Which groups define you? Which groups overlap? How do groups misdefine you? How do you resist those definitions?

Memory

Knowing a few things about how memory works helps me teach kids how to interpret their memories. If they know, for instance, that certain moments stay with us because they are important, then kids can speculate about *why* they are important. Recent theories, posited by neuroscientists and psychologists, show that memory, rather than being like old photographs or records stored in file cabinets in our brains, are made up of perceptions constructed in our cultural, historical present. To remember, we do things to our present consciousness such as relax, close our eyes, or look at photographs or objects. Memory is an active process: we have to actively *reconstruct* some image or fragment of time into a story. It's not as if we can reach into our brains and pull out an intact, as-it-truly-happened event.

Memory is something we construct. Rather than feel frustrated by its inexact nature and bound by dates, details, and dialogue we can't possibly remember, we can become artists and make our stories match our own truths. Judith Ortiz Cofer writes in *Silent Dancing: A Partial Remembrance of a Puerto Rican Childhood* that she "faced the possibility that the past is mainly a creation of the imagination . . . although there are facts one can research and confirm" (1990, 12). But her purpose in her memoir *ensayos* (rehearsals or exercises) was to connect her *self* to the "tapestry that is [her] memory" and to the lives that touched hers. Freud believed that emotions are essential to the act of remembering, so that indeed, the things that touch us, that have personal significance, are the things that we remember best. We can help young memoirists sort through the lists of facts and tidbits of story to find the moments that make their hearts soften or their hearts race—the moments that feel big.

Self and memory are the building blocks of the memoir, but they are not automatically a part of what young writers put down on paper when they first start out. Most kids define themselves first with their name, age, or what grade they are in at school, and on the other side of the question "So what?" there is a giant question mark. So the next step is to teach kids to write about their lives from any number of lenses or perspectives, to interpret their memories, to look into a mirror and say back what they see there.

Interpreting Our Notebook Writing

In the rest of this chapter, I will list and describe numerous questions, frames, activities, and prompts to give to students doing interpretive work in their writer's notebook. Items from these lists form the content of my minilessons and writing conferences during the one- or two-week-long selecting, collecting, and layering phase of the memoir study. If students are working with memoir buddies or in small writing response groups, you can frame their work together by using the questions and prompts that I list here, plus any that the groups might devise. These questions stimulate some deep thinking and may prove difficult for some kids; they bear repeating and responding to more than once. In response groups, kids may word the question in such a way that a writer finally gets it or may ask it in a way that elicits a different response than the one you got from the writer. Some students may feel more comfortable answering their peers than answering the teacher and will be able to talk through some of the more difficult interpretive questions with their friends. Finally, as in instances when there are multiple reader-interpreters of a text, a partner or response group may help the memoirist see multiple interpretations of his life that were not apparent before.

At this point in the process, students have read independently at least three memoir models and possibly had some read out loud to them. They have made multiple entries in their writer's notebook about places, persons, and events from their past. Still working in their notebook, they now *select* a focus for their memoir. They *collect* more information about that focus, gather more memories—other events that connect to the focus, perhaps the stories of other important persons, maybe some specific facts like street names, and so on. And then they *layer* this new material with interpretive questions and ideas, in effect looking at the stuff of their life from multiple perspectives. I save the bulk of the interpretive work for the selecting, collecting, and layering stage of the process, after my students have filled their notebooks up with times, places, and people and are ready to dig in deeper with an interpretive lens. For most children, the interpretive work is the hardest part, and I find myself pushing them to reflect on their memories even as they are writing their first, second, and final drafts. The struggle is worth it, however, because this reflective work layers the material with rich meanings and insights.

Looking Inward: Seeking Themes in Our Notebook Writing

On the first day of this new stage of the memoir writing process, I ask my students to reread all of the entries in their writer's notebook that are memories to find emerging patterns and themes *in order to write more about them*. This is crucial. If I don't emphasize and demonstrate how to write more about a selected theme, my students would simply choose one notebook entry or one event, copy it onto draft paper, fix some spellings and punctuation, and call it done.

Strategies for Discovering a Theme

Reread, Seeking Big Ideas

In the minilesson, I demonstrate exactly what I will ask kids to do that day: I skim over all the entries in my own notebook, reminding myself what this one and that one are about, and then I think out loud about some of the different big ideas I see, and I list them on a piece of chart paper. I notice that my notebook contains many entries about the landscape of New Mexico, so I write, "NM landscape." I notice that Nana appears in every other entry, so perhaps that is an important relationship I should write more about. I write "Nana" on the chart. And, wow, I notice that there is not a single time, in any of my entries, where I talk! My mother talks, my teachers, my best friend, even total strangers talk, but I haven't written any words that *I* might have uttered. I write, "Silence/talking." I purposely sweep across many entries, formulating big ideas that are almost outside of the printed words, hoping this will help my students push past simply choosing their favorite entry or one isolated memory. I accomplish this by looking at my *past* through the eyes of the *present*. Virginia Woolf realized that to write about one's memories and include one's current ideas about them can actually influence the structure of memoir: "It would be interesting to make the two people, I now, I then, come out in contrast," she writes (1976, 75). Truthfully, we are simply not able to remember the past purely, without coloration from the present moment, so we might as well include "I now, I then" as a structure.

Then I say to my students, "I have two choices of what to do next: I could decide which of these big ideas I want to select to be what my memoir is mostly about. If I do that, I will spend the next five days thinking, writing, and adding on to that topic in my notebook. Or, I could hold off on what my memoir will be mostly about until I have done some writing in response to the questions and ideas from the list I'm going to give you. If I try out some of these different angles and lenses, I might see the entries in my notebook in a way I hadn't even thought about."

Sometimes, I don't give students options but simply demonstrate the second approach. That is, I ask them to hold off on selecting a topic so that they can practice interpreting their memories from a variety of perspectives. This way, students don't just leap at the first idea that occurs to them. Of course, even if they do select a topic right away and begin to layer more writing onto it, the topic can certainly change a number of times in the course of revising. The main function of this week's process is to write about their memories from a variety of angles and vantage points, layering on that reflective aspect that defines the memoir genre.

Ask Hard Questions of Your Entries

During a minilesson on Tuesday or Wednesday, I demonstrate with published memoir excerpts or samples of student writing the concept of looking at a memory in order to interpret or have big ideas about it. For example, in a passage from *Growing Up Inside the Sanctuary of My Imagination*, Nicholasa Mohr (1994) writes about the death of her father when she was quite young. She writes honestly about feeling almost emotionless at his death; he was a great deal older than her mother, had fathered her six older brothers, and had never shown much affection or interest in her at all. Shortly after his funeral, Mohr found a dead sparrow and she made a little coffin, and with her two friends, she gave the bird a burial ceremony complete with songs and prayers. She felt grief-stricken about the dead bird, thinking of how it would never fly or sing again. Then, as an adult writing about this memory in retrospect, she had this insight about these events:

> By personally performing a ritual for the dead sparrow and lamenting its demise, I was finally able to mourn for my father. I used the sparrow as a symbol in order to connect with the reality of death. Somehow the ceremony and burial of the bird was the bridge that allowed me to imagine and grasp the death of my father. For the first time since my father had died, I began to cry in earnest. It was only then that I understood that I would never again see Papa sitting on his favorite chair, reading his copy of the *Daily Worker*. He would no longer sit at our table or take us to the park on Sundays.
> "Papa's gone . . . " I cried, and was able to mourn and accept the loss. (72)

Mohr writes here about how she understood that her grief over the dead bird symbolized the grief she was not able to display at her father's death. I tell my students that Mohr may not have truly understood that when she was little, but in the act of writing about it later, she came to this insight. Perhaps in her writer's notebook she asked herself something like, "I wonder why I was more crushed by that bird's death than by my own father's death?" This bit of text and passages from other memoirists help me demonstrate to my students the idea of asking reflective questions to arrive at a possible theme.

Connect Unconnected Writing

On Thursday, I use a piece of student writing to demonstrate how bumping seemingly disparate notebook entries against each other can often lead to fascinating interpretive thinking. Young people love to look at other students' writing, and they learn easily from it, so I try as often as possible to use student writing alongside adult or published writing. Figure 5–1 contains a passage written by a student named Eduardo when he was about thirteen years old.

My sister Fernanda is seven, but she's still like a baby to me. I try to protect her and take care of her. We walk to school together and when she goes to her class I worry about what might happen to her. For a few minutes after I leave her I am nervous. Sometimes kids are mean to her and me too. They yell at me, "Mami, Mami, go get your baby!" I guess they never saw a guy take care of a little kid before.

•   •   •   •   •

Once when I was eight I saw a baby girl standing by herself in the street. She was crying because she had cut her foot. I didn't know what to do because I didn't know where the baby's parents were. I stood by her and held her hand. I tried to pick her up but I couldn't carry her. Finally, her mom came along and took her. My sister was four years old then, and the baby made me see I always worry about her.

•   •   •   •   •

I feel scared for small things. We used to have a hamster. It got out of its cage and died behind the couch. For a few days when I didn't know where it was, I felt scared for it all the time. It was like I knew how scared it was. It's like that with my sister, when I am not with her and she is not bugging me. I think about her feeling afraid or hurt or crying, and I try to hold her hand in my mind.

•   •   •   •   •

What patterns or themes are emerging in my memoir entries?
When someone is small, you have to take care of them. It's easier for them to get hurt, and I worry about things that can get hurt. I mean, when my hamster was lost, I kept trying to picture it in my mind. Where was it? I pictured it inside the walls in my house like a mouse I saw in a cartoon. I pictured it getting outside and being scared of the cars. I can't stand if anything or anyone, not even a hamster, feels scared on the inside.

I think about how my hand is so much bigger than little kids' hands. That baby's hand was tiny. It's not like holding my girlfriend's hand, where our fingers go between each other's. A baby's hand is just inside your hand. My sister's hand is in between those two, small like a baby's but not as small. It's funny that I can make myself feel those different hands in my hand just by thinking about it.

I don't talk about this that much with my friends, because some of them think that things like taking care of babies is for women. Not all of them. Some of them have little sisters and brothers and they have to take care of them and they worry about them. To me, if you think about protecting something or someone, that means that you're strong. But it does not feel like being strong when you are worried.

Maybe I should work on cars when I get older so I don't ever have to see anyone bleeding or a baby crying. But machines make me bored. I would rather teach little kids for a job. I want to have a lot of little kids of my own when I grow up. And I won't ever hit them or leave them like my dad did.

Figure 5–1   *Eduardo Connects Separate Notebook Entries with Patterns or Emerging Themes*

After I read Eduardo's piece, I ask my students to talk about what they think he did to make the facts of these memories lift off the page to become something bigger. Students have noticed that Eduardo bumps at least three different events up against each other to find out what they have in common. That is exactly the kind of work a memoirist does to find rich layers of meaning in experience. Eduardo may have begun from an ongoing theme or issue from his life—how he has a persistent impulse to take care of the vulnerable—and then searched his memory for examples to support that thesis. Or he may have reread his notebook entries and noticed that there was a pattern emerging in the events he wrote about: they all seemed to revolve around small things, taking care, being a good big brother, worrying from the perspective of those weaker than he is. Either way, he did not let these events stand isolated, but instead he wove them together with the threads of vulnerability and care.

Talk with Those Who Know You About What They Notice

Sometimes viewing the material of their life through a friend's or family member's eyes helps students discover themes or patterns of behavior that they can develop, if they so choose, in their notebook. In Barbara Clements' sixth-grade class, Mark had written an entry about the first day of third grade and his self-conscious efforts to figure out which desk was his (Figure 5–2).

Most children would recognize and relate to Mark's shyness, his desire to get things right in front of a group of strangers, and not to get branded as lost or incompetent by the rest of the children. When Mark read his entry out loud to a few children, his friend Camille, who has known Mark and been in classes with him for several years, noticed that this particular entry provided a glimpse into an ongoing pattern or theme in his life. "Mark is the kind of person who tends to be nervous about things going well," Camille said kindly.

It would have been possible for Mark to use his friend's insight to frame his memoir. He could have looked back then at the rest of his entries to see if there were other stories about feeling nervous or needing to appear competent and secure. If other entries didn't fit this framework, he could have decided to proceed, in this collecting and layering stage of the process, to remember and write about other times in his life that this tendency to get nervous showed itself. When was the first time he remembered feeling nervous? Were there other settings or circumstances in which this tendency appeared? Were there circumstances in which he felt relaxed and sure of himself? Mark could have

The first day of third grade had to be the scariest day of my [3 year old] life. I usaully worry about every little thing but this was a big thing and I was freaked out.
   The first order Mrs. ___ [(my) teacher] dished out was "Find your desk your nametag is on it." I thought alright this is something I can do, so I searched around for my desk but without much luck. As I circled the desks I began to get worried. There was no desk with my name on it. I started to get the feeling I actually might not be in that class and I went to the wrong room. I feverishly searched again but with no luck.

I felt blood rushing to my head and I couldn't think straight. I was to scared to ask her so I just stood behind a vacant desk and waited. After a while she noticed I was still standing up. She asked me why and I simply replied that I couldn't find my nametag. She looked at me and then down to the floor under the desk and up at me again. Then she bent down and took it from under the desk I was standing at. She gave it to me and I felt really stupid.

Figure 5–2   *Mark's Notebook Entry About Searching for His Desk*

also thought and written, over the course of several days' entries, in response to this question: What from your past do you think caused you feel this way about yourself?

Not all children will be able to explore their psyches to this degree of depth and intensity. For various reasons, they may not feel safe enough to reveal their innermost selves, or this level of abstract thinking may not feel comfortable or familiar. For others, however, these questions can fuel pages of writing and even provide an organizing frame or structure for their drafts.

Looking Outward: Trying on Themes from the World

Another way to help students interpret their life narratives is through the narrowing scope of one abstract or critical idea that stands outside of the personal self, that turns the memoirist's gaze to the social world she resides in. Some theorists call these ways of considering the world lenses, as in a feminist lens, and some call it taking a certain stance on the material. Journalists might refer to the angle of a story. Some teachers feel more comfortable using the term *theme* to refer to such big ideas. Whatever term you use with your students, you will want to present it so that they understand that they should look back at the stories of their life to interpret them through one or two big ideas about the social world. Formerly unrelated and unconnected memories will now feed into this developing idea, connected by the larger lens or theme. This lens will color everything. It's rather like those proverbial rose-tinted glasses—when you put them on, everything turns pink.

What follows is a short list of possible critical themes or lenses that your students can apply to the material they have collected so far in their notebooks. Usually, I ask my students to choose two from my list and to write an entry about how they could think about their life from these perspectives. Throughout this selecting, collecting, and layering phase of the process, I also invite them to invent their own themes and lenses, and I add those to a chart called "Possible Themes for Our Memoirs."

Strategies for Discovering a Theme

Explore Ideas About Class, Gender, Race, and Ethnicity as They Relate to Your Life Stories

Many contemporary adult memoirs take one or more of the following critical lenses as themes: class, gender, race, and ethnicity. Even in young adult memoirs, these are becoming crucial frames through which to view a life history. Nicholasa Mohr (1994) writes honestly about being part of the only Latino family in a largely Anglo neighborhood in New York City in the 1950s, where her home was vandalized and her family called derogatory names. Her teachers in public schools were verbally abusive and racist. Mohr's response to all that hatred and bigotry, she believes, was to work harder to achieve and to prove her talent as an artist and writer to the world.

Powerful themes connected to race, ethnicity, and class are stories about emigrating from another country and perhaps becoming an American citizen. While many memoirists write gratefully about their safe harbor in the United States, there are also, clearly, stories that describe feelings of loss and grief for a homeland and culture, feeling unjustly treated because of skin color, and the overwhelming difficulties of learning a new language and losing the old one, living in what Judith Ortiz Cofer calls "two worlds" of language. In *Silent Dancing*, Cofer (1990) describes feeling constantly torn as a child between her two homes in New Jersey and Puerto Rico and never being completely at home in either one. In *Hunger of Memory*, Richard Rodriquez (1982) writes poignantly about losing Spanish, the language that his mother whispered to him as a little boy, and about the increasing emotional and psychological distances that grew between him and his family as he became more fluent in English.

Young people tend to have a great deal to write about gender issues. Females especially write easily about instances of oppression, verbal abuse, and stereotyping without thinking much about it. With my students, I try to complicate the accepted rhetoric, the social language and conventions, of our time a bit, to open the gender lens for the males in our group as well. I read the story "Everything Will Be Okay," by James Howe (1996), about how he was desperate to save an injured kitten, but his brother easily put it to sleep at the vet's (Dr. Milk's) office. I ask my students what they make of his last lines: "I will never work for Dr. Milk. I will not go hunting with my father. I will decide for myself what kind of boy I am, what kind of man I will become" (48).

I also read the picture book *Saturdays and Teacakes,* by my friend Lester Laminak (2004). I tell them how Lester performed this book for a group of literacy educators one evening, and he prefaced it by saying that he grew up in a tiny Alabama town where being a boy meant "everything [he] was not." He dedicated this memoir to his grandmother, who, he said, helped him feel normal. I ask my students what they think Lester meant about not feeling normal.

The males in the group were adamant that boys should not be spending Saturdays making teacakes, whatever those are! "I mean he's normal for riding a bike and mowing his grandma's yard, but not making cakes!"

"Who says?" I ask. Of course, the more we dig into this topic, the more boys begin to melt, admitting that they have a favorite stuffed animal from when they were little, or that they wish they didn't have to play football in the one-hundred-degree Texas afternoons, but their family and friends expect them to. Gender (and sexual preference) naturalizing exists as ferociously for males as for females in our culture, and I believe that getting young people to think and write about themselves in particular ways instead of as stereotypes will help broaden what it means to be human beings.

Defining Yourself as a Member of a Social Institution (Family, School, Church, Scouts, Sports Club) or as an Outsider

Although most memoirs mention or elaborate on the author's experiences living with family, attending school or church, and belonging to some kind of club or social organization, some explore these critical social identifications more than others. Again, no human exists in isolation from others. And as I mentioned, we affiliate with some groups by choice and others by life circumstance.

Family, for most people, is a group we belong to by circumstance. Family plays a hugely significant role in most memoirs. Writers describe their family identity, as in "We were the kind of family who . . . talked about social injustice at the dinner table; went on camping adventures; demonstrated love through small acts of service rather than with words or hugs." Other writers relate how they were abandoned or elected to leave their birth families and, as adults, have carefully chosen friends and loved ones to call family.

Memoirists might also define their self-identity inside the family group, for instance, as being the oldest, middle, or youngest child; an adopted child; an only child; or one of a large family. A main focusing theme of Ralph Fletcher's memoir, *Marshfield Dreams* (2005), is his identity as the oldest of nine children. He documents the obviously comical episodes, like when all nine fell ill with the mumps, and he recalls episodes that happened away from the house teeming with people, and away from his job, as the eldest, of taking care of the babies.

In "Scout's Honor," Avi (1996) writes about joining the Boy Scouts when he was nine because he worried that he "wasn't tough enough." "Scouting, I thought, would make a man of me" (123). The rather inept attempts he and his best friends made to move to second class by going on an overnight hike in the country proved that though they signed up for this group, they were not going to be able to belong, if roughing it was a necessary feature of the group's identity.

The point of setting one's life history in the context of one's social memberships is to recognize and reflect upon their influence in a critical way and to understand that groups can give individuals power as well as a sense of identity and belonging. But they can also, as in the case of cliques in schools, create profound feelings of personal rejection should one not "qualify" for membership because of skin color, size, disability, or other perceived inequalities.

Set Your Life Inside of or Against a Period of Social History and Write About Its Influences on Your Identity

Young people can't possibly distance themselves the way adult memoirists can from the social period of history they are living in. Time grants the necessary distance from periods of history, such as the Vietnam era, the civil rights movement, or the 1950s postwar baby boom, that allows historians and sociologists to name and define them. But some students might wish to set their parents or grandparents inside a social, historical, or political frame. They might do a bit of reading about the 1970s, for instance, and then have something to say about how their parents' lives were affected by the times they grew up in. Or the most adventurous of students might even attempt a kind of cultural study of their own social milieu, finding things to say about the politics, arts, fashions, and entertainments of the decade they grew up in.

Some good memoirs written for children that make excellent read-alouds or book club selections for this type of historical, sociopolitical writing are *The Circuit* (1997) and its sequel, *Breaking Through* (2001), memoirs about migrant farm workers in California, by Francisco Jimenez; *The Red Scarf Girl*, a memoir of the Cultural Revolution in China, by Ji Li Jiang (1997); *Rosa Parks: My Story*, about the bus boycott in Montgomery, Alabama, by Rosa Parks (1994); and *No Pretty Pictures*, by Anita Lobel (1998), *Kindertransport*, by Olga Levy Drucker (1992), and *I Have Lived a Thousand Years*, by Livia Bitton-Jackson (1997), memoirs of the Holocaust.

Exploring and Developing Selected Themes

Besides offering models from my own notebook, from published texts, and from student writing for how students might rework the material from their notebooks with an interpretive stance, I also provide a typed list of the following questions and activities for them to respond to in their notebooks. These questions ask for fairly sophisticated kinds of thinking; they directly call for writers to reverse their thinking, argue with their preconceptions, sweep across numerous entries searching for patterns and connections, and apply abstract concepts or metaphors to their self-identity.

I don't think of this as a checklist of items to march through; instead, I decide which questions feel accessible to a particular group of students to tackle, and I develop mini-lessons about those. The rest remain as options for students to work on during class and/or for homework.

As you read through the following questions and activities, you might notice that some will make more sense for students who have already selected the focus or theme for their memoir while other questions may help students discover a theme, as Sinnae did, where none existed before. (See Figure 5–3.)

I've finally decided on a theme.
It's time, the changes, the adjusting,
the memories I have of being outside
and time just seems to RUN through
your fingers. A lot of my life just
revolves around time, and I want to
show that. It can be about how fast
time seems to travel, or how it seems to
stand still at certain times.

Figure 5–3   *Sinnae Settles on a Memoir Theme*

- Look back at all the notebook entries you've collected for this memoir study. What patterns or themes are emerging? How could all these entries go together? If students feel overwhelmed by all the material in their notebooks, you might have them write in response to one of these prompts: "What I most want you to know about me is . . . " or "The reason I need to tell you this right now is. . . . "

- Make a list of five abstract concepts or ideas and see if any of them apply to the memories you have generated in your notebook. Are there one or more entries that can fit into this larger thematic concept? You might help students come up with their lists of concepts by giving them a running start on a few. Here are some examples my students and I have come up with:

defiance	loss	perfectionism	fear	conceit
disability	nervousness	anger	difference	illness

- Notice if there are patterns of behavior, thought, emotion, or physical activity that appear across your notebook entries. What meaning do you make of this pattern? Some examples:

obsession with a TV show or video game	counting steps while walking
a need to be a good girl (or boy)	getting angry at little things
being teased continually	coming alive at certain times, in certain places
wearing baggy clothes to hide your body or a hat to hide your face	giggling nervously or laughing at the wrong times
feeling like an outsider or a misfit	needing love or attention

- For each event, memory, and feeling that you have written about in your notebook, ask how it fits in with your idea of who you are and write an entry about what you figure out. "The time I got lost in the woods behind our house shows how much I love to pretend. Like, instead of getting really scared (well, I was scared too!), I just pretended I was a unicorn, all alone, like unicorns always are, waiting for a fairy to find me and ride me back home. I got so interested in my little story, that it helped pass the time till my uncle found me. How does this fit in with who I am? I guess it says I am creative and a dreamer. I want to become an actress or writer or painter or famous figure skater."

- Take the idea you have been developing about yourself and turn it on its head. Argue with it. "I have only wanted to play football since I was four. Football rocks! You get to ram into other kids and not get in trouble for it! And when you win, everybody makes a big deal about it. My parents take us kids to our favorite restaurant to get lobster and cheesecake for dinner whenever we win a game. Every boy in our school and town is supposed to play football, so I guess that's why I love it so much. [Now argue with that]: But sometimes, I wish I could play the guitar. If 'my boys' knew that, they'd call me a sissy."

- Ask the same kinds of questions of your own life that you would ask about a character in a book or movie: What kind of person is this character (yourself)? What angers, excites, terrifies, saddens this character? What has she or he wanted, and what are the conflicts or obstacles he or she has faced? What roles do other characters play? What importance does place have?

- Try reworking some of your material using the concept of *memory* itself as a theme. What role do you notice that memory plays in your notebook entries? What kinds of things seem to stand out most in your memory: people, objects, colors, places? Do you have trouble remembering a certain period from your life? What do you make of that?

- Think about how your life could be told metaphorically through a myth or fairy tale or comic book hero's story. If your life is like Spider-Man's, how so? If you feel like Cinderella, what are the situations and who are the people making you feel like that? Variation: Compare yourself with a character in a book; compare your memories or life situation with a fictional situation.

- Look at one memory from the points of view of other people who were involved in the event. What would they have been thinking and feeling during this event? Use your imagination and pretend to be inside the mind of the other person(s). Or interview them to ask how they witnessed the event and what they were thinking.

   Sinnae wrote about a moment she remembered from when she was four years old in three different ways. First, as the memory itself, then as her current self reflecting on the memory, and then as what she imagines her father might have been experiencing at the very same moment (see Figure 5–4).

- If you already have a theme, angle, or focus for your memoir draft, here are some more questions you can apply to your theme:
   1. What are your thoughts and feelings about your theme?
   2. What images, metaphors, or visual symbols can you make for your theme?
   3. What does your father/mother/sibling/friend/grandparent have to say about your theme or angle?
   4. What is the history of this theme? When in human history, or the history of the planet, did this happen?
   5. What is the science of this theme? What is the physical, concrete cause and effect of your theme?

1

She held her daddy's hands, small and chubby, and as he tensed himself to enter the elevator, she screamed and cried with a tangy edginess in her voice. He begged on the pavement as passers-by looked on in bemusement, *little girl so stubborn and unrelenting, father so kind and generous*. The minds of onlookers quickly dodged to other subjects as they walked on. She never let go, and mother back at home jokingly says, "People must've thought he was kidnapping you!"

She never lets herself be lured into painted walls and clinking machinery.

2

When I think of this memory, I think of bright grey and the senses that grey brings. Cool yet not confident and watery, that would be the best description for pavement-under-new-sunlight. I can see myself thrashing, and then, again out of my own eyes looking in the small "lobby." I can feel warmth from the sun above, and the sun is trying to correct me and my actions, but I am no regular Prometheus and I could not have looked ahead. I feel like I'm being put under the spotlight by all the passers-by and my father, who, in vain, is trying to put an end to all this. Since I was a little child, I did not understand human emotions that were a little less sharper and a little more blunt. So I didn't know how I was embarrassing my father. I felt very small, probably because I was in a dress, and that makes me feel small. I wasn't intimidated in any way, just afraid and aimlessly directing my fear to my father who tries to grab my arms so I should not hurt myself.

3

My daughter, Sinnae, has been very strange. When I took her to the back entrance of 119, she screamed and threw a fit on the street. She yelled and she used all her strength to stop from being moved. I was so frustrated when she wouldn't move, and afraid that something might have been wrong with her. But I told her and explained and as we walked away, she calmed down and didn't yell anymore. But I'm still quite shocked because I've never seen her acting this way. Never seen her throw a fit, except maybe the Rocking Horse Tea Party Incident. She is usually quite . . . careful. Not very quiet, actually very talkative, but also sensible on how to present herself to others.

Figure 5–4 *Sinnae Writes About One Memory from Three Different Points of View*

In this notebook entry, Sinnae tries out a metaphor for her theme and also describes the physical manifestations of anger:

Anger

For me, anger is like a calendar. It ends quickly, like the sheets flying off in the wind, until the end of the year comes closer. Maybe it's the rush that ends quickly, not the effect. Maybe it's that horrible buzzing in your ears that disappears after a few minutes, the red you see when you close your eyes even in the darkness. The distance, the words that come from my mouth not being mine; that all ends soon.

But it's the throbbing pain, the stones in my chest being thrown at my ribcage and shattering the bones—that stays with me for hours, days. Even years after I can feel the heartbeat slower and more deliberate, I can feel the fists at my side.

All the questions and activities in this chapter that attempt to push writers to take on critical, interpretive angles and lenses can be quite challenging for many young people. Not every student of mine has been able to step outside of his or her life to look at it through any eyeglasses, rose-colored or not. Instead, some have preferred to simply write the story of what happened—first this, then that. But in writing conferences with these students, I still ask them to help me understand the answer to a question all memoirists ask themselves as they write: *So what?* What is the significance of the memories they have chosen to write about? What does it all mean to them now? I put the words *So what?* on our chart of the elements of memoir because I want all my students to try to figure out what's important about their story and to make that be a part of their final memoir draft.

Seeing what was not apparent before, making more of something than it seemed at the time, making connections between formerly disconnected events, and finding deeper meanings in our memories—this is the stuff of interpretation. This process describes what writers do and readers do. It really describes how we learn deeply about anything.

6 Shaping the Story

Possibilities for Structure

Why memoir? It means the world becomes yours. If you don't do it, it drifts away and takes a whole piece of yourself with it, like an amputation. To attack it and attack it and get it under control—it's like taking possession of your life, isn't it?

—TED HUGHES

Ever wonder why humble office supply stores have blossomed into superwarehouses, the size of mega–home improvement stores? It's because they understand that humans seek order and structure. People need colored folders and big, plastic bins to put things in. We need files with labels for the piles of paper, and ceramic bowls for the fistfuls of paper clips, before all of it threatens to engulf us. Once we put papers and supplies in their proper containers, we can sit down in our cleared-out space, perhaps light some incense, and proceed to find the larger meaning of all that stuff.

Words on paper need a structure also. When we read words that are not placed into organized categories, or into some logical, pleasing shape, we don't know what to do with them in our minds; we don't know how to get to their larger meaning. Warning: organizing can be a hard move! Here we are, writing lovely little splotches of things as they occur to us, with no responsibility toward the audience, no need to make logical sense from one thought to another, and now we have to structure it and make it flow? We need some plastic bins and file folders!

Fortunately, the contemporary memoir as a literary genre is still fairly young, allowing it some freedom from rules and boundaries. It reminds me of the current explosion on the Internet of blogging, that kind of free-form, journal-like, yet public writing that thousands of young people read and respond to daily. The memoir genre is evolving, and so it encompasses multiple forms, styles, images, and sounds. I believe we can thank the startling experimentation of several literary geniuses of the early twentieth century—Virginia Woolf, James Joyce, Robbes-Grillet, Gertrude Stein, Samuel Beckett, and others—for opening up what is possible for narrative structures. Artists also redefined their genres in the last century. Picasso and Braque fractured objects, seeing in them the geometric planes and shapes of cubism. Seraut represented the world in tiny dots of color and white space. Contemporary memoirists borrow from other writers, from visual artists, even from music composers for the shapes of their memoirs. Memoirists now employ stream of consciousness, shifts in points of view and time, fractured narrative, divisions into *movements,* and the use of mixed or multiple genres to relate how the world appears to them and how life feels to them. As with a poem, the form of a memoir carries its meaning—history might be represented as a continuous sequence, as a series of vague impressions, as a story interrupted, or a scene unraveling backward in time, depending on the meaning an author wishes to convey (Morris 1966, 11).

In this chapter, I describe several structures that kids write in most successfully and also some ideas about how to teach those forms. I provide examples of particular structures from published memoirs so that these can become models for your students to emulate. I begin by discussing the umbrella category of narrative and then break that down into manageable chunks for helping students write various forms and shapes with confidence.

Components of Memoir Narratives

First, I need to reiterate that in this book and in my classroom, I am teaching how to write memoir as *nonfiction.* This means that for the most part, what happens in the memoir text is the truth. Names may be changed to protect certain identities; some details may be imagined because of the writer's vague and imprecise memory; dialogue may be invented and events exaggerated a bit in order to dramatize a scene and reveal characters' personalities; and there may even be some interesting play with other genres— myth, poetry, playwriting—whose forms best convey the memoirist's meaning, but essentially, memoir is *not fiction.* That said, however, the most pervasive and, some might argue, most inviting and interesting form of memoir writing to read is the narrative, or story, form.

The narrative form, most broadly defined, follows a sequence of events over a period of time. It starts at a certain point in time (not necessarily at what we might call the beginning, say, the author's birth); it proceeds through time (possibly with flashbacks and foreshadowing—see "Framing with Time" on page 134); and it ends at a later point in time (again, not necessarily at what we might consider the end, like the day the author put the manuscript in the mail to the publisher, and certainly not at the author's death!). Inside this story that travels through time, characters (the author and his family and friends) do things and say things to each other that influence, hurt, heal, and mean a great deal to the author.

For some lucky writers, memory might actually reveal itself in a narrative form. Patricia Hampl (2004) argues that "memory is an automatic formulator of story" and that everyone remembers in narration, perhaps even Hampl's dog, who remembers where he was the last time he got a treat from her! For most people, however, memory does not unfold as a neat story structure. Rather, it reveals itself in fits and starts, as if in a fog, as if underwater. In visual images and sound bites. In vague, irretrievable whiffs, like a passing scent of some long-forgotten perfume. Fortunately for that kind of mind, there are dozens of shapes, tones, and designs of texts that allow for the briefest description or explanation of events in a life. I will offer several of those possibilities later in this chapter.

Like most stories, a great memoir narrative can express a sense of discovery as time moves along. In the best examples of this narrative form, there exists a slight feeling of suspense or mystery, so that to read this life feels like reading a good novel. The main character (the author) is driven by desire or the need to find something out or to live out some inexorable fate. Obstacles exist along the way to meeting that need, and this causes narrative tension. The content is organized into scenes and moved forward by dialogue and action. Woven throughout will be reflections and interpretations—some thoughts about *how the character changed because of this* or *what this all means to her now*. Finally, like most literature, the narrative structure of memoir contains a heightened emotional quality, and it can have an ending that invites more questions than it gives answers. The reader gets caught up in the memoir's characters, the struggles they face, the dreams they pursue. The reader comes to care deeply about the main character and is anxious about the outcome of his story.

Young or unpracticed writers of memoir often feel frustrated that they can't remember enough to flesh out full scenes containing dialogue, action, and description of place. Here again, we need to remind students that memoirs are not legal documents; they do not need to contain exact, certifiable truths, but only the *felt* or *emotional truth* as experienced by the author. Beyond that, authors must borrow some of the tools from the fiction writer's tool box to help make their story flow like a delicious novel. Two of the best-selling adult memoirs of all time, *Angela's Ashes*, by Frank McCourt (1996), and *The Liar's Club*, by Mary Carr (1995), got the full narrative treatment from their authors. Carr and McCourt constructed minute, narrative details, the blow-by-blow depictions of action, and dialogue that sounds completely right. They are both exquisite storytellers, and their books make terrific models for teachers to study for their own knowledge of narrative.

So what are some elements of narrative writing that *do* make memoirs exciting to read, which we can teach kids to attempt as they write their own? I'm going to focus on three components of narrative: scenes (including dramatic action), dialogue, and conflict.

Scenes

Although the fit is not exact, our students can learn some things about how to craft a dramatic scene from watching television or films. Certainly, children understand the concepts of action and dialogue when we relate them to their favorite movies or television shows.

I ask students to think of a TV sitcom. In fewer than twenty minutes, a new minidrama emerges that manages to begin and end in a way that feels satisfying to viewers. In between commercials, scenes unfold, during which people talk, conflicts arise, and something happens to resolve everything at the conclusion. Once we've found a common language and understanding of scene from discussing a popular TV show, I can move along to analyze excerpted scenes from written texts.

A major difference to notice between written texts and television shows is that in texts, there is a lot of writing that does not contain any action or dialogue, but just solid blocks of description and explanation. This kind of writing, usually called exposition, narration, or summary writing appears before scenes of dialogue and action in order to set them up or after scenes to explain what just happened. In fiction, narration or summary allows the writer to move through a lot of space and time quickly and smoothly and provides important information that establishes locations, times, and characters' thoughts. It gives writers a chance to write lovely passages of description and introspection, and it gives readers a little break. Constant action and dialogue are hard to digest in a written format and they don't give the reader or writer any opportunity to reflect on what is going on. For the memoirist, summary provides an even more crucial function as a place to do the reflective work that defines the genre—showing the action and conversation and then explaining what meaning it holds for the author. Exposition acts almost like a camera lens in a movie or TV show: using words, an author can tell where the story happens, can describe the external details that a camera shows with pictures. But as I tell my students, writers are so much luckier than cameras, so much more powerful! Writers can go where no camera can: to the thoughts and feelings inside people.

Learning how to work scenes and exposition into a well-paced rhythm takes a great deal of time and practice. One way to learn how to construct a scene is to study a good one from a published text. I copy an excerpt, such as this short bit from "In the Blink of an Eye," by Norma Fox Mazer (1999), onto a transparency so my class can study it together. In this scene, the author is trying to sneak into the house after having tried her first puff of a cigarette:

> My sister is waiting for me, standing near the Sternfelds' front porch, a kind of concrete apron with two pillars. Upstairs, right above it, we have a better porch too, where my mother lets us eat in summer. My sister puts her hands on her hips. "Where were you? What were you doing?"
>
> "Nowhere. Nothing." I talk through tight lips.
>
> "I was calling you."
>
> "I know."
>
> "Mom is home from work. She wants you for supper."
>
> "I know."
>
> "Were you with someone?"
>
> "Who?"
>
> "That's what I asked you."
>
> "What?"
>
> "Don't be fresh. Who do you think you are, Wonder Woman?"
>
> "Yes, yes, I'm Wonder Woman!"
>
> I forget to keep my lips tight, and she leans close and sniffs, her nostrils drawing up in disgust. "What's that nasty smell?"
>
> I run around her, up the wooden steps into our apartment, and down the hall: past the room that I share with my little sister, past the door to the back stairs, then the living room and the kitchen, and into the bathroom. (23–24)

Notice the exposition before and after the dialogue and action. Imagine this as a play that has a live person narrating, setting the scene with the big sister waiting on the porch, shutting up to let the actors take over to dramatize the moment, and then narrating again to get our main character into the bathroom to rinse her mouth out. Notice that a well-written scene has a nice balance of action and dialogue and that the dialogue moves the story forward: we learn from the sister that Mother has come home (uh-oh!) and dinner is waiting (better hurry!). Again, if characters are not moving like actors on a stage, it's exposition. If characters never talk to each other as they move around, it can still be a scene, but too many such scenes will become monotonous.

Mazer's is only one way to craft a scene. Some writers advise using more dramatic action right up front and dispensing with all that exposition. It depends on what kind of tone a writer is aiming for. More action and dialogue fits a very action-packed story. It's fun to study different kinds of scenes with students and decide what tone the writer aimed for.

Notice that scenes often crescendo to something semidramatic, or at least to a point where something, or someone, changes. Some writers believe the cardinal rule of scene writing is to have something change. I'm not sold on that, but I do think that writers should work toward a feeling of *tension* in a scene—Mazer has built up plenty of that in her scene— otherwise it can feel flat and unnecessary.

Tools for Crafting Scenes

Choosing Meaningful Moments

For a first step in scene writing, I ask students to choose one event or one important memory from their collection of notebook entries. Choosing a meaningful event is crucial to the success of this exercise and ultimately to the whole memoir. The point is not to write indiscriminate scenes; instead, each writer needs to choose which moment in his memoir bears dramatizing. In *Writing the Memoir: From Truth to Art*, Judith Barrington (2002) likens scene writing to a camera zooming in for a close-up on two people sitting at a table, drinking tea and talking to each other. Memoirists might reserve scenes for showing when something happened differently one time, something so important that the writer needs to slow time and zoom in on facial expressions, to capture every word of dialogue. Barrington says that a narrative memoir needs to intersperse that kind of close-up shot with writing that summarizes events that happened pretty much the same way for years and years. She compares the summary kind of writing to a camera's long shots, where in one swoop, the camera takes in the scenery, the time of day, the street, what the houses in the neighborhood looked like, the city, and so on. This summary writing can cover great spans of time, can scatter quickly over settings, and can establish a lot of the historic, factual territory of the memoir so that the close-up scenes stand in relief.

Writers create some scenes to dramatize turning points in the story, the events that hold deep meaning, and they might also develop a scene in such a way that it stands for all the times that things happened in a certain way. In my own memoir, for instance, I wrote a long, detailed scene at the dinner table of my childhood. The scene does not describe one particular night, but rather just about every dinner scene, as I remember them, when my mother was likely to do such and such, and my father always said so and so, and I always felt the same way at the end of it.

In contrast to that kind of habitual scene that encapsulated many dinner-table episodes, I placed this scene about a dramatic event in my childhood:

When I was nine years old, my Girl Scout troop visited an aviary in the South Valley of Albuquerque. It was owned by a man we called *Viejo*, which means "old man" in Spanish. This place looked like a chest of precious gems, all those brightly colored bird feathers, tucked into the brown desert valley. Inside the sprawling adobe hacienda, I noticed fireplaces and books in every room. Birds, strange tropical breeds, flitted from room to room, and owls roosted on the bookshelves.

Outside, acres of sage, yucca, and mimosa trees, and more birds, of every variety—some in cages, some free to roam around his land. He had a dozen peacocks, dull-colored females, and several spectacular males. We tried to coax the males to spread their colorful tail feathers for us. "Come on boy, come on, let's see your pretty fan!" Some of the girls became bored with this and began to chase the geese, swans, and ostriches around the yard. The owner was very angry with us; if we chased the ostriches, he shouted, they would kill us with their necks, which were as thick as young tree trunks.

We spent hours at this house, while he showed us all the different birds and told us interesting facts about them. I hated to leave this magical place. I loved the birds, and I wished I could run away from home and go live in Viejo's house. I could be his *hija*, his daughter, and help him take care of the birds. As we began to move toward the gate to board the bus back to the school, I followed last, slumping along, wishing they would leave me behind. Suddenly, I felt a heavy thud, like the blunt end of a rifle, then a sharp stab, on the top of my head. Stunned at first, I started running and screaming. I reached my hand up to my head and touched the giant claws and talons of a bird. I could not imagine what was happening to me, so I ran even faster to escape it. As I ran, the bird dug its claws deeper into the skin of my skull.

Viejo yelled out at me, "Stop running! Stop running!" I stopped, and the old man snuck up behind me with a broom. I heard the thwack of the broom on the bird's body, and then a shrill, high-pitched screech, almost like the sound of a girl screaming. I felt the claws release from my head with a violent thrust. The bird flew up to the roof of the hacienda. I began to cry, but as I looked up, I saw him, a huge, male peacock, strutting across the rooftop, fanning his feathers out for me.

The old man held me in his arms and whispered to me, "It's your beautiful, long, golden hair. See?" He pointed up to the breathtaking fan of turquoise, purple and blue. "He is calling to you with his tail. He wants you to love him."

In this scene, I use more exposition than dialogue, but that fits my memory of this event. I lived inside my head as a little girl, speaking to few, and I wanted to re-create the lonely quality of my childhood. But people (and birds) move around, and I tried to create some dramatic tension in the scene by taking time to build it up, using sensual details, and even adding a tad of foreshadowing about those dangerous ostriches.

To help students write scenes, I first ask them to choose a moment or a situation that deserves slowing down and zooming in, and then I ask them to close their eyes and try to re-create the scene, to "make a movie in their mind" of what happened. On a fresh page in the writer's notebook, or a new blank piece of paper, I ask them to write out a draft of that scene, exactly as they see it unfolding in their head. As with all first-draft writing, I think writers need to put down their first words and trust that they can go back to write it better later. The early draft of a scene might simply set the time, place, people, and events just as they appear in memory. Fine-tuning the scene to make it more dramatic—to add tension or to make the dialogue more interesting—can happen in revisions. For homework, or during writing workshop the next day, I ask students to choose another event or memory and again write the scene as it unfolded. After we have worked closely together as a class on developing a couple of scenes, I add "scenes" to our repertoire chart for elements of the craft of memoir.

Depending on how much time you wish to devote to this aspect of narrative development, you might try the following concrete and terrifically fun strategies that help kids craft scenes. The first is to create a time line, the second is to draw a storyboard, and the third is to act out the writing. (See Chapter 8 for more ideas for using outlines, drawing, and acting out during other phases of the drafting and revision process.)

Creating Time Lines

I use informal time lines during writing, reading, and actually in all areas of the curriculum. It's a powerful tool that helps kids see and manipulate the sequence of events and ideas. Obviously, the length of the time lines, as well as the beginning and end points, vary depending on what chunk of time they represent. A time line can be as humongous as all of human existence or as miniscule as what happened during the last five minutes. The function of the time line is to order events in time.

We can even choose one big topic or idea and find its plotline in our life. In her chapter about memoir in *The Art of Teaching Writing*, Lucy Calkins (1994) says she could make a time line just for the topic of her relationship, a lifelong struggle, she notes sadly, with her *hair!* There are endless topics for time lines, Lucy realizes, and "Because each dot on each timeline . . . contains endless stories, a timeline of any one of these strands can function as a table of contents for many future entries" (412).

For scene work, I ask students to make a time line and start it at the moment the first person walks in or the first person talks or the first action occurs. The end point comes when the last person walks out, the last person talks, or the last action occurs. This is the easiest way to fix the large events of the scene on a time line. Once the events are mapped out along the time line, writers can choose any point along the sequence to begin writing the scene.

Next, students might write the scene exactly as it happened—step one, step two, step three—or you might invite them to play with the order of events or begin writing the scene with something that happened in the middle of things. In my childhood dinner scene, for instance, I might begin the scene with the action of myself setting the table, worried about remembering the proper placement of the plates and utensils. Or I might begin with my four family members already seated and eating, and I might have my mother say something and then have me react to that. Or I might begin with the final event, which was always my mother leaving the table, going to her bedroom, and closing the door. The scene could then rewind in time to try to figure out what the inciting moment was that caused that to happen. Who said or did something that upset her so?

Drawing Storyboards

Like the time line, a storyboard fixes a sequence of events, but in this case, the drawings add color, shape, mood, and visual embodiment to the words. Storyboards look something like comic strips; they sketch out the physical details of each moment in a script.

Film and television directors use storyboards to plan out scenes before they film them. This step saves a great deal of time and money, since actors know what they will be doing in each shot, and camera operators know where they should be aiming their lenses. For writers, the visual representations can help determine sequence as well as help generate more visual descriptions about a particular event. Students who think and work best using visual images find that these tools help them generate and then order their ideas and memories.

I show students how I would storyboard the scene with the peacock landing on my head. I make a few rows of squares, about three inches by three inches. I talk out loud about what happened that day as I *sketch* (this is key—I don't let kids belabor these drawings; they are meant to help them think and plan, not illustrate) figures and buildings, trees and birds into the first few boxes. I use colored pencils or Cray-Pas, adding quick splashes of color so that I can write about colors in my scene. The important move happens next: I look back at my sketches to decide if I need to cut up the boxes and move the order around. I also notice some physical details that I have drawn and tell kids that I'm going to go back to this scene in my notebook and add them to my writing.

Acting Out

For helping students visualize and dramatize their writing, there is no tool more powerful than drama. In the process of embodying a scene—of deciding where and how the actors should stand, sit, move, speak—kids discover all sorts of necessary details that need to be added to their written texts before the scene looks and sounds right.

One crucial narrative device that young writers need to practice is dramatic action, and the first big lesson for memoir writing is that action doesn't mean "Zap!" "Pow!" and blowing things up. In daily life, our actions are fairly simple, peaceful, and redundant: brushing hair, lifting forks and spoons to our mouth, changing channels on the TV. While many kids feel they have a firm grip on action, especially when they are re-creating video games and scenes from Japanese anime, for instance, they would be shocked to find out how weak their descriptions of character actions are if someone acted out their writing in front of them.

Kids are by no means the only ones who struggle with dramatic action. It's one of the major obstacles that separate me from writing the great novel or screenplay I just know I have in me. I'm forever coming up with the wittiest (to me) ideas for skits that might appear on the television show *Saturday Night Live*. They usually come flying out of the blue as Randy and I are walking our dog. I'll say something like, "Hey, I just thought of a great idea for a skit on *Saturday Night Live,*" and then explain the gist.

Randy says, "Yeah? Then what happens?"

"I don't know!" I whine. "It's just such a funny idea!"

Randy is right, of course. In a successful play, movie, or story, usually, something has to happen. It's the most basic writing advice: show, don't tell. Characters need to move. They have to climb, sit down, eat, strike out, kiss, do something. Not only that, but action, along with dialogue and narration, advances a story to its coherent, believable conclusion. I bring lessons in portraying action to life by having students act out their writing with friends. Kids understand that in a sitcom or a play, actors can't just stand there. So they learn how to manipulate their characters on paper by making them move first in a skit or in their storyboard sketches as described earlier.

Learning how to craft scenes benefits all writing genres, so I tend to carve out several days during the drafting phase for this work. As always, I rely on published memoir excerpts of great scenes to use as models we can analyze and refer to. I ask students to mark with sticky notes scenes in their independent reading that they think work well and want to use as models. I want every student in my class to have the experience of writing dramatic scenes, whether or not he or she winds up writing a strictly narrative type of memoir or one of the other myriad forms available to the class. Ultimately, students may decide to fold one to three of their crafted scenes into a longer narrative. As they decide how to play with time in their narrative, they may rearrange the order of scenes or purposely begin their memoir with the last thing that happened. (See page 134 for a discussion about playing with time in the memoir.) Or students may decide to expand just one major scene while interweaving reflections and ruminations until the original scene fills pages and pages of text. Or they may of course decide to dismantle the scenes altogether, crafting instead a montage or pastiche of memories that truly feel like little poems written in prose.

Dialogue

A second crucial component of narratives, whether they contain recognizable scenes or not, is dialogue. Done well, dialogue works miracles in a story. It reveals a character's background, values, and personality. For instance, in the delightfully humorous story

"Scout's Honor," Avi (1996) brings his two best friends to life through dialogue. Max is usually full of information, a Mr. Smarty Pants kind of kid. The friend named Horse always asks, "You saying . . . ?" as if challenging anyone who speaks to him:

> Horse, envious, complained he was getting hungry.
> "Eat some of your canned beans," I suggested.
> He got out one can without ripping his pocket too badly. Then his face took on a mournful look.
> "What's the matter?" I asked.
> "Forgot to bring a can opener."
> Max said, "In the old days, people opened cans with their teeth."
> "You saying my teeth aren't strong?"
> "I'm just talking about history!"
> "You saying I don't know history?'
> Always kind, I plopped half my sandwich into Horse's hand. He squashed it into his mouth and was quiet for the next fifteen minutes. It proved something I'd always believed: The best way to stop arguments is to get people to eat peanut butter sandwiches. They can't talk. (128–29)

Avi provides a handful of perfectly timed examples of Horse responding, "You saying . . . ?" so that this character becomes funnier because he repeats it so often. Also notice that Avi drops part of the verb from the question so that it sounds even more like a real person talking: "You saying . . . ?" instead of "*Are* you saying . . . ?"

Tools for Crafting Dialogue

Studying Real Conversation

Dialogue can explain what happened before this moment and look forward to what might come later in the story. In memoir, it carries the weight of evidence, proof of what people are truly like. Done poorly, dialogue makes characters sound like robots or idiots or like boring, boring people giving long speeches. It's worth spending time helping young writers learn to write dialogue because they will be able to use those lessons in everything they write. Here are some things I've asked students to try to practice dialogue:

- Read like a wolf. (I echo Gary Paulsen. It can't be stressed enough.)
- With some friends, act out chunks of dialogue from the book you are reading. How does the author make the dialogue sound real and believable?

- Write down overheard conversations in your writer's notebook, and use bits or even whole chunks from them in your writing.

- Write out some dialogue from a scene you are working on. Give the dialogue to some friends to act out. What works and what sounds awkward, silly, or robotic? Take suggestions from the actors for making it better.

- Listen hard for your characters' (which in a memoir will likely be people in your family or friends) personal speech habits. Does one person talk in a kind of formal way, always saying "yes" instead of "yeah" or "uh-huh," like most people? Does another person speak only in half-formed sentences so that you can almost hear ellipses (. . .) after each utterance?

- Listen hard for the words, phrases, and utterances that important people in your life say over and over. Does your father always call you little pet names, like Toots or Smoky Boy? Does your little brother say things in a whiny way, like "That's not fair! You got more than me!"? Does your best friend always use the latest cool words, like "You're the man, dawg!" (That was cool in 2005 anyway!)

Studying Written Conversation

I make an overhead transparency of a scene from a memoir that uses strong dialogue. Sometimes I also make copies for students to keep and mark up. I pick a scene from the book I am currently reading aloud or one that has been a past hit with my students so that we can focus on the dialogue and not on the story. Then I try these activities in a minilesson or over the course of a few days, using different excerpts:

Step One: I read the scene once, using a dramatic voice to sound like different characters or to impart the emotion and meaning being conveyed.

Step Two: I ask students to volunteer for different parts. As they read their bit of dialogue, I encourage them to emote and express as I did. They practice several times, and I coach right along until we can hear differences in the way the actors use their voices to express meaning.

Step Three: I ask kids to sit with a partner and practice reading the dialogue again. I listen to as many partnerships as I can, again coaching them to read so that it sounds like real people are talking.

Step Four: I ask what students notice about the different ways the characters talk. How did the author make each person come alive on the page? I write down what kids say on a chart titled something like "How to Write Good Dialogue."

Following are some things students notice, or that I add to the list if they don't. (The excerpt from Avi's story demonstrates most of these characteristics of dialogue.)

- Characters talk in short sentences, phrases, or even just one word.
- There are lots of words where the narrator is describing something or the character is thinking something, and then there are a few lines of dialogue.
- Sometimes, the words are spelled differently (kids might say "spelled wrong") to match how a person really talks. For example: June Jordon spells her father's West Indian dialect as it sounds: "Listen to me, girl. Mon to mon: You see? You have to be tink to you'self about *everting*. You can' go through life like a nincompoop. You have to use you coconut!" (2000, 67) David Almond's spelling gives his childhood friends a dialect that is probably specific to a certain geographic area of England: "Daft dog!" he shouted. "Look what ye've done to me dinna!" (2003, 6).
- Writers most often use "he said/she said" after someone talks.
- Sometimes there is just the dialogue, without telling who said it. (Writers try to make sure it will be clear from the sequence of dialogue or the context of the words who is speaking.)
- Sometimes the dialogue is all there is to a scene. Somehow the author has made something happen just in the talking. (We call such authors masters of dialogue.)

Conflicts and Consequences

When students are writing a memoir of some length and complexity, they need to find the overarching *desire* that drives the story. As they draft and revise, they will be developing their own *self* as the main character. Throughout the story, that character wants something special, though likely something intangible. Or that character needs to make an important choice in order to move on. Or something needs to happen as a consequence of a choice he or she made at another time.

Conflict, or tension, is the engine of story. Tension comes from a desire that faces obstacles, which can arise from external or internal forces. William Faulkner said the best meaning in stories comes from "the heart in conflict with itself." Suspense and tension occur naturally as the "I" makes decisions and moral choices. Readers wonder what the consequences of those choices will be. We feel anxious for this character at the same time that we hope for better outcomes.

Tools for Crafting Conflict

Studying Tension in Literature

Learning to compose this kind of story arc requires the same kind of analyses of published texts that I've already demonstrated during whole-class reading discussions and in writing minilessons. To pursue this new purpose, however, we turn our eyes toward interpreting the big ideas, what the authors of those texts desire and what obstacles or conflicts they face.

In *Breaking Through* (2001), the sequel to *The Circuit* (1997), his first extraordinary autobiographical novel for young adults, Francisco Jimenez and his siblings fight to remain in the United States and not get deported back to Mexico. Jimenez writes about their daily life using details fraught with danger and difficulty. We read this story, rooting for Francisco, devastated when he gets caught and deported, rejoicing when he gets to come back home to his mother and his beloved schooling in California. This is an example of a character's desire set against extreme social and political forces, but even in less dramatic stories, tensions exist. E. L. Konigsberg wants to maintain her "station" in life as the youngest child and straight A student in "How I Lost My Station in Life" (1999). Circumstances conspire to pull the rug out from under both those identities. In the funny and sweet story "Food from the Outside," Rita Williams-Garcia (1996) describes the desire shared with her siblings for food cooked by anyone other than her mother. They devise an elaborate plan to thwart the house rules against eating "from the outside," and of course, there are consequences for disobeying "Miss Essie," their mama.

Reading Desire into Your Writing

Students can look over all the entries they made during the generating, collecting, and layering phase and pretend that they are reading about a character in a book. What does this person want in life? What are his desires? Her dreams? What gets in the way of what this character wants? How does he work through the conflicts? What are the consequences of her actions?

When the writer has thought about and written in response to these questions, she might be ready to map out how the story will go so that it will be sure to include the process toward a fulfilled (or perhaps an unfulfilled) goal.

Structures for Narrative Memoirs

Now I'll describe several ways to structure the memoir using narrative frames. I teach these particular structures because they are the most accessible forms for students to take on as models and learn to write well. They offer useful alternatives to the extended, novel-length memoirs, especially for those students who find remembering or controlling large amounts of text difficult. These structures still fit under the large category of narrative; that is, they tell a story in time. But they are much shorter than novel-length memoirs, containing only a few full scenes or consisting of *vignettes* (tiny stories), or of moments strung together, like beads on a string. They provide imaginative ways to frame or contain the contents of the memoir, using shape, contrasting elements, or time.

Framing with Shape

One Event
Probably the most popular structure for picture books, this shape relates one meaningful event or memory. Like the scene, the shape of the one event will probably follow a story arc where tension builds, then something happens, and then all the pieces fall into place. James Howe, in "Everything Will Be Okay" (1996), and Joseph Bruchac, in "The Snapping Turtle" (1996), stay tightly inside a single past event. In both stories, by staying so close to one memory, the authors capture the magnificent, heartbreaking poignancy of the child's perspective and make it immediate.

Other examples of this structure focus primarily on one event but also make detours and digressions into related events or other times this kind of incident has happened. Adult memoirists can easily control this more complicated structure, but so can many kids if they have an example or two to guide them. In the first volume of *When I Was*

Your Age, stories by Laurence Yep (1996) and Katherine Patterson (1996) demonstrate this technique. The major event in Yep's story, "The Great Rat Hunt," is going after a rat in his family's store with a rifle. But the deeper lesson he learned that day was that his father loved him despite his lack of athletic ability. Yep helps us feel the importance of that realization by digressing from the main action to explain his physical weakness from asthma, his hatred of killing, and some things about his father's childhood fears of coming to America from China.

In "Why I Never Ran Away from Home," Patterson diverges from her main event of almost running away to tell about a number of instances when she was made to feel ugly, stupid, and useless as the youngest child in her neighborhood and the baby sister of smart, pretty Lizzie. The anger and loneliness Patterson felt when she was seven years old, enhanced by examples of other times she felt like this, led her finally one evening to just "walk away" from everyone.

For a minilesson, I copy several pages from these stories onto overhead transparencies. I read through the excerpts (having already read the full stories out loud at a different time), asking kids to help me mark the places where the narrative strays from the main event. We talk about *why* the author digressed: possibly to show that certain behaviors or actions were consistent patterns or to contrast another event or time with this current event, for instance.

If kids choose to write their memoir about one main event or memory, they will need to know why *this* event or memory. What does it reveal about who they are? What changed because of it, or what did they realize as a result of it?

Graphic novels and picture books   When I first began teaching memoir, I had a narrow concept of what to expect from students as their final project. It took a comment from Tony, who asked why he had to read so many *picture* books to learn how to write memoir and then had to write so many *"long words"* on notebook paper, to open my eyes wider. Great question. The reason I use picture books with older students as model texts is that they are short. It's easy to teach some aspect of writing or genre when the text can be read and discussed in one sitting. But before Tony complained, I had rejected the idea of my students making picture books because we were not studying the picture book genre. I did not want to have to go into graphic design lessons when my focus in the memoir genre was discovering meaning in our life stories.

But Tony convinced me that he could make a text that fulfilled all my wishes for the memoir as well as his incessant need to draw. He was an artist, and since his memoir was *about* learning how to draw, it seemed ridiculous not to let him draw his memoir. I suggested that he read *The Art Lesson*, an autobiographical picture book by Tomie de-Paola (1989) about a little boy who becomes an artist despite the rigid, prescriptive lessons he is given at school.

After that experience, I began to offer graphic texts as an option for my students. In the baskets of memoir books, I included one that looks like a comic but is called a graphic novel. *Persepolis*, by Marjane Satrupi (2003), is a moving account of the author's experiences growing up under an oppressive regime in Iran. *Maus: A Survivor's Tale*, by Art Spiegelman (1986), is another extraordinary example of this genre, though it contains quite gruesome scenes of the Holocaust and may not be suitable for elementary-aged children. Surprisingly, not that many children have wanted to make picture books or comics. Usually, it is the kids who are passionate about art as well as some reluctant writers who see an opportunity to put fewer words and more illustrations on the paper. Of course, when we confer with children writing a picture book memoir, the lessons are the same: finding the heart of the story and portraying the self.

A short, contained period of time   Similar to the one-event container, this frame focuses on a *time period* rather than an *incident*, and that length of time will be longer than it would take for one event to happen, so it might contain several incidents. A period of time might be "my year in third grade," or even "the time it took to learn how to shoot a basket," or "the hours from 3:00 P.M. to 6:00 P.M., when I am alone in my house with the door locked until my mom gets home from work."

We might imagine writing about situations such as waiting in an emergency room or playing outside on the last night before summer vacation ends by making the felt experience of how time passed become almost the subject or main character of the piece. For kids, a time period, whether hours or years, provides a tidy container for the content of memories and reflections. But as with all choices of what to write about, there should be strong meaning and purpose behind the time period selected. For instance, perhaps in third grade the writer discovered basketball, and now he is reflecting on how that opened a new world of physical activity for him. Or perhaps the years at middle school pointed the writer on a life mission: it was during that time she discovered the violin and now she wants to grow up to play in an orchestra.

Series of Events

Vignettes   Every time I teach a memoir genre study, the self-contained, one- to two-page *vignettes*, each poetically titled, such as in *The House on Mango Street*, by Sandra Cisneros (1989), become the most popular way for kids to structure their memoirs. That makes sense. It's challenging even for adults to sort through the material of their lives and restructure it to make it controlled, coherent, and enticing for others to read. Many young people prefer books that are episodic or filled with short vignettes for their independent reading, and naturally, they look again to these texts to mentor their own compositions. While the authors of the following texts may not have called their writing vignettes, that is what I call them when I demonstrate this way of shaping memories.

Childtimes: A Three-Generation Memoir, by Eloise Greenfield and Lessie Jones Little, with material by Pattie Ridley Jones (1979), is one of my favorite examples of this structure. The organization of this book is complex, so I draw concentric circles to show students how the book is put together. The largest organizing structure, dividing the book into three parts, is generational: grandmother, mother, and daughter (Eloise) each write their memoir. The next circle of structure is chronological: each author relays events as they happened loosely, across time. The innermost circle is topics or events. Each woman writes short vignettes about topics or events that stand out in her memory, with titles like "Papa's Jobs," "Hot Rolls," "Clothes," "World War II," and "Black Music." All three sections are united by the larger theme, which they call the "Landscape," of life in the United States for African Americans since the 1880s.

The House on Mango Street, by Sandra Cisneros (1989), is an autobiographical work of fiction that is written in first person and has all the elements of memoir that I want my students to understand and attempt in their own writing: specific detail, reflection, portrait of the "I," and dialogue. Read this book first before giving it to your students. Certain vignettes that deal with sexuality may not be appropriate for elementary students. I excerpt several vignettes for younger audiences. Of course, some of my fifth-grade students bought or checked out the book from the library because they loved it so much. Students in middle and high school can certainly handle reading the entire book, and many high schools include it as required reading in English classes.

The individual vignettes add up to an overarching story of a girl who desires to move out of her house, with its "windows so small you'd think they were holding their breath" and its crumbling bricks and swollen front door, to bigger and better things. The book focuses on a span of childhood from about eight to thirteen; the vignettes are ordered chronologically, and the narrator gets older in the course of the story. Many students are most impressed with the superbly poetic style of the prose. Cisneros is a poet, and she writes with lovely, surprising images.

Marshfield Dreams, by Ralph Fletcher (2005), is suitable for young people of any age to read and to use as inspiration for their own stories. For each year of his childhood, from age three to thirteen, Ralph includes several vignettes, marking the most important people, places, events, and memories that happened that year. Some vignettes are about the tiniest, most ordinary moments, yet he writes about them as the monuments they felt like when he experienced them. He captures life in his family of nine children, hitting just the right voice and perspective of an inquisitive, loving, sensitive young boy.

"Statue" is a breathtaking little piece about a game Ralph's parents played with him when he was a toddler. He captures his parents' warmth and love in a surprising way, and in so few words. I use this vignette to teach dialogue, action, and description of familial love that doesn't sound pat or cliché.

Snapshot structure   The snapshot structure is similar to vignettes, but the individual stories are even smaller, with a shorter time frame and less of an overarching story. I use various metaphors to describe this way of framing the memoir: as snapshots in a photo album, beads on a necklace, pattern blocks on a quilt, freight cars on a train, cards in a deck. The bits and pieces should be related by topic, theme, or time frame (the photo album, the train, the card deck). Its subject might be something obvious, like summer vacations or holidays, or something more surprising, like "the times I've seen my father cry." Students can easily imitate this structure because they don't need to provide much in between the beads or the freight cars except the thinnest line of narrative thread.

Cynthia Rylant's picture book *When I Was Young in the Mountains* (1982) provides an instantly recognizable model for the kind of snapshot structure I'm talking about. On each page, the "I" relates some memory, a tiny moment, of being with her grandmother and grandfather at their rustic home in the mountains. These are truly individual pearls on a string: what happens on one page does not affect what comes next, and it seems that one could rearrange the little moments and it wouldn't make a big difference in how we understand the book as a whole. Rylant strings the moments together by repeating a phrase at the beginning of each little snapshot—"When I was young in the mountains . . . "—and that constitutes her narrative thread.

In *Looking Back: A Book of Memories*, Lois Lowry (1998) makes literal use of the snapshot structure. Like a photo album, each page holds a photograph of Lowry or some family member and a snippet of text about each picture. Although the book begins with a chronological structure, she breaks from it frequently in the final third of the book, organizing the snapshots by topic (dogs, her children, books) rather than by time.

Events presented in this naked, unadorned way need to work double time to be interesting. It would make dull reading indeed if the memoirist just wrote: "On my first birthday I got lots of clothes. On my second birthday I got some clothes and a giant teddy bear. On my third birthday . . . " That type of list can be made interesting by adding a dramatic twist, a time when something different happened. (See the section on the "Every day/One day . . . " structure.) Again, looking at examples of texts written with this string-of-events-type structure will help you teach children how each little moment needs to shine like a jewel.

Circle Structure

When the last words, paragraph, or image of a book repeats or echoes the beginning, some call this a circle structure. The end brings the reader's mind back to the first image in order to emphasize it, to remind of its importance. Usually the end, though it simply repeats the beginning, takes on deeper meaning because of all that has happened in between.

Many picture books use the circle structure, so you can fill your classroom with great models. Three of my favorites are *My Mama Had a Dancing Heart,* by Libba Moore Gray (1995); *The Rolling Store,* by Angela Johnson (1997); and *When I Was Nine,* by James Stevenson (1986). It's an immediately recognizable structure, and kids love finding examples of it in their independent reading. It's one of the easiest structures to imitate, so some kids settle on it just to be able to wrap their writing up neatly. I confer with students to ask if they really intend the meaning that the circle structure imposes on their memoir. If looping back to their mother's adoring gaze or to watching the sunset over their favorite mountain underscores the overall theme, then it makes sense. If there doesn't seem to be a strong reason to repeat the beginning, then I encourage the writer to try another ending.

Framing with Contrast

Every Day/One Day . . .

If there were such a thing as a classic story structure, it might bear some resemblance to this cartoon version: "Everything was going along just fine and dandy, same ole this, same ole that, but then WHAM! Trixie McDougal moved to town, and nothing was the same after that." When you're reading a story out loud to kids and some of them pipe up, "Uh-oh!" you know this structure is working its magic; something is about to happen, and everything will change because of it.

To teach this structure during writing minilessons, I turn to several stories in volumes one and two of *When I Was Your Age*. In the story "All-Ball," Mary Pope Osborne (1996) spends six pages setting up the importance of a ball: how lonely she is until her father gives her this ball before he leaves for service in Korea; she names it All-Ball; she plays with it constantly, even sleeps with it. Something is bound to happen to that ball. We know it because she sets us up by giving all that attention to it.

This structure works well for students who decide to focus on one major event or memory from their past. The "every day" part covers a lot of territory to set up the status quo, against which X occurs. In conferences, you will probably need to remind students working on this structure that the description of life before X has to be laid on thick, so that life after X feels different and so that the reader can also recognize that, indeed, things changed after X.

Then and Now

All memoir texts are written from the standpoint of *looking back* at something that happened in the past; it is the default position of the genre. The one who thinks, writes, and talks about the past *now* is inherently a different person—more experienced, more educated, happier, sadder, *different*—than the one *back then*. So a deep internal structure of then and now will exist within the memoir, even if the writer does not intentionally use those words to name it. While many memoirists keep their stories located in the voice and perspective of the child they once were, others purposely expose themselves as the adult, or the older person writing now. In *The Moon and I*, Betsy Byars (1991) establishes herself as an adult writer of books for young people who is sitting at her typewriter in her study when she sees a snake. This event in the present reminds her of the first time she saw a snake when she was seven. Byars moves back and forth from adult writer to child throughout the book.

Michael Rosen comments on his child self from the adult perspective in "Pegasus for a Summer" (1999), from the second volume of *When I Was Your Age*. In one emotional moment in this beautiful story, the twelve-year-old Rosen throws his arms around his horse's neck. The adult Rosen writes about this recurring visual memory as if he were watching himself from above: "This image of myself, stunned and weeping in the middle of that meadow. And while that twelve-year-old boy and, no doubt, that mythic horse, are long gone, I now can see—rather than the sun, woods, or other riders—my own reflection in that cloudy, uncomprehending, sparkling eye of my horse. It's not so different from who I am today" (124–25).

Some students may find it useful to purposely set up a contrasting structure using *then* and *now* or *before* and *after*. They might write half the memoir describing who they were in the past and the other half from who they are now. Or they might alternate chapters, paragraphs, or even sentences within paragraphs. In the hands of a talented writer, the forced contrast can have a strong effect, much like the humorous comparisons in Judy Blume's *The Pain and the Great One* (1984), which is a book I always use to demonstrate contrasting points of view.

Inside Me/Outside Me

Many memoirists describe having felt in childhood a profound disconnect between what the world saw and took for granted, the external features and behaviors of their child self, and what they experienced internally. Because I was horribly shy as a child, I rarely spoke in public, especially when asked a direct question. Year after year, teachers expressed to my parents their concern that my intelligence was questionable because I seemed unable or unwilling to perform or participate in most classroom activities fluently and vividly. This drama of the split self—outwardly mute and timid, inwardly daring and creative—took decades to resolve.

As I discussed in Chapter 5, a person is not one solid, unchanging self, but a kaleidoscope of shifting selves. For many memoirists, this tension between the inner and outer selves was the most painful part of growing up, especially when the adults in charge of them seemed ignorant or oblivious to the difference, or worse, insisted the child maintain a false self. I think children may sense a distinction intuitively but feel helpless to argue when the world boxes them in, labels them things like "good girl" or "clumsy" or "bad speller." Helping your students write well about this very normal part of growing up is important work.

In a minilesson, I give pairs or small groups of students copies of a memoir excerpt. I ask students to mark and discuss places where the author describes feeling different from what others say about him or her or names multiple selves. Here is an example from *Bad Boy: A Memoir*, by Walter Dean Myers (2001), that demonstrates the contrast between external and internal selves:

> I realized I liked books, and I liked reading. Reading a book was not so much like entering a different world—it was like discovering a different language. It was a language clearer than the one I spoke, and clearer than the one I heard around me. What the books said was, as in the case of *East o' the Sun*, interesting, but the idea that I could enter this world at any time was even more attractive. The "me" who read the books, who followed the adventures, seemed more the real me than the "me" who played ball in the streets. (46)

Practiced writers move so seamlessly from external to internal that it's hard sometimes for kids to track the changes and even harder for them to figure out how to do that in their own writing. Some students might find it helpful to create a contrasting structure, again, as in Blume's *The Pain and the Great One*, to describe first their external self, the public mask, or at least what people say about that "outside me," and then turn their attention to their inner thoughts and what feels true internally, or vice versa.

It helps some kids when I give them separate pieces of draft paper and write on one page, "The outside me looks like, says, does . . . ," and then ask them how a stranger would describe what she sees on the outside: "long black hair; athletic build; a boy who makes good grades; a girl who talks a lot in class." On another page I write, "The inside me looks like, says, does, is, feels . . . ," and then I ask what would surprise the world to know about them. What kinds of things do they say and do that don't match how they truly feel? For example, "I talk a lot in class, but that's because inside I'm terrified that if I don't say something, no one will ever notice me, like I will be invisible."

Not all kids are aware of or sensitive to any discrepancies between the external and internal, and some are not willing to admit what they do notice. I would not push this structure on any student; simply offer it as one more in a world of possibilities.

Framing with Time

The contemporary memoir, unlike real life, is not a prisoner of time. In fact, manipulating time or making huge narrative leaps back and forth in time can become one of the memoir's most conspicuous features. Time can even become, like the topic of memory, a major theme in the retelling of a life story. I'm going to present a few possibilities for organizing time in the memoir, but again, studying how writers do this in published texts can yield even more examples for students to imitate.

Using Tense

While it seems obvious that a story about events that occurred in a person's history would appear in the *past* tense, there's no rule about that. Many memoirists write in the *present* tense at times, as in "I am sitting next to my father on the bench. It's cold outside and I do not have a coat on." The present tense makes the situation immediate; it places the writer inside the memory, as if he were reexperiencing it right now or watching it unfold in front of him. That unfolding quality makes present tense a useful tool if the memoir is about discovering a mystery or a secret. Present tense can also provide a sense of continuous action or states of being, so writers often use it to describe those "over and over" scenes, such as the dinner-table scene I mentioned from my own memoir.

Skipping Around

Most contemporary memoirs skip around in time, beginning at age eighteen, for instance, then going back to age five to illustrate some point, then moving to the present adult, and finally going back to a different past incident. I show students how authors play with time by drawing a time line for a story on an overhead transparency and marking the leaps on a time line and then asking them to do the same with a few other memoir texts they have read, to see how many possibilities exist for manipulating time. Here, for example, is rough time line for the story "Flying," by Reeve Lindbergh (1996):

Present (at time of writing) ⟶ past (brothers and sister learned to fly) ⟶ different past (brother skydives) ⟶ present (dislike of loud noise) ⟶ farthest back so far (mother learned to fly) ⟶ past time (when Reeve got to fly with her father) ⟶ past time of the main event (when Reeve and father almost crash) ⟶ present reflection on what she learned about her father.

In a writing minilesson, I show students a few ideas for framing with time using the following time lines to get them started, and then I invite them to play around with at least three different ways they could structure their memoir by using time lines (or whatever graphic representations they prefer).

A - Z

Story begins at logical beginning, somewhere in the past (A), and ends sometime further on (Z). This structure stays, for the most part, as a narrative of the past.

Z - - - - - - - - A - Z

Story begins in the present (Z) as an introduction; then it goes to the past (A) and continues along a regular time line to the present again.

A - - - - - Z - - - - - A + 1 - - - - - Z + 1 - - - - - A + 2 - - - - - Z + 2 - - - - ⟶

Story begins in past (A), is interrupted by a present reflection (Z), then goes back to past (A + 1), then returns to the present (Z + 1), and so on.

Z - - - - - - - - - - - A - - - - - - - - - - - B - - - - - - - - - - - C - - - - - - - - - Z

Story begins in the present (Z), goes to a time in the distant past (A), then to a completely different past time (B), and then to yet a different past time (C) before returning to the present.

The number of ways to manipulate time is limitless. Some students may find it easier to stay focused entirely on the first time line structure: the story begins in the past and works sequentially and chronologically to end at some later time. But other students may experience great power and meaning from manipulating time. It is yet another way to signal control over one's self-narrative: "I am the author of my life."

Drafting the Memoir

I explain to students that preplanning their memoir draft using some kind of shorthand or visual diagram saves work, paper, time, and, in the case of making art or directing television shows or making movies, lots of money. And since, as in "the best laid plans of mice and men," plans often change, it's much easier to change a few words on an outline, or make a new diagram, than to rewrite pages and pages of text, although writers do that frequently as well.

Perhaps it's the frustrated architect in me, but I love to shape text. I love to draw different structures for text: pyramids, concentric circles, dots and lines, big square boxes and thin rectangles. As I stated earlier, the structure of a memoir, or any text, gives the text meaning. So, for example, if I end my story in the same place it began, I mean to say that this is how life feels to me, like a pattern, a repetition, a coming back home. If the opening image is a positive one, then "Hallelujah, here we go again!" (If negative, it's more like "Damn! Here we go again. . . . ") Visually, that structure can be depicted on an outline, a storyboard, or a time line, simply by using an arrow to loop the last section back to the beginning section.

For many children who like to think things through visually, drawing possible structures works well for planning the draft of the memoir. Just as builders construct from blueprints, chefs cook from recipes, directors film from storyboards, and teachers plan what to teach by day, week, month, and year, writers benefit from making a plan before they begin to write. When I learned how to make an outline in high school, there was only one way to do it, and it involved Roman numerals, capital and lowercase letters, and something called parallelism that never quite worked out right.

Having suffered through the old-fashioned outline, I want to be sure my students have a variety of methods to plan how their writing will go. I demonstrate how to make webs, maps, diagrams, lists, storyboards, time lines (both vertical and horizontal), and even informal outlines, with numbered sections and dashes or dots beneath each section. Educators refer to these tools as graphic organizers and use them in every area of the curriculum. Unfortunately, most of the ones we see in school are prefabricated, made with the assumption that everyone's material should be structured in the same way. I suggest teaching children how to make a variety of graphic organizers and then inviting them to invent their own, making up ways to organize that work well for them.

At this point in the journey of the memoir genre study, students have been reading memoir texts—chapter books, picture books, excerpts from adult and young adult memoirs—independently or in pairs or book clubs; listening to you read aloud from a lengthy memoir text; and discussing the features of this genre, which you are displaying on charts for them to refer to as they write. Students have generated multiple entries in their notebook, sometimes as lists of memory topics, sometimes as two- or three-page entries about a memory or some aspect of their life. Finally, by now, most of your students have settled upon a theme, angle, or slice of life and have explored that stance in their writer's notebook for several days to a week. They have circled around their theme, layered it with more insights and memories, come at it from different points of view. They have planned, sketched out, and rehearsed some possible structures. The day to commit to a draft has arrived: Draft Day! On Draft Day, I ask all students to follow these procedures:

1. Reread everything you have in your notebook that relates to your chosen theme or angle.
2. Put your notebook away.
3. Take a piece of draft paper (I supply lined and unlined paper in abundance in various baskets around my classroom).
4. Begin the draft.

Inevitably, someone will moan that she doesn't know how to start her story. I tell the kids it doesn't matter one bit how they begin because the story will change anyway! By the time I introduce the memoir genre to my students, they are familiar with my song and dance about revision, and they know that whatever they put down first will most likely change and change again. If your students have not had plenty of practice revising, from this day forward, begin teaching how to do it in your minilessons. (See Chapter 8 for detailed descriptions of what to teach in revision minilessons.) The idea right now is simply to begin so that they will have a working draft to take through several major revisions.

At first, I ask kids to put their notebook away because I would like them to recompose their memoir, to think, explore, and discover anew in the process of spilling words out on paper, according to their plan, time line, or diagram, and not to simply copy wholesale from their notebook. All of these little tricks—a change in materials, a blank piece of paper, and a new pen—serve to wake up the mind, add energy to the process, and pull different kids into the process. After they have a working draft, by all means, they should go back to their notebook to see if there is material in there to patch into the draft.

When I taught kindergarten years ago, I had a big table in the classroom that I filled at various times with sand or water (to which I sometimes added bubble bath!) and numerous measuring spoons and cups and quart and gallon jugs. I loved watching the little ones play: there was no end, apparently, to the fun of filling those containers, holding them up to the light to study the contents, pouring from one vessel into another, emptying them, and filling them again. As I said at the beginning of this chapter, people love having containers in which to store their stuff, and now that students have considered possible shapes for their memoir, and poured their memories into the draft containers, they are ready to hold them up to the light of revision, to empty and refill them with new language.

Recognized Lives

Secrets for Conferring Successfully with Children Writing Memoir

Many people are longing to be in conversation again. We are hungry for a chance to talk. People want to tell their story, and are willing to listen to yours. People want to talk about their concerns and struggles. Too many of us feel isolated, strange, or invisible. Conversation helps end that.

—MARGARET WHEATLEY, *Turning to One Another*

Randy and I have finally figured out to take backpacks when we travel anywhere for longer than one week. The memory of dragging our ocean liner–sized suitcases over ancient cobblestone streets in Italy a few years ago still causes us pain. In many ways, we have come to know ourselves better as travelers each time we've stepped outside our familiar work–home–school–grocery store routine. While we don't need spalike luxury, and while we want to immerse ourselves as much as possible in the local culture of the places we visit, we do relish restaurants, hot showers, a quiet night's sleep. I think we fall somewhere between so-called armchair travelers, who merely read about exotic places, and travelers like our friends Kate Montgomery and her husband, Dave Hackenburg, who spent their honeymoon sleeping in a hammock on a beach in Mexico on their way to Africa to begin two years of service in the Peace Corps. In fact, there is a name for the kind of travelers Randy and I are, even a website for souls like us, called "Slow Travelers." We like to plant ourselves in one spot, and to feel as if we have experienced life, however briefly and superficially, in that place.

But no matter how you travel, unless you are made of stone, you experience an expansion of self. That's why I travel. I go to feel my expectations explode and biases dissolve. To discover that I am capable of learning a new language, of eating foods, like spicy grasshoppers, that would normally repulse me, of trusting total strangers with my money and my life, of deflating the cushion that I put between myself and the world. And finally, to find connections between myself and the history and cultures of the world.

I think I may have experienced one of my greatest highs as a teacher on one such trip. We were in Mexico City, a place I had longed to go to since I saw a picture of the pyramids in Teotihuacán when I was in elementary school. We climbed to the top of the Pyramid of the Moon. The stone steps were steep and the treads so narrow that I often had to turn my feet sideways. I have read one theory that the Mayan priests, in their religious ceremonies, climbed up by walking sideways on the treads, like a long snake slithering and winding its way to the top. The risers on these steps, all two hundred of them, were about a foot and a half tall, and the air in Mexico City is famously thin and infamously polluted, so I felt as if I were drawing the absolute last shred of air left in the world as I ascended this enormous structure. But I made it. At the top, I was able to see for miles in all directions. I could see how the shapes of both the Pyramid of the Sun and the Pyramid of the Moon echoed the mountains behind them. The sky was overcast, the air a perfect seventy-four degrees.

To my right were three little girls, about eight years old. I smiled at them in a way that seems to signal, no matter what country I'm in, that I love children. A smile was all it took for one of them to say *"¡Hola!"* to me, and when I said, *"¡Buenos Dias!"* back, she asked: *"¿Como esta mi nombre en ingles?"* (What is my name in English?) Her name was Perla, and I said, "Oh! That means Pearl in English."

That got the other girls going: "What about Carla?"

"Es lo mismo" (It's the same in English), I said, but I said her name with a *gringa* accent, heavy on the *r* instead of rolling my tongue and saying a soft, trill-like *r,* and the girls giggled hysterically at that. How about Azucena? Fortunately, I happened to know that meant "lily" because I had once had a student in Austin, Texas, with that same name.

More girls joined our little conversation, there on the top of the Pyramid of the Moon; some were only six or seven years old. They were on an *excursion,* they said, the word in Mexico for a field trip, to the pyramids. They crowded around me asking all sorts of questions, like if I had children of my own. They giggled when I pointed to *mi esposo,* Randy. I told them I am a teacher, and they were thrilled with themselves for having guessed that because, they said, I was "so nice!" I gave them my notebook and pen, and they wrote down Spanish words, wanting to know the English words for them.

We practiced colors. They pointed to my eyes and said *"ojos verdes,"* and I said "green eyes." They taught me the word for curly—*rizoso*—as they played with my hair. They conferred among themselves, amid much giggling, and then leaned in close and whispered, "What's the word for *corpiña?*"

"I don't know that word," I confessed. They tried to act it out for me, screaming with embarrassment. I finally figured it out and showed them a tiny peak of my bra strap. "Do you mean this?"

"Yes!"

I spelled in Spanish *bey-erray-ah*, "bra." More shrieking. At this point, their *maestro* (a male teacher) signaled that it was time for them to go. We hugged and said *"Mucho gusto"* (Pleasure to meet you) and waved as they descended, way too fast for my heart, the steep, steep steps of the pyramid.

I was ready, for several hours after that, to sell all my belongings and move to Mexico to teach. In his wonderful book about conferring, called *How's It Going?* Carl Anderson (2000) tells us that when we confer, we should feel like we did when we fell in love for the first time. That's exactly what I experienced. For the rest of that afternoon, I kept trying to find those little girls again. I felt deeply recognized for who I think I am—a teacher, a nice lady, a lover of children. The girls and I had looked into each other's eyes, and we had asked each other the questions that most people want to, but are too shy and grown-up to ask.

To feel recognized means to feel seen and understood. Feeling recognized means someone has heard you, listened to what you had to say. It can seem as if the other person knows the secret, inner you; it can even feel like falling in love. When you sit, squat, or kneel beside children to talk with them about their writing, you are recognizing them. Conferring with a child about any kind of writing he is doing—poetry, fiction, letter writing—will make him feel seen and known. But having a conversation with a child who is writing about her life stories, her self-identity, creates a profound connection that has the power to illuminate, to lead her to understand deeply something about herself or about how to compose her self on paper. Learning about a student in the midst of a conversation can alter the way I teach him from this moment forward. It can have the effect of an earthquake with aftershocks.

We call this situation a writing conference. It sounds clinical, yet it is anything but clinical. It should be named something like "a special time when it seems as if you are all alone in the room with each other, and you are paying attention only to each other," but that would be too hard to say all the time. The conference is suffused with anxieties on the part of both the teacher and the student. It holds both the teacher's expectations for the child's learning and the child's wish to be seen, heard, and understood by the teacher. Its structure—research, decide, teach (see Anderson 2000; Bomer 1995; and Calkins 1994)—can sound formulaic. Yet since we are talking about conversations with children, who often respond in unpredictable ways, the conference is anything but formulaic. What formula would tell you, for instance, how to respond to a six-year-old who shows you two envelopes covered with cartoon characters beautifully drawn in colored pencil and tells you he is writing about how he learned to draw from his father and his uncle, both of whom are currently incarcerated in the same state prison? A formula could never help you know what to say in that conference; only your humanity will suffice.

Many of my professional colleagues learned how to confer from Lucy Calkins. Decades ago, when I was a student in her graduate class at Teachers College, Columbia University, she conferred with me about my writing. Lucy pulled a chair up next to my desk one day and in her quick, direct way, said: "So tell me what you're thinking about as you write."

I was terribly put off by that question at first. What was I *thinking* about? Writers don't divulge their thinking processes! It's supposed to be a big mystery how writing goes from inspiration to published book. It happens as if by magic. And only to certain, very special people!

But Lucy had learned how to confer from a superlative teacher of writing, Donald Murray, who absolutely stripped naked the notion of a special secret life of writers. Murray had opened wide his notebooks—daybooks, he calls them (1987)—had published his earliest, messiest drafts of pieces, had even written off the top of his head, on an overhead projector, right in front of audiences full of teachers. He explained that to teach writing, you have to listen to the writer's intentions or to her questions about writing, and then you have to teach into those plans and questions.

So Lucy pushed me to make my own writing process concrete in order to know how to help children do the same. I learned how to talk about the choices I made for organizing my writing, how to name the strategies I used to revise, how to talk about the books, essays, and poems that mentored my writing. I still turn to Lucy's books, as well as to Anderson, Murray, and Donald Graves, to remind me how to let the writer speak first, how to teach into the writer's intentions, and how to "put myself out of a job," as I've heard Lucy say.

Conferring with Children Who Are Writing Memoir

Part of the craft of conferring involves paying careful attention to the messages we give writers with our voice, or body, and the character of our listening. While the basic structure of the writing conference remains the same, no matter what type of text a child is composing, we need to pay even more attention to our tone of voice, body position, balance of talking and silence, and the quality of our questioning when a writer is composing the story of his life.

In *The Call of Stories*, Robert Coles (1989) writes about his residency in the psychiatric ward of Massachusetts General Hospital. His supervisor gave him a tool that changed the course of his professional life, and that tool was to ask the patient to "tell her story." Instead of rushing, as doctors are wont to do, to "fix" the patient, to administer a diagnosis and prescribe a treatment, his supervisor suggested that Coles take the time to listen as his patients told "the truth of their lives." When Coles tried this strategy on a particularly recalcitrant patient, he stumbled over this new procedure at first, but in his conference with her, he asked her to tell him the story of her life—"moments in it . . . that [she] remember[ed] as important, as happy or sad." Then he sat back and waited. "She was utterly quiet long enough for me to get anxious. Should I say something? Had we reached an impasse? Should I try to break it? Rewording one's questions or interpretations is a handy way of giving the patient time to think, then speak" (11).

For a therapist, it is interesting, revealing even, whether the patient fills the space with words or with silence because both mean something. I find that useful to think about as I confer with young people: silence is rich. Silence might mean reluctance, fear of being wrong, or fear of disclosing information. Or silence might simply mean the writer needs time to relax, think, travel back in time. I try to read which of these reasons might be the case for a student and let her lead the way in the conference. Most of the time, waiting invites the writer to talk. Coles' patient remained silent for a long time, perhaps because for her too, this was an entirely new kind of therapeutic procedure, but ultimately, "her story poured from her" (13–14).

In conferences with children who are writing memoir, teachers might practice a similar strategy. Rather than inundating children with specific questions about where they were, who they were with, what the weather was like that day, our first utterance should simply be "Tell me your story," and then we should sit back and wait. Bill Moyers, a gifted journalist and interviewer, said he learned that "extemporaneous listening is as important as extemporaneous speaking." The "climate" of the interview is critical, he said, and asking another question immediately after the first question makes the person's mind "richochet like a pool ball" to another topic. "So sometimes I will just be silent . . . and the guest will come forward with the next thing that's just below the surface of articulation" (Buchholz 2001).

I think these images of waiting and silence seem foreign to most classrooms these days. Teachers feel frantic to move students along, to prepare them for the tests or for the next level of schooling. I remember feeling terrified when an administrator suddenly appeared in my room, strode over to my plan book, and checked to see if what my students were doing at 9:52 A.M. coincided with what the plan book said they would be doing and that the plan itself matched the mandated learning objective, number E5a. Hardly a climate for silence and waiting. But I remained prepared to justify the moments of meditative silence, waiting for children to think of the next thing just below the surface, as necessary for thinking, learning, and especially writing. The conference should never become a timed formula guaranteed to produce measurable results, but rather a template into which we pour our fully attentive selves as we guide students in writing the truth of their lives. Let me share some of the images that I use to keep myself open to whatever each child brings to the conference and to avoid turning it into a formulaic procedure.

Confer as if you are traveling in another country

Prepare to learn something new here. You know a little something about this country because you've watched movies, or read about it, but the experience of it is altogether more illuminating. You are more alert than usual. Signs, labels on bottles, menus are endlessly fascinating. You sample the spicy, fried grasshoppers. You take time to examine those blue flowers you've never seen before in your life. You try to understand things in this culture, some of which might make you cringe, and you do not judge. You are a guest here. Prepare to be changed when you leave this country. Prepare to be changed when you leave a writing conference.

Listen as if the mysteries of the world will be revealed by this child

If we truly thought of the writing conference as a conversation, we would keep in mind several rules of conduct: our tone of voice would be friendly, casual, highly interested. We would look at the other person with steady, alert eyes. We would take turns talking. We would say back what we understand the person to be saying, and we would ask questions about things that confuse us, or things we want to know more about. And if it was truly a conversation, we would leave feeling closer than ever because that child had revealed something, let us in on some secret, and we had taken the time to understand what things are like for him.

This part is easy. I believe everyone has a story to tell, and I want to help him or her tell it. Strangers tell me their life stories, and then say, "I've never told anyone that before!" If I had been raised Catholic, and, well, if I were a boy, I might have been a priest! Or I might have chosen to be a psychologist, except that I have no answers, no good advice to give. I just love to listen, and I try not to judge.

Margaret Wheatley, author of *Turning to One Another* (2002), believes we could change the world if we would actually learn how to listen to one another. Listening, simply listening, without trying to fix someone or give advice or convert him, is one of the most healing acts, Wheatley says. "I have seen the great healing power of good listening so often that I wonder if you've noticed it also. There may have been a time when a friend was telling you such a painful story that you became speechless. You couldn't think of anything to say, so you just sat there, listening closely, but not saying a word. And what was the result of your heartfelt silence, of your listening?" (88). While our job is to teach children, and the writing conference is a place to do that, I wonder if we often rush to that teaching moment without simply listening first. I know that when I force myself to stay silent for a few minutes, children will often fill that silence with words that can become part of their memoir writing.

The tone of a conference during memoir writing must be a tone of rapt attention, with a complete lack of judgment. In his travel memoir of Mexico, called *Oaxaca Journal*, Oliver Sacks writes about being completely awestruck by the temple ruins of pre-Hispanic people. People created feats in mathematics, astronomy, architecture, and art that surpass our "advanced" civilization, and they did it "in a pre-wheel, pre-compass, pre-iron age" (2002, 151). Yet they built structures that have withstood centuries, and tremendous earthquakes, while modern buildings crumpled. We simply cannot assess another culture by the standards of our own or any other culture, Sacks writes; the terms *primitive* and *advanced* are simply inapplicable. I try to remember that code of conduct when I travel in the world and in conferences with my students.

In a writing conference about memoir, I try not to bring a prescribed set of standards to this particular student. This person has mysteries to reveal, and she knows more than I will ever know about a lot of things. On the other hand, I do have content about writing that I want to teach students. I have images of the memoir craft and writing conventions that I expect students to work with and produce, so my job is to listen attentively, without judgment, and then to teach them how to write.

Confer as a seeker of honesty

Ask, "What do you want me to know about who you are?" That works better sometimes than the more direct "What do you remember?" Memory is so slippery. The beginning memoirist thinks she has to write the exact truth of a memory—what day it was, what her mother was wearing, or what exact words were said. But she can't actually remember, so then she gets nervous and becomes too paralyzed to write. You can help open her memory by asking: "What do you want me to know about your life?"

I've asked that question many times in workshops with children and adults. Adults might say to me: "I want you to know that I hate writing." Or "I want you to know that my mother died recently." Young people might say: "I am shy." Or "I love Japanese animation." Or "I can think only of bad memories of my childhood; I don't want to write a memoir." In a conference, I say to all of those writers: "Write about exactly that: write about what makes that so important to you." Sometimes they respond: "Oh, that's too personal." Or "That would be too boring. Who would want to hear about that?"

"Anyone," I answer, "if you write honestly."

In Mexico City, we went to the painter Frida Kahlo's *casa azul* (blue house), which is now a museum, left very much like it was when she lived there. I had seen the movie *Frida* at least three times and read a biography by Hayden Herrera (1983) and also the memoir of her husband, Diego Rivera (1992), called *My Art My Life: An Autobiography*.

So going to Frida's house was like going to a friend's house. I felt as if I knew her also because her paintings are so autobiographical. She painted dozens of self-portraits throughout her life, never afraid of being too personal. What the world loves about her paintings is their raw honesty. She painted her pain, physical and emotional. She admitted that while Diego Rivera painted the history of Mexico and its people, she painted her own reality.

Look at one of her paintings. There are aspects of the experience that she obviously remembers vividly—the color of the walls, the shape of the medical instruments used in dozens of operations on her crushed pelvis. Yet other aspects are more like symbols than reality. She re-creates her deepest truth; she finds a language for pain that people can understand and relate to, even though many of the images come from her dreams.

Of course I don't require my students to be as deeply confessional or personal as Frida Kahlo, but even at the most basic level of self-disclosure, students need guidance to reach deep inside, to express their own reality. Writing can feel so intensely personal, like standing naked on a stage in front of strangers, or as if we have cut out a little piece of our heart and now hold it out in our hands, saying, "Here I am, please be careful with me." Knowing that even adult writers feel this way, we must be extra supportive of our youngest writers who are just learning to trust the process and trust that readers will not take the stuff of their lives and crush it. We must create a classroom that is, as Vivian Paley says, "A place to tell the truth about yourself, where you don't feel ashamed." And then sit beside this writer, prepared to cup your hands around his truth and hold it carefully.

Confer as if you have forever

Maybe the main reason I love to travel is to reacquaint myself with time as a river flowing. Time as a mystery with no immediate solutions. I purposely leave my watch at home when I travel. I eat when I'm hungry and sleep when I'm tired. I let time become a flower unfurling. In Mexico, we took time one night to stand on the street corner and watch a hundred geckos gather around a lightbulb. It looked like a gecko convention. As we watched, they devoured, in one gulp, whole bodies of mosquitoes. Suddenly, we understood why, on summer nights, when we're watching TV in our den, the window screen crowds with geckos. We had never bothered to look long enough to see them eating the bugs attracted by the lights in our den.

In our modern, high-tech society, time has become linear; time has become something to march through. History is marked by wars and elections. People tell about their lives in milestones: birth, graduation, marriage, divorce, second marriage, children, death. Virginia Woolf suggests that another way to look at history and at time passing is to focus on the subtle moment of human contact and nurturing. Sometimes, when you are conferring with a young person about her life, time has to unfurl. You have to give the conference the time it needs. If we fully interact in a conference, as one human being to another, it might not feel so much that we don't have enough time. Instead we might feel more full—as if something big and important has happened. And it has.

What if on that particular school day, you aren't able to confer with five or six children? Know that conferences don't always happen within the confines of the writing workshop. Especially with memoir writing, conferences can take place in the oddest moments and places. "Dani," I said to one of my first-grade students out on the playground one day, "remember at the beginning of first grade, when you were crying because you had blisters on your hands and you said you were never, ever going to get on the monkey bars again?"

"Yeah! But then you told me, Ms. Bomer, that's part of getting good on the monkey bars—to make those thick bumps on my hands. See? I have 'em now! Remember you said to me, 'Don't give up!'?"

"Right! And you never did, and now look at you! You're skipping bars and going backward and learning new tricks every day. You know, that could be part of your memoir, how you're the kind of girl who never gives up!"

And it is also true that writing conferences can build and build over time. It took more than two hundred years to build the Pyramid of the Moon in Teotihuacán. The base is some seven hundred feet square with two hundred steps to the sky. It was built from large stones dug from the area and hauled to the site. How? No one knows. Without wheels to roll the rocks, without even beasts of burden (horses and donkeys would be brought from Spain after the conquest), human beings built this astonishing triangular structure. The people who worked on the base, the largest tier, never saw the triangular shape of the pyramid. They had to trust that their work was crucial, and that without it, the pyramid would never rise to the moon.

The best conferences I have are ones that build on all the time we have spent together, and all the work that has gone before, when I can say, "Remember when you got hurt on the field trip and you were so brave about asking for help? You really know how to take care of yourself." Or when I can say, "Remember what we talked about in our last conference?" Or "It makes sense that your memoir is all about nature—you love spiders and snakes so much!" Or when I can say, "Oh, here's that image of the sun again. You love to use that image in your writing, don't you? Maybe you should explore what the sun means to you and think about making it a recurring or repeating image in your memoir."

The best conferences are like a deep, layered history between myself and each child. Now, if we were only having a conversation, I could simply leave and say, "It's been fun hearing about your life, *ciao!*" But my job is to teach. So I'm not afraid to go ahead and propose something: a way to revise, a book that might be a good model text, something I've tried in my own writing that might help this student.

Confer (once in a while) as if you are a Broadway director

Ninety percent of the time, I want children to make independent decisions in their writing after having learned strategies from my minilessons and from reading published memoirs, so my conferences refer to something I know they have learned from those sources. But 10 percent of the time, I pull out the stops. I confer as if I am directing a movie. From what my student has written or said out loud to me, I can envision the whole powerful piece. I can use my student's words to brush the air, to pitch how the story might go, as directors and screenwriters do for film producers in order to get financial backing. The writer becomes like an actor in these moments. The material is there, in the actor's mind and in the actor's hands, and with a director's light touch, and the editor's cutting and rearranging, the film becomes whole. All writers have been given such visionary direction, from editors usually, or close writing friends.

I taught English at night to parents who had children in my school in Texas. I decided to help them practice English by asking them first to tell stories from and then write about their lives. One night, one of the women in the class wrote about being only sixteen when she crossed the Texas border from Mexico. It was just one line, but it raised so many questions in me. What were the details that would help all of us experience this story with her? I asked her if she would tell more about it. She talked about being very poor and deciding, with her family, that she would come to Texas to take care of her baby cousins while her aunt worked. Her aunt would pay her a little bit of money, and she would send this back to her parents in Mexico.

Living in the Southwest, in one of the border states (Texas, New Mexico, Arizona, and California), one lives with stories on the nightly news and guarded references to what is commonly called *the crossing*. For many students in my classes in Texas, the stories are not rumors or journalism but real-life dramas that are often, for security purposes, never spoken of. *The crossing* refers to the drama that ensues at the border between the United States and Mexico, a difficult, dangerous line if you are Mexican and wishing to come into the United States for an opportunity to make money for your family. Esteban, another member of the class, decided also to risk writing about his coming to the United States. In a writing conference, as soon as I said that familiar, loaded phrase, "Tell me about the crossing," Esteban opened up and spoke more than he had all semester long. This was apparently a story he needed to tell.

"There was a big light. They told us, 'Look for the big light.' We walked for five days and nights. We walked only at night so the helicopters don't see us. We were so cold at night. And hungry. We were just skinny kids. My parents still stay in Mexico—we just come alone. We were lost, and we keep walking to that light. But we never got there. We never got to that light."

"That's an amazing image!" I shouted and jumped up from my seat. I think I shocked him. "Please put those very words in: a big light. Lost. Walking toward the light. Repeat it just like you said it. When you repeat it, I can feel how desperate you were to reach it."

I've read many memoirs, possibly several hundred by now. I can hear in my head the sounds of the ones I love. I have a sense of what makes a good story, and Esteban had one right in his mouth, ready to commit to paper. When we confer with young people about their writing, we sometimes realize we actually do know a lot about how stories go. We've even written some of our own. When we teach kids how to write a letter, we don't get all coy about it; we don't say, "Hmm . . . I wonder what a person could put on that first line, to address the person they are writing to?" We just come right out and tell them: "Letters almost always begin 'Dear so and so, comma.'" So there are times when I become rather like a director, and I say: "Oh, you must be sure to write it like that!" Or "The ending just needs to shout your message from the rooftops!" Or "Your story deserves the kind of ending that whispers and sends shivers down the reader's spine. I remember you have those kind of words in your writer's notebook. Let's find them and see if they fit here."

I asked my niece Brianna the other day what she remembers about being my flower girl in my first wedding. She was only eight years old, and now twenty-eight, she remembers quite a few details about colors and decorations that I've forgotten! She remembers that she and I danced together at the reception, even that the band was down in the basement of an old lodge. Then she casually threw in, "I remember I got sick later that night, and my dad sat with me in the corner, watching everyone dance. I was hurting, but I didn't ever want to leave that party!"

To me, this is an interesting part of the story, an insight into Brianna's personality, at such a young age. And if she were writing about it, and if I were conferring with her about it, I would go ahead and mention that. My memory of her at my wedding is the image of her little face, expectant and excited, in her ivory flower girl dress with a fuschia satin sash that matched the bridesmaids' dresses. She was pale as plaster because she became terribly sick that night with what turned out to be appendicitis, and she had to have surgery later. But there was not a chance, despite illness, that she would miss even a second of her favorite aunt's wedding! Perseverance is part of her character even now as an adult, the way she sees things through to the end; she doesn't give up or give in.

I kept asking Esteban to concentrate on the sensual details of his walking into this country and also on what he remembered of his interior life—what he was thinking and feeling. Week after week we worked on it, in Spanish, and then in the English translation, always with me inviting him to "see it again; walk it again." When Esteban felt finished, he told me so. "Are you sure? We still have one more week together. . . . " I was wishing he would still include more of the specific details he told me orally, but he was satisfied. He was the ultimate author of his life story, as it should absolutely be.

And isn't that just like our conferences with our students? They sometimes fail to follow our brilliant direction! We must not worry about the parts of conferences that don't get into the writing; they can still be some of the most important moments of our teaching. You know how sometimes, you think you've given someone a superhot bit of advice, where you've said to yourself, "Whoa! That was a great conference!" and then you come back to visit the writer later, and she has not followed one bit of the advice you gave? Well, don't despair, because that same writer might come up to you three months later and say, "Remember when you told me that the beginning of my story sounded like I was just getting a jump start and that I could try cutting off the first part and starting right in the middle of my piece? Well I tried that and it really works!"

The Most Oft-Repeated Memoir Conference and a Cheat Sheet for Five More

Some days I feel that I should carry a tape recorder of myself conferring and just push "play" because I find myself teaching one point over and over in conferences about writing memoir. I've presented versions of this lesson to the whole class in several mini-lessons, but I try to find other ways to teach it when sitting next to writers struggling with some aspect of the process of remembering, reflecting, writing, organizing, and revising. Let me define this lesson in detail and give a couple of ideas I use to teach it in conferences.

Memoir does not simply tell about something that happened in the past; it reveals something about the person it happened to

From 1920 to 1936, Virginia Woolf and a group of writers who called themselves the memoir club met monthly to read their memoir drafts. Woolf wrote to her fellow memoirists about her developing ideas of what memoir is. She claimed that the failure of so many memoirs is that "They leave out the person to whom things happened. They describe the event, but forget what the human being was thinking, feeling, knowing" (1976, 65).

The memoir should not be merely a laundry list of events—"We went to the beach every summer. We moved when I was five. My grandma moved in with us until she died." It goes beyond even a *poetically written* laundry list of events: "In the prime of my young life, I drifted to the pale, green sea. I swam with the mermaids and the whales, and they sang their sea songs to me." No, memoir is not only about the thing that happened but also about the person who experienced it. A memoirist reflects on the event with a particular stance that only he could have on that event. In her stunning memoir, *Not by Accident*, Samantha Dunn (2002), an accomplished equestrienne, describes quite graphically being trampled by her own beloved horse. But that horrific event occurs very early in the book. The largest portion of the book is reflection on that life-changing event. Dunn seems to discover, almost as she is writing the book (a mark of excellent dramatic and essayistic writing, in my view), that her life has been full of accidents, and she wonders what purpose those accidents might be serving. Ultimately this memoir is about healing—about becoming a person who no longer needs to get hurt to be able to feel her life. So when I confer with someone writing a memoir, I try to help her do what Samantha Dunn does in her memoir, to find what meaning she can in the patterns of events in a life.

Not all memoirs have that reflective, analytical aspect to them. Many function well simply as narratives, telling a story or stories of the past. But for unpracticed writers, what often gets left out of a story about the past is any sense of the *particular* child, the "I," the main character of the story. Things happen in the story, but to what effect? All good stories succeed because we fall in love with the main characters; we ache for them; we root for them; they live on in our consciousness.

In my conferences, I ask some version of this question to help draw out the *character* of the memoirist: "*Who* is the person this story is happening to?" Or "Where are *you* in this piece?" Or "What are you *really* trying to say here?" I usually ask these questions in the conversation and wait for response. After kids talk to me a bit about what was going on in their heart and head, I tell them to open their writer's notebook to a clean page, write whichever question I proposed to them at the top of the page, and spend a few more pages answering the question. To help some kids get closer to the effect or meaning of their story, I use a visual tool—I ask them to draw a line down the middle of their notebook page and label the left- and right-hand columns as in Figure 7–1. On the left side, they write a brief summary, even just a word or phrase to identify the event or memory. On the right side, I ask kids to choose one of the sentences from column two that will help them reflect and write about that memory.

Their answers shouldn't sound like columns in the finished piece of writing. It would sound awkward, if, for instance, I were to write: "How going to Mexico fits into the pattern of my life is. . . . " Instead, while writing about Mexico in my notebook, I questioned what it is that I love about traveling to another country. Then, as I was preparing this chapter, I thought about what kind of metaphors I could use from my Mexico writing that would help me explain conferring. I circled around the idea of traveling, and how it affects me by expanding my experience of people and places. I looked at travel as a metaphor for talking with children as they write.

Now, if you ask a child to do this in his notebook, and the right-hand side of the paper has nothing on it, the writer has probably not gone traveling inside his own life to find those moments that vibrate in memory. Or she might be writing on the left-hand side what she thinks are the exciting parts of her life—getting twenty stitches, or getting Playstation 2 for her birthday. Suddenly, she realizes she has no special meaning to

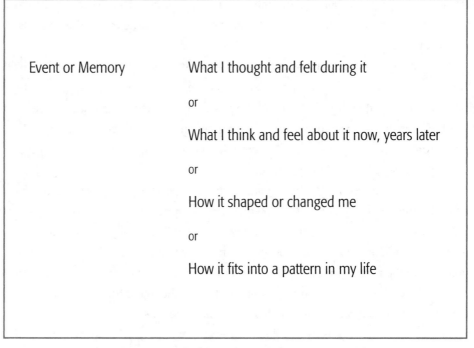

Event or Memory	What I thought and felt during it
	or
	What I think and feel about it now, years later
	or
	How it shaped or changed me
	or
	How it fits into a pattern in my life

Figure 7–1 *Two-Column List: A Tool for Reflecting on the Meaning of a Memory*

make of those moments except to say that they were exciting. You may need to direct her to read more memoir books to notice how other writers seem to put themselves back into the memory to relive what words they said and how they felt during exciting times like these.

Another possibility for students whose writing lacks specificity is to point out that memoirsts find the tiniest, most subtle or ordinary moments to help them tell the world who they are, not just the "action-movie events," and then they paint the picture with images or build a scene with dialogue and small actions. In his memoir, Ralph Fletcher describes how, as the oldest of nine children, he had to help feed, diaper, and entertain the babies in his house. Nothing earth-shattering here, just a collection of gestures and precise details. We get a picture of the "I" as a person who loves babies and children, and that absolutely describes the adult Ralph to a tee.

Mom barely had a second to breathe what with doing laundry, answering the phone, cooking supper, or nursing the new baby. So when the baby started crying, I helped out. We all did. I knew how to pick up the baby and tell if its diaper was dirty or clean by how spongy it was. I knew how to change dirty diapers (and avoid the messiest ones), to pin the cloth diapers without poking the baby. I was good at telling the difference between *I'm-really-hungry* crying and *I'm-just-bored* fussing. I loved the taste of baby food (and always sneaked a few bites when Mom wasn't looking). I knew how to warm up a bottle of milk in a saucepan on the stove, and squirt a little on my wrist to make sure the milk wasn't too hot. I could pick up the baby and walk around with it, cocking my right hip, so the baby would have a nice little ledge to sit on while I held it snug with one hand and rummaged through the cabinet for a teething biscuit with the other.

With the eternal Fletcher baby sitting in the play pen, year after year, I sort of became an expert on the subject. (2005)

Ralph didn't realize that he was "an expert on the subject" when he was a little boy; he came to that realization by reflecting on the moment much later, and by asking himself to remember how he felt back then and what meaning those events held for him now as he composed his memoir.

Most of the predictable roadblocks on the journey of memoir writing arise in the five categories that I list in Figure 7–2. I include three typical conference questions or suggestions that I use beneath each category.

I have been wanting to write this book about teaching memoir for fifteen years. It's ironic, or perhaps it makes perfect sense, that I'm finally getting around to writing it now. For many reasons, memory is a subject that fascinates me. I feel a pressing need to write about it as my father becomes increasingly confused about where I live, to whom I'm married, even, at times, my name. I gave up hope that he would remember that I am a teacher and a writer years ago. When I speak to him on the phone lately, he asks two or three times where I am. "I'm in Texas, Dad."

He remembers, in the odd way that people with certain kinds of dementia can sometimes, back seventy years ago: "Texas! I spent some time in Texas! Used to live there in Galveston when I was, oh . . . 'bout seventeen, eighteen? Think I lived in Fort Worth quite a few years too."

Each time we go through this routine, I try to make light of it, when deep down it scares me to feel myself being erased from his memory. "I know Dad. I lived in Fort Worth with you. Remember? I went to high school there?"

And now, also trying to make light of what surely terrifies him—losing whole chunks of his life—he becomes stupid; he guffaws in the silliest way and says, "You did, did you? Well now, how 'bout that?" Then he asks a fourth time: "Where you livin' now?"

Before his memory is completely gone, I want to have a writing conference with him. I will tape-record his recollections because he can't write anymore, but I'll ask the same questions I would if he were writing his memoir. I want to travel in the country that is my father. I want to know how things affected him. What changed him. I want to take all the time that we have left, before he no longer recognizes me, to put his life down on paper. That is how I will know him.

If the Focus Is on Finding Memories . . .

- Don't think about remembering anything today. Reread the entries you already have in your writer's notebook to see if they spark some ideas.

- Write about some people who are important to you. Who are they, what do they look and sound like, and why do they mean so much to you?

- Make your mind like a hand and actively reach back for a memory. Don't make any judgments about it; just write it down in your writer's notebook.

If the Focus Is on Expanding a Memory . . .

- Close your eyes, breathe deeply, and put yourself back in that moment. Pretend it's happening right here, right now. What do you hear? What do you see? What's happening in your body?

- Make a little research project of this memory. Talk to some other people who were with you and write down what they say about it.

- Listen to some songs from that time, or think about what you watched on TV. Write about what else was going on in the world around you.

If the Focus Is on Crafting the Text . . .

- What was happening to the inside you while this other thing was happening outside you? Look in your draft and see if you can find at least three different places where you could insert some sentences about what you were feeling on the inside.

- How are you thinking that you will play with time? Let's make a time line together. First we'll make one that goes step-by-step in time. Then we can try cutting it up and moving the parts around.

- Which parts are you going to zoom in on to slow down the story and make it drip with detail? What parts will you summarize in a sentence or two? Let's circle the "slow scene" parts in one color, and the "fast summary" parts in a different color.

Figure 7–2 *Memoir Conference Cheat Sheet*

If the Focus Is on Fine-Tuning Language . . .

- If you were going to repeat a certain word or phrase because that phrase meant something big to you, what would it be? Where are some different places in your draft you could put that phrase?
- If you were going to go in and make some parts of your draft sound lovely, like a song, which parts would they be? Let's find those spots and look closely at changing the words to sound like poetry.
- Let's look for places in your draft that you could turn narration or description into dialogue and gestures so that it sounds and looks like real people in a play or movie.

If the Focus Is Using Knowledge of Their Life Story for Other Writing Situations, Like Tests . . .

- When you think about all the memories you've been gathering, which are the ones that you'll always remember and could easily retell to anyone who asked?
- As you reread your writer's notebook, be on the lookout for kernels that you will be able to write into great little scenes or narratives.
- What are some different frames, angles, or lessons you could write from one memoir narrative? Try out a few with me right now; for instance, "The person who has most influenced my life is . . . ," "A time I realized I was really good at something was . . . ," "My biggest fear in life has always been . . . until one thing changed all that. . . . "

Figure 7–2 *Continued*

Revising a Text, Revising a Life

Five Sledgehammers and Nineteen Nails
for Making a Memoir Even Better

My advice to memoir writers is to embark on a memoir for the same reason that you
would embark on any other book: to fashion a text.

—Annie Dillard, "To Fashion a Text," *Inventing the Truth*

Finally, after all the remembering, collecting, layering, and planning, your students have begun writing drafts of their memoirs. Of course, they would like to
be finished now. Who can blame them? They've been working hard! But it's not
over, for now we begin my favorite part of the writing process: revision. During writing
workshop, whenever my students profess to be done or complain that they don't like
what they've written on the page, I say, "You don't like what you wrote? No problem—
you can revise it! Get back to writing!"

Revision is hope. We live our "one, wild and precious life," as Mary Oliver calls it,
only once, but we get to *reconsider* it dozens of times along the way. We can change our
clothes, hair, interests, friends, and mates, if necessary. We can change careers and
neighborhoods. We can change our minds and beliefs. We can even change identities,
especially as we write about ourselves in a memoir.

Revision is like the layers of soil in Italian vineyards, like the layers of ancient civi-
lizations beneath modern cities, like the layers of DNA in the oldest variety of grape,
grafted by vintners over centuries into new varieties of grape, always in pursuit of the
finest wine.

Revision is a second, third, fourth, even a twentieth chance.

We can revise our life. We can revise our teaching. We can revise the way we operate in the world. Think about revision in the largest sense, of imagining things as if they could be otherwise, as Maxine Greene says.

Revision is forgiveness.

When you revise memoir, you become the *author* of your life. How dare you change the sequence, the names, the dialogue, the *true facts* of your life? Well, you *do* dare because you are revising to make your life mean what you want it to mean. You enlarge the story; you enlarge your life. You layer your memoir like thick layers of paint on a canvas. In Italy, we saw a painting, and a special X-ray machine revealed that underneath the picture of a fully clothed standing man, there was a seated, naked woman. Don't you wonder who or what made the painter revise that work?

As you write and remember and add layer upon layer to the stories of your life, you begin to realize this frustrating truth: that your life, anyone's life, is so thick and complicated that it can never be fully revealed. Revision helps us shape, regroup, and make sense of all those complexities. Ted Kooser (2005), the U.S. poet laureate appointed in 2004, says that he revises heavily, sometimes up to thirty or forty times for a single poem (16). Kooser, who also won the Pulitzer Prize for poetry in 2005, says that he wants to revise from complexity toward simplicity and order. You can begin to chip away at the chaos of experience by sharpening some of the tools of revision. I wish I could devise an original metaphor for revision strategies, but seeing them as tools just fits so perfectly. Two of my favorite books about revision—*The Revision Toolbox,* by Georgia Heard (2002), and *The Poetry Home Repair Manual,* by Ted Kooser (2005)—talk about the tools of revision, so I know I'm in good company when I use this image. A draft is like a field waiting for a plow to turn the rich soil over. A draft is like a lump of clay that requires the sculptor's tools—the sawtooth carvers and ribbon cutters—to chip, scrape, and cut it to get to the essential work of art. The draft is a building that needs the builder's tools—hammer, saw, nails, trowel—to raise the roof. All craftspeople use tools to make things, and the memoir writer is no different.

I offer the following five ways of reseeing the memoir draft as the big pickaxes and sledgehammers of revision. In my classroom, I present these demolition moves early in the writing process and come back to them repeatedly in minilessons and writing conferences. Revision, as practiced writers understand, does not happen as an afterthought to writing, but rather in the midst of thinking about, adding on to, and composing drafts of a piece of writing. Smaller, finer tools will be needed for the detail work that can be applied when there is a substantial working draft, and I name those in the second portion of this chapter.

Five Revision Sledgehammers

1. Revise by answering this question: Where am I in this story? What is happening inside of me? What does this story say about who I am as a person?

In a student memoir draft, we might get a full rendition of an event, but the author might forget to clue us in to how he was thinking and feeling during it. This problem occurs often, so I display these questions on a chart for students to use while revising:

Where are *you* in this story?

What is happening inside you?

What did you learn from this event?

What changed as a result of this event? (For the youngest children, you might word this question a bit differently: What do you want people to know about you in this story?)

These are perhaps difficult, sophisticated questions for anyone to answer, but they are the soul of memoir. (Telling a good story may be the heart.) Memoir, at least as I define it in this book, is *memory* plus *reflection*. As the memoirist looks back over her draft, she might find that she has written the outline of what happened.

First, we drove for about a zillion miles to get to my grandma's house. Then when we got there, we were already too late for dinner and I was starving. My Granma brought me a special tray with little kid-sized dishes full of my favorite foods: whole wheat crackers with peanut butter and sliced bananas, a little bowl of cream of chicken soup, and a little slice of her vanilla cake with chocolate frosting.

This is a wonderful little moment in this writer's memory of her grandmother. Teachers would be delighted with the descriptive details of "kid-sized dishes" and the foods. But to revise it toward memoir, the writer might ask, "What am I trying to say here?" or "What does this memory reveal about me, or about my relationship with Granma?" Perhaps she remembers the little tray with her favorite foods made her feel special, seen and known in the midst of a houseful of grandchildren. Perhaps this kind of demonstration of her grandmother's love stood in marked contrast to how she felt treated in school.

In Italy, Randy and I stayed for one glorious week at an ecotourist farmhouse in Tuscany. In the mornings, I would sit on our little terrace with my caffe latte, watching the owners water, pick fruit, sweep the walks. I wrote in my notebook:

> This morning everything feels so fresh and new. Every breeze brings a sweet jasmine smell and bird songs I've never heard. I try to paint this view with my watercolors—I can't. I don't know how to mix colors to get all these shades of green. The leaves of trees sparkle in the sun. The white gravel roads glow. Nothing detracts from the earth: all the buildings grow out of the ground in tans and terra cotta colors. Even the pool mimics the sky today.

I looked over this paragraph in my notebook, and I was not happy with it. It may have been fine as a casual observation of the surroundings, but I knew my noticings were unoriginal, and I also knew I was avoiding what was really going through my mind that morning. Fortunately, I knew it was just something I jotted in my notebook and that I could revise it. Patricia Hampl says, "Writing a first draft is a little like meeting someone for the first time. I come away with a wary acquaintanceship, but the real friendship (if any) is down the road. Intimacy with a piece of writing, as with a person, comes from paying attention to the revelations it is capable of giving, not by imposing my own notions and agenda, no matter how well-intentioned they might be" (1999, 28).

So I asked myself about this little notebook entry: What do the details of what I'm describing reveal to me? Not much, yet. I needed to turn the writing over and over like tilling a field before planting the grapevines. So I pushed my hoe in deeper, turned up a new layer of ancient dirt. I wrote more honestly, always a sure way to improve one's writing through revision. As this was merely a notebook entry, I knew that since I couldn't remember the full Dante quote (now in quotation marks) that suddenly came to me, I could just put "Dante" and look it up when I got back home:

> Coming to this gorgeous place in my 45th year, like Dante, I am "midway on my life's journey, I have found myself in dark woods, the right road lost. To tell about

those woods is hard—so tangled and rough." I watch that young German woman sunbathe nude for hours by the pool. She loves her body. No self-consciousness whatsoever. Her body is like a flower stem. I watch also the older American woman outfitted to fight off age—sun hat, zinc oxide like a white mask over her entire face, giant black sunglasses—exercising in the water first thing every morning. Her body is the full, round flower, and she covers it with a towel the second she rises from the water.

Why do we worship the young green stem and not the full flower?

OK, I liked this better, but if I wanted to make this a memoir piece, I could go back to possibly the deepest layer of myself, to reveal the embarrassing truth: that much of the time in Italy, when I wasn't studying Renaissance art and architecture, or painting landscapes, or talking to locals about the voting system in Italy (all noble pursuits), I was gripped with jealousy, watching all the young, beautiful Italian girls in their short, short skirts and leather jackets, their impossibly high heels, zipping around on their Vespa motorbikes, just beginning the night's adventures as I was heading home to sleep. I felt envious of the young Americans studying art in Florence for a year. Why hadn't I tried something like that? I was mourning a life I feel slipping away, and then I beat myself up for being so incredibly shallow and unsatisfied. But I knew that beneath jealousy and nostalgia there had to be some true compost, some live organisms, some heat, so I kept digging, and I found three more truths: (1) I am afraid of getting old—afraid that I will miss something I was meant to have or to experience, something life-changing. Beneath that is (2) a lifelong struggle to feel happy and satisfied with the gifts I have been given of a full and happy life. And I face that struggle because (3) I have not forgiven the adults responsible for me, and not thanked them either, for giving me life. There. After a great deal of reflection, I was able to reach some level of truth. As I revise, I now have the option of weaving those revelations into my original observation or just letting them inform which details I choose to put in and which to leave out. This exercise reminds me of the second big way to revise.

2. Revise by telling the truth

Not the truth as in who was sitting around the table when you threw up your Thanksgiving dinner that time. Not as in the exact words you said to your brother when he took your bike and wrecked it. Not the names of each and every ride you took at the amusement park. But the truth about what you were feeling at the time. Or the truth about how you feel *now,* reflecting on something that happened *then.* The power of memoir resides in what might be called an emotional truth. This is critical because the images and feelings that linger inside us might not coincide with what others claim to be the truth. When William Zinsser's mother read his memoir chapter about his lonely boyhood on Long Island, New York, she wept because his memory of his childhood was "less golden" than her memory of his childhood (1987, 12).

In *The Seven Sins of Memory,* Daniel L. Schacter (2002) assures us that we all recall the past through our current biases and beliefs. It is impossible for humans to give a clear, concise, accurate account of what happened in the past. For memoir writers, that should come as a relief. We can use noncommittal phrases like "I think it was . . . " or "It seems as if . . . " or "I don't remember exactly, but. . . . " In fact, such phrases help earn the trust of your reader, who doesn't remember her past very clearly either and will be sympathetic to your foggy memory.

Memoir writing is probably the most risky kind of writing for postulating truth. Fiction and poetry, of course, are exempt from telling the truth, except that the events, situations, and feelings of the characters have to make sense within the world of the text and within some kind of world order that people can accept. Characters can't suddenly have an about-face, a change of heart, unless there has been provocation enough to make it happen. Unless it is a science fiction novel, green, slimy creatures can't come to dinner. Unless it is a fantasy novel, children probably can't fly through the air on sticks.

Some kinds of expository writing, such as journalism, academic writing, and feature articles in magazines, posit truths that must be backed up with evidence: facts, statistics, verifiable quotes and references to other texts, names, dates, numbers. But memoir hangs out there like a loose kite. You think you can still see it up there, tiny against the clouds, but you can't pull it back, you can't tie it down, you can't follow it, it's moving too fast. Memoir is suspect and subject to scrutiny and to multiple points of view. Have you had the experience of sitting around the table, recounting some old family story, when your brother said, "That's not how it happened!"? Or perhaps your mother said, "I don't remember that. You must be mistaken!" Sometimes it seems as if we grew up in entirely different households.

Truth, in memoir, is ultimately between the writer and the writer's conscience. The memoirist tries to be honest, tries to turn a memory over and over, tills the soil to find where the central theme is, tries to reflect on the event in a way that reveals something that seems a bit risky, a little on the edge. You almost blush from saying these words, yet you decide to go ahead and say them. Writing memoir should feel almost as if you were diving from the highest platform into the deepest pool of water. Or as if you were watching a video of yourself teaching your class. You know that feeling—"Oh that can't be me!" But it is you.

Why do I have to make myself feel like that? you might ask. Why do I have to be *that* honest? And especially, why would I ask my children to feel that way? Because the unspoken contract between the memoirist and the reader demands honesty. People who enjoy reading memoir read it presuming that the author is telling the truth. They want to know how this person, this particular writer, sees the world and makes sense of his life. What he learned from experiences that might be like the reader's own. Finding out that a memoirist was telling barefaced lies causes a breech of trust, and it chisels away at the writer-reader relationship for future memoir writers. If it happened too often, one could imagine memoirists becoming people who, like politicians, are largely distrusted and ignored by their audience.

The memoirist has the responsibility to develop her "I" in the memoir. The "I" cannot be too full of itself or too positively in the right and in the know about things. Unlike politicians, memoirists should not be making grandiose promises or holding themselves up as the best and the brightest. The memoirist should concede to not knowing a lot of things, to not remembering exactly, to being right about some things and very wrong about others, to making mistakes, and especially, to having twenty-twenty hindsight. Often, the most interesting parts of a memoir lie in the reflection, the process of looking at the past through the lens of the present. "Now that I think about it . . . "; "If I had only been able to . . . "; "I used to think . . . but now I think. . . . "

On the other hand, you can try the third large revision strategy.

3. Revise by telling "lies"

Embrace your aging memory! Daniel Schacter assures us that there is next to nothing we can do about the common memory problems we all, young and old, face. We are absentminded; we misplace our wallets and keys; we think about too many things at once. We block certain things, like someone's name, and then we all experience that "tip of the tongue" feeling. We mistake words or faces that look similar. Our memories are open to suggestion. We see the past through our current biases and beliefs. Bad memories persist and good memories fade with time. Rather than bemoan these memory problems, we can revise to compensate for what we can't remember.

Move events around in time. Make something the climax of your story that in reality played only a small part. Change names to protect the innocent (and the guilty). Don't fuss and fret over details of what the place looked like, which exact intersection your car broke down in, or what color of shirt your father had on that day. Make up details that will create the world that seems *most true to your experience*.

> *It was a stormy night—so black after flashes of lightning that I thought someone had thrown a wool sack over my head to blind me.*

No.

> *It was a close, muggy night, and the mosquitoes kept me awake with their high-pitched whining around my ears.*

No, actually . . .

> *It was the kind of night when you never want to go to bed because the air feels so sweet on your skin.*

It's useful in the draft to try to get to the truth, to the heart of the matter, and then make up details that help your memoir be a better piece of literature, a more finely crafted story, a more moving narrative. Of course all writers can get carried away with descriptive detail or with facts and events that drift away from the core of the story, so they need to know that they must also use sledgehammer 4.

4. Revise by leaving things out

Russell Baker said that while the biographer's problem is that he never knows enough, the autobiographer's problem is that he knows *too much*: "He knows the whole iceberg, not just the tip" (1987, 49). Just because you have the floor, so to speak, in your memoir, it doesn't allow you to blather on about this and that, to "hang on the reader's arm, like a drunk" (1987b, 68), as Annie Dillard so deftly puts it. A writer who sounds drunk had best learn the power of silence. Poets know the power of silence and use it often in the white spaces of their poems. The subjects not mentioned, the occurrences left out, the feelings alluded to but not dissected to bits—in the hands of a skilled writer, this reticence becomes aesthetically pleasing, a quality of good writing.

The best advice we can give any writer is to learn how to cut things out of his text, and most writers cut ruthlessly. The memoirist might have a particularly hard time letting go of actual parts of his life, but the craftwork, according to Dillard, is "to fashion a text," to figure out "what to put in and what to leave out" (1987b, 55). Figuring that out is difficult, especially for young or first-time memoirists. Teachers of writing hear the same complaint year upon year from their students: "But that's what really happened!" The details of exactly what happened are not the point, however. The point, in fashioning a text, is to tell a great story that makes the reader care to read it.

Deciding what to cut, deciding what to leave out, deciding what to reveal and what to conceal becomes an art, and it takes years of practice. Do not expect children to know how to do it without a great deal of support from you and time to practice it again and again.

5. Revise by telling another side of the story

In Italy, we saw possibly thousands of frescoes, paintings, and sculptures depicting the same Bible stories and the same lives of the saints and monks, the bishops and popes. Each work of art was more breathtaking than the last, but they all shared the same theme: the unquestioned and unquestioning religious piety of medieval Europe.

But there were other stories as well. At the Museum of Torture in Siena, you can look at instruments, paintings, even handwritten journal entries documenting the details of certain men of the church who tortured anyone who did not bend to their beliefs. The tools of torture are some of the most brilliant objects I've ever seen, and the most hideous. A sign at the entrance of the museum reads: "No one under 14, or the sensitive." I should have heeded that warning.

For Christians, this is a very hard story to think about, and yet if it doesn't get told, we are letting masses of people die without graves.

My student William was having trouble writing about his family because he was so angry at his father for ignoring or making fun of his children and for eventually leaving home. He told me he didn't want to write anything about his childhood at all because "none of it was good." When I asked William if he could think about why his father might have acted toward him as he did, William decided to revise his memoir by including another side of the story, one about his father's childhood. William's father had been adopted by a white couple who had stripped him of his Dominican culture and language. They wanted his father to "dress white, talk white, and act white." "I think that's why he criticizes the way I talk sometimes," William wrote. "He says I'm talking like a 'Spic.' I guess he didn't really have anyone to teach him how to love someone for who they are and talk nice to them."

Revision may not have led William to forgive his father, not yet. But it helped him imagine his father's side of the story, and that may be the first step toward forgiveness. I think that forgiveness can come from imagining what were the social, political, and psychological conditions of the people responsible for us that would allow them to ignore or even encourage things to happen the way they did. Once you look critically at the social conditions surrounding your life, you angle your memoir out of yourself toward the world.

The Finer Tools of Revision

Once students have selected a topic or theme for their memoir, collected more information and layered the story with interpretive lenses, and attempted some of the large tools of revision, we can approach a list of serious nuts-and-bolts strategies for revising the memoir draft.

For at least one week prior to taking drafts through final edits for spelling, grammar, and punctuation, I ask my class to help me generate a chart of things to do to change their drafts. If students have been writing for several months, or have been in writing process classrooms before mine and tried writing several different genres, I encourage them to begin our "Memoir Revision" chart with activities that worked well for them in the past. I also add strategies that I know work particularly well for the memoir genre. I type and copy this list for each student to paste into the writer's notebook, and during the week or more of revising, I require students to tackle at least two items from our list of revision strategies during class or for homework.

Usually, they do this revision work in their writer's notebooks, which are like workbenches. These activities should feel liberating, eye-opening, as fun as letting loose a giant bundle of helium-filled balloons into the sky. Some of the work they do in their notebooks over the next week or two will find its home in the final memoir draft, but some of it will not. The value is in the exploration and finding out that writers fiddle and muck about and play with language a lot until they find the exact right words for what they want to say, which has the effect of hitting a nail smack-dab on its head.

Draw a section

Draw part of the memoir. Talk about what you drew with a partner. Are there things in the drawing that can be added to your draft? What were you thinking about as you drew this picture?

After you talk for five minutes with your partner, go write down in your notebook what you talked about so you won't forget it. Then, look over your draft to see where these new pieces of information will best fit.

Act out a section

Get together with a partner or small group and act out a part of your memoir. First, give your partner(s) the portion of your memoir that you want to see performed. It should be a section that has some dialogue and action, or else there's nothing to act out! Ask someone to play you and others to play any other characters. See if they can come close to what you had in mind when you wrote the piece. If not, revise your writing to make it come closer to what you had in mind. Your partners may have some great ideas for how to improve this scene!

Make various outlines for a section

Once you have written a draft of a memoir, try making at least two different outlines of the major sections. In your outlines, rearrange the parts. Move the chunk you currently have at the end up to the beginning. Move what is currently in the middle to the end, and so on. Think about how reorganizing the sections would change the draft, and be open to finding a new and better way to organize the major parts of your draft.

Cut up big sections and rearrange

Make sure you have a copy of your draft before you do this. Cut the draft at the large sections. Rearrange the parts so that what used to be in the middle is now at the beginning, and so on. Think about how reorganizing the section changes the draft; you may need to write a new opening paragraph or a new ending to match your new arrangement.

Study published lead paragraphs

Look at the first paragraph of five published memoirs. Read them out loud to yourself. Notice how the author invited you, the reader, into his or her story. What did the author do to catch your eye? Is this something you can try in your beginning? Here are five beginnings to study:

I remember the first time I got really bad news. (Mary Pope Osborne, "All-Ball")

I grew up riding a rocket. If legendary rocket man Wernher von Braun could have harnessed the power of my meteoric temper, we'd have beaten the Russians into space by a good six months. (Chris Crutcher, *King of the Mild Frontier*)

When I was your age, I was flying. I wasn't flying all the time, of course, and I didn't fly by myself, but there I was, nonetheless, on Saturday afternoons in the 1950's, several thousand feet in the air over the state of Connecticut, which is where I grew up. (Reeve Lindbergh, "Flying")

"Guess what?" That's all my nine-year-old sister Lizzie had to say to get me excited.
    "What?"
    "You'll never guess," Lizzie said. And I wouldn't. Lizzie was too smart for me. (Katherine Patterson, "Why I Never Ran Away from Home")

My sister, brother, and I didn't have a dog, but we sure could have used one around dinnertime. Our dog would never have had to beg for table scraps, for we promised sincerely in our mealtime prayers always to feed Rover the main course. It wouldn't have been so much for love of dog, but for survival. (Rita Williams-Garcia, "Food from the Outside")

Write five leads

Write at least five different beginnings to your memoir; then choose which one you like best. See how your memoir would change with each of those possible beginnings.

Study published final paragraphs

Look at the last few paragraphs of five published memoirs. Read them out loud to yourself. Notice how the author "leaves the page." What did the author do to make the story sound finished (without saying "the end")?

[My father] was persuading and coaxing and willing the plane to do what he wanted; he was leaning that airplane, like a bobsled, right down to where it could safely land. He could feel its every movement, just as if it were part of his own body. My father wasn't flying the airplane, he was *being* the airplane. That's how he did it. That's how he had always done it. Now I knew. (Reeve Lindbergh, "Flying")

The rest of that night I slept sweetly, peacefully, for the first time in I couldn't remember how long. I slept deeper than the voice of Howard Bruce's father, a sleep that might have come all the way from Heaven. (Karen Hesse, "Waiting for Midnight")

Swimming now in the clear-water lakes of Wisconsin, where I live, I sometimes imagine my mother riding the waves of the sea, cresting over the top and falling gently without ever hitting bottom, laughing her easy musical laugh. She could be right next to me: we are separated only by glimmering water. (Kyoko Mori, "Learning to Swim")

It is from that moment that I stop crying. Although I don't know it then, sitting in that chair in our living room, I have passed over a line—the invisible line between childhood and whatever it is that comes next. Not adulthood, not that quickly, but the beginning of the long, long walk into another world. (Norma Fox Mazer, "In the Blink of an Eye")

"We'll leave her," Grampa said. We turned to get into the car. When I looked back over my shoulder, she was gone. Only ripples on the water, widening circles rolling on toward other shores like generations following each other, like my grandmother's flowers still growing in a hundred gardens in Greenfield, like the turtles still seeking out that sandbank, like this story that is no longer just my own but belongs now to your memory, too. (Joseph Bruchac, "The Snapping Turtle")

Write five endings

Write at least five different endings and choose which one you like best. Notice that if you change your current ending, you will probably need to change other parts of the draft, even the beginning, to fit the new ending.

Tell someone your memoir

Call someone and tell him or her what you are writing about in your memoir. Have the person take notes, or tape-record you, so that you can add some of the new and different things you say to your friend into your draft.

Describe the internal you and the external you

Choose two or three meaningful events or memories from your draft. Rewrite them to include what was happening to the external you and then again to include what was happening to the internal you.

Write more about one sentence

Find a part of your memoir where you write only a sentence or two about something important. In your writer's notebook, write that sentence up at the top of a blank page. Then squeeze and squeeze your memory to write two pages all about that sentence. Pretend the sentence is the door you open into a museum. Go exploring to find out what is in that museum.

Turn a difficult part into a list or poem

For a part that feels overwhelming because there is just *too much* to say, or it is painful to say it, try just writing about it in a simple list, using only a word or phrase on each line of the list. Or try writing this section as a small poem.

Write a section in third person

Think (without looking at the actual draft) of a paragraph or a scene from your memoir that is written in first person. Write that small section over again in your writer's notebook, using the third person.

Now compare the two versions, and notice what is different. See if there is anything in the tone, the word choice, the details you recalled in the third-person version that you can add into your draft.

Study five favorite published titles

Find five titles from published memoirs that you admire and try writing a few like those. Are they funny (and long), like Chris Crutcher's *King of the Mild Frontier: An Ill-Advised Autobiography*? Or is the main title one strong word, like *Soldier*, by June Jordan? Are they poetic, like *The Air Down Here: True Tales from a South Bronx Boyhood*, by Gil C. Alicea?

Write five different titles

In your writer's notebook, write at least five different possibilities for the title of your memoir. A good title makes a reader want to read your piece. So you won't just make it a boring old title like "All About Me" or "My Life Story." Instead, you might want to use a phrase that sounds like poetry: "Pink Mountains and Pearly Moons." You might want a title that gives a tiny bit of information about you, but in a mysterious-sounding way that will be explained inside the memoir: "Girl at the End." (The end of what? At the end of a line? At the end of her patience? At the end of time?)

Writers often find a meaningful word or phrase inside their piece that will make a good title. Look inside your memoir to see if there is a great word or phrase for your title. Perhaps you write about a pattern in your life that would make a good title: "Always Right" or "Laughing at All the Wrong Times." Perhaps you found a theme that can now become a title: "Family First, Video Games Second" or "Alone but Never Lonely."

Find five things to name with proper nouns

Look back over your draft and find five things you can give a proper-noun name to: not just *cookies*, but *Nutter Butters*; not *my street*, but *the corner of Colorado and Mossman Place*; not *an old lady*, but *Mrs. Muriel Olafsen*.

Read your memoir out loud

Read your memoir draft out loud to as many people as you can. As you read, listen for places that your voice might stumble over. Maybe some words need to get rearranged in the sentence, or perhaps there are too many words in that spot. Be ready with your colored pen to change words, add things, or delete things right there, as you are reading.

You can also ask someone else to read your memoir out loud to you. Again, listen as if you have never heard it before, and you are ready to be critical of it. Make notes on a piece of paper about things you want to be sure to change when you get the draft back.

Type your draft

If possible, type your draft or ask someone to type it for you. Seeing your words "in print" can help you find places where the writing feels weak.

Put the draft away for a while

Finally, put your draft away for a few days. There is nothing better than the passage of time to help a writer look at his or her work with new eyes and revise some weak parts.

Revision's tools are power tools. For the memoirist, the ability to change even the few words of a title can result in a new way of thinking about and telling a life story. Revision allows the memoirist to stand back, stand apart from the work she created to see it again, to see it anew, and to make it even better than it was before. How many things in life do we get another chance to make better?

Answering Test Prompts by Drawing on Best Memoir Writing

T o move from talking about revising memoir as a way to gain perspective on one's life to talking about preparing for school tests seems like a move from the sacred to the profane. It's sad but true that our students compose their lives within a school system that continually wants to measure whether they are good enough to continue progressing through those lives.

The good news is that spending four to six weeks studying the craft of memoir writing can help students perform exceedingly well on writing tests. I believe that most of the essay prompts on writing tests call for some type of autobiographical or personal narrative response. So learning how to write honestly, from the heart, about an event from their lives—learning how to craft scenes and vignettes, how to layer with sensual details and precise dialogue, how to control narrative time, how to make beginnings that grab readers by the throat and endings that leave them in tears—will directly improve students' responses to standardized test prompts.

More good news: students can use the best of their memoir writing that they have already shaped, layered, revised, and edited to plug into almost any test response! There is never a need to face blank test paper and invent something to write out of thin air! In this chapter, I'm going to show you how to prepare students to face almost any test prompt, armed with their lovely prerehearsed memoir vignettes, which can be twisted and tweaked to fit any occasion.

Teachers who care about the quality of their students' learning have learned to protect the important work they want to do with their students by carving out a unit of study that prepares students for the tests they are required to take. In this test genre study, students approach their state or district writing test as they would approach any other text—they read it, discuss it, and write in response to it. As they do with feature articles and poems in other genre studies during the school year, students question this text's author and purpose; they name its genre-specific elements and features; and they even try to make their own writing tests just like this one in order to master the genre.

I had to administer writing tests to fourth and fifth graders in New York City and in Texas, and I know how much practice and preparation students need for them. I have also graded the writing portion of exams against a holistic, criteria-based rubric, using numerical scores from 1 to 4 or 1 to 6, so I know how scorers are trained to evaluate students' writing. In preparing for this chapter, I have examined the writing prompts used in exams from many different state tests, in grade levels from fourth to tenth, and noticed that most of them require autobiographical responses. I have conducted a study in one fourth-grade classroom to further test out some of the ideas in this chapter about using a memoir study to teach students how to respond to personal narrative prompts. From these experiences, I have developed some ideas and activities that might help children perform better on the composition portion of the tests than they would without these efforts.

In the first portion of this chapter, I lay out a plan for a monthlong writing test genre study that helps prepare students for the specific tasks they will perform on whatever writing test your district offers, and I describe how I set that up in my fourth- and fifth-grade classroom. In the second part of the chapter, I analyze sample writing prompts from various state tests to see what kinds of response they are asking for. Next, I demonstrate how to help students twist and tweak the material of their lives, the terrain of topics that they know inside out, to make it fit whatever test prompt gets thrown at them. I finish with a detailed portrait of how my students and I set up simulated testing conditions in the classroom and practiced for a week before taking the actual test.

Let me sound the first warning bell here, and then I promise to ring it again throughout the chapter: the practice I describe here is strictly for helping the students who will be taking certain types of tests. This study is limited in time and scope. It is not a viable occupation for students who do not have to take a writing test, nor is it an educative way to spend most days of the year in a classroom. For most days of the school year, students should spend ever increasing amounts of time reading and discussing their reading; writing and revising their writing; thinking, exploring, inquiring, making connections, discovering, becoming, and having the time of their lives.

Studying the Test as a Reading and Writing Genre

When I was a fourth- and fifth-grade teacher in New York City, facing district and state standardized tests, I was part of a study group that developed the idea of teaching the test as yet another genre with its own rules, elements of craft, purposes, and audience. That inquiry resulted in a book called *A Teacher's Guide to Standardized Reading Tests: Knowledge Is Power*, by Calkins, Montgomery, and Santman (1998). I recommend that book for more information about treating tests as a genre to be analyzed and for descriptions of strategies for studying standardized, multiple-choice reading tests.

In many states, the "writing tests" given to particular grade levels contain from one-half to three-fourths multiple-choice questions about grammar and usage, followed by one or sometimes two compositional writing tasks, usually requiring an autobiographical narrative response. Later in this chapter, I will offer strategies to help children improve their responses to autobiographical narrative prompts, but first I wish to describe how I conducted a test genre study in my fourth- and fifth-grade classroom.

For one month before the scheduled testing days, usually around March and the beginning of April, my classroom buzzed with test research. Reading and writing workshop were given over to examining sample test questions and writing practice responses, and our discussions generated strategies for success. I copied as many sample tests as I could get my hands on for study purposes. Part of the challenge for many students is getting past the graphic structure and visual look of the tasks, so the practice items must look as nearly like the actual test as possible. When there were no exact replicas of the test to practice with, my colleagues and I made them ourselves. When my students practiced responding to writing prompts, they used special test paper, which I made by copying the pages allotted to writing straight from a sample test booklet.

In small test-prep groups, my students studied what this test genre comprises: how the test is put together, what the questions ask for, what patterns appear across tasks and items. Just as they had studied short stories or poetry, looking for the elements and criteria of those genres in order to make their own stories and poems, they read the tests like writers. We listed properties of the test genre on charts and then matched them to a new batch of practice items to see how the criteria held up and what else could be added to the list.

Evaluating Sample Essays

After reading many test items to determine their qualities, we examined four student responses to test questions from previous years. (Some student essays were provided by the district; others I copied from former anonymous students.) We studied responses that had received each of the four possible scores, from the lowest, a 1, to the highest, a 4. Again, we charted what we noticed about each sample essay. So, for instance, my students noticed that the 1 essay was short, had "simple words," and was "kind of boring." The 4 essay was longer, used "fancy" words (that's what one group of students called metaphorical, lyrical language, or simply a vibrant vocabulary), and said a lot more about the topic.

Next, I put a copy of the district's official evaluative rubric on an overhead transparency so that we could all read and discuss the scoring criteria together. I provided each student with a copy as well. We matched the district's rubric with what we had already noticed about the different levels of response, and then we studied the essays again with the rubric beside them. My purpose in this exercise was to allow students to first develop a felt sense of a rich essay response compared with a more skimpy one and to compose their own language about what made one response better (according to the rubric) than another one. The official rubric simply validated what they had already noticed and also added some complexity and terminology to their critical judgments.

For the next step, I copied more sample responses by former students and also wrote a small batch of essays myself, trying to provide examples of writing at each level of the rubric, from 1 to 4. With their personal copy of the rubric in hand, students read at least five essays and assigned a score to each. Then in their groups, they compared their scores and debated with each other when there was a discrepancy between scores. (This is exactly how test scorers operate as well. A typical process is this: Each essay has two evaluators, and the score is averaged between them. If there is a wide discrepancy, a third reader is called in to settle the score.)

Making Our Own Test Prompts

After reading, deconstructing, and scoring essays written by me and former students, the next step in our unit of study was for my students to write their own prompts and submit these to self-evaluation and group critique.

As I wrote in Chapter 3, about reading memoir, when children become makers of a certain genre, they become better readers of that genre, and vice versa. In order for my students to truly understand the tasks they'd be presented in the test booklets, I asked them to write their own essay prompts. Here are some student imitations of the personal narrative prompt:

- Write about a time you got hurt the most on the inside or outside.
- If you could go back to one day in your life and live it over again, what day would it be?
- Tell about the best Christmas present that wasn't a toy that you ever got.
- Who is your biggest hero in life?

In truth, their questions were sometimes more interesting than the real test prompts, but many of their questions would also be considered biased or not universal enough for a real standardized test, so we had to reject those. We managed to develop some sympathy for how hard it is to construct a test during this exercise.

Making Practice Responses

I selected those prompts that were most like the questions on the actual test and typed these into a format that matched the official test booklet. During writing workshop or at night for homework, students responded to these prompts on the special test paper, using the material from one of their memoir vignettes. The next day, they exchanged essays with one preselected test buddy (see next paragraph), and they scored each other's essays using copies of the official rubric. The amount of practice my students got from writing, reading, and evaluating these test essays went a long way, I think, toward helping them write what the district or state evaluators were looking for on this particular task. They had multiple opportunities to hold their own and each other's essay attempts up to the evaluative mirror of the rubric and to decide if the attempts did or did not fit the established criteria.

When I explain this practice with teachers in workshops, they often wonder if having students grade each other's essays is a nice thing to do. I think that depends upon the tone of the learning community. I paired my students with one other person whom they told me they felt comfortable with, someone they trusted. I tried to make the pair as close as possible in their test-taking abilities, but even if they're a bit uneven, both will benefit from the exchange. The good test taker will develop a critical eye for weak responses, and the weaker test taker will have an opportunity to review more competent essays. I talk frequently to my students about being a team against the test makers (those poor, anonymous test makers!), who are trying to "get us." Our job, as we read each others essays and offer helpful comments, is to make *everyone's* essays shine. The kids put on their "test maker eyeglasses" as they read each other's essays and then wrote comments such as, "You really captured what it feels like to be embarrassed!" and "You have not used enough details about your most exciting day! I can't see it in my mind! Did your heart beat extra fast? Did your head feel like it would explode?" By this late date in the school year, my students have helped each other in every area of the curriculum, and especially they have brought their writing to each other for comments and constructive criticism, and during this exercise, they feel like they are helping each other combat an external force.

Some teachers may simply decide to have students evaluate their own essays against the rubric. What gets missed, however, is the level of learning that comes from looking critically at writing that is not their own. We all know how helpful, and yes, scary, it can be to hear someone else's opinion about our writing. We also know how easy it is, even for adults, to miss words and punctuation marks as we write. Professional journalists, even famous writers, depend heavily on the critical eyes of writing friends and editors to help them see what they can no longer see because they have become too familiar with the work. Ultimately, of course, it is very important for students to bring that critical stance back to their own writing because they will have only their own pair of eyes looking back at their test essay to help them revise and edit it.

Making the Material Fit the Test

In this portion of the chapter, I describe in detail the typical autobiographical test prompts and how to help students craft delightful responses from the best writing they have done during the school year.

Any writer will tell you that he often writes to a perceived or explicit need, to someone's query, to a gap in literature, and to requests from editors and publishers. He will also tell you that no prompt or question is impossible to write about if the writer can apply what he has written about before, and has rehearsed and revised, to this new question. The trick is figuring out a sentence or two that appears to answer the question directly and then slanting the material the writer already had in mind to write so that it fits the new topic. Politicians, in press conferences and political debates, do this without blinking an eye. Many don't even try to sound as if they are answering the reporter's or moderator's question.

Ideally, students will have spent many hours writing about topics and ideas that matter to them. They will have written about these meaningful subjects in a variety of genres—as poems, feature articles, fiction stories, letters to the mayor and the editor of the local newspaper. They will have had opportunities to share their writing with multiple audiences and to get meaningful response. When this is true, students are, literally, practiced writers, nearly as fluent as hard-boiled journalists. Given a prompt, they pick up a pen, think for a few moments, jot out a plan for how to structure their response, pull an old piece from their storehouse of material, and make the material fit the question.

We somehow fear that tests require children to invent answers out of the blue, but invention doesn't start when they first look at the question. Instead, it begins every day in the writing process classroom, when a student tries out a new genre or learns something new about her passion—music, football, animation, skateboarding—or discovers a different way of looking at the world from a classmate.

Students are able to do these things, but we have to give them the time and space to get there. What I am proposing as a way of preparing for writing tests requires letting kids write all year long about what they know, rehearsing it until it becomes almost memorized. Then they can take the material they know best and that they have written about, perhaps in various genres, in prose and poetry, in fiction and nonfiction, and reshape it to fit any number of writing prompts.

Studying Test Prompts Up Close: What Do They Want?

Before we figure out how to tweak best writing to fit test prompts, let's look closely at several questions typical of most state writing tests for elementary and middle school students. From studying these prompts we can notice what type of response is required.

Typical Prompts for Elementary Students

1. *Think of a time when something scared you.* Maybe it was something that scared everyone around you or maybe only you were scared and no one else noticed.

2. *Think about a time that you taught someone how to do something or someone taught you how to do something.*

3. *Tell about a sport or game or performance or hobby you have participated in.*

4. *Tell about someone who was a hero in your life.* Describe how that person changed your life.

5. *Write a story about getting a present.* Describe what it was, who gave it to you, and why it was important to you. In your story, be sure to include a title, a beginning, a middle, and an end to your story, and details to make it interesting.

6. *Write a composition about the worst day you ever had.*

7. *Write about a time when you heard something really beautiful or something really interesting.* Describe what you heard so that the readers can understand why it was beautiful or interesting. Use specific details.

Typical Prompts for Middle School Students

(Notice that a few of the following prompts include quotes from famous people about generalized topics such as pride, perseverance, doing the right thing, and so on. If your state writing test asks students to respond to a quotation, you can help your students learn how to incorporate the quote throughout their response while staying grounded in personal experience, or memoir, as the italicized words of the prompt ask them to do.)

8. Write a composition *about a time when you learned a life lesson.*

9. Some people admire another person's talent or intelligence; some admire a person's clothing or car; and some admire the other person for having qualities like courage, kindness, and compassion. *Think about a person you admire and what you admire about them. It can be someone you know* or someone you have heard or read about. Write a composition describing this person. Explain in detail at least two reasons why you admire this person.

10. Helen Keller wrote, "We can do anything if we stick to it long enough." *Have you ever stuck with something for a long time until you finally succeeded at it?*

11. President Abraham Lincoln said, "Every man is proud of what he does well." *In your own life*, have you found that statement to be true? *Write about a time when you felt proud of something you did well*. Be sure to be specific.

Notice that in each item, the question calls for an autobiographical response, for memoir material. (I italicized the request for memoir material in each question.) Notice also that some of the wording in the prompts signals exactly what kind of response is required. If the test calls for a personal narrative response, that means the writing should tell a *story*, probably in chronological order, just to be safe. Some writing tests signal the need for a narrative response with words like *Tell what happened*. Other prompts flat out require a "story" with "a beginning, a middle, and an end."

There is no reason that prompts like these should feel to students like a shock to the system, as if they're entering a whole new galaxy when they open their test booklets. What I teach my students, in fact, is to apply the life material they have already worked over and over during various genre studies we have been doing all year long to a series of practice prompts. I want them to feel so familiar with and comfortable in their life stories that they can write them, with some modifications at the beginning and end, to fit any prompt. The first step in that process is to ask them to review their material from the year.

Filling the Storehouse: Students Get to Know Their Life Material

The first thing I do during the monthlong test genre study is ask my students to review all of the writing they have done so far this school year. Students spend a day reviewing all the material about their lives housed in their notebooks, as well as the finished pieces—the memoirs, short stories, poems, and feature articles—stored in their writing folders or portfolios.

The next step of the test-preparation process is to take a few pieces of this life material and begin to shape it into well-written vignettes. Students might choose vignettes they have already written for the memoir genre study, or they might decide to work up some material from their writing notebooks or from poems, for instance, that now has to be written as prose. The point of this exercise is to prepare one or two memoir nuggets that will be fine-tuned and shaped to fit practice test prompts.

Crafting Test Responses

When I've spoken with people who score student writing tests, they've let me in on a few predictable preferences: for instance, they don't care for responses that sound as if they were written by a machine, the kind in which you can see straight through to the five-paragraph formula, with its precise placement of thesis statement and topic sentences, using the same five transitional phrases. Scorers love essays that make them smile, that have a young person's voice, with words and phrases that pop out from the mound of papers, phrases like "It stung my behind!" They also appreciate a response that brings tears to their eyes, or that makes them remember their own childhood, or that makes them see the world in a new way. How can students write these kinds of responses? By knowing the material they are writing about so well that they have already invented crowd-pleasing language and structures for writing about it.

Let me share a process that I have used for helping my students prepare well-written test responses. The first step was to have my students write from one to three perfect little memoir vignettes that could be tweaked to fit whatever prompt the test makers invented. Remember that I had spent the entire school year so far asking students to write about subjects and events that mattered to them. But even if the ideal has not been possible for everyone, we can help students craft one or two memoir vignettes during the month before the test that will knock the socks off those scorers.

In Chapter 6, I offer some suggestions for how to write and structure scenes and vignettes. My students and I studied several of the well-written models for vignettes that I refer to in that chapter (Fletcher [2005] and Greenfield [1979], for example) during the memoir genre study, and then during the month of test practice, we turned to our favorites again to learn how to craft a tidy vignette.

Once my students had crafted a couple of successful vignettes, we practiced tailoring them to fit some test prompts. For many narrative pieces, all that might be required to make it seem as if they were written expressly for a certain prompt is a few sentences at the very beginning and a few at the end. This way, the prompt acts as the frame, and the language from their memoir illustrates the point expressed in the frame. I think this is the safest structure for most children in the testing situation.

More sophisticated writers may be able to weave a test prompt question throughout their narrative or essay, pulling and tugging at it as if they were thinking about it right on the page. The prerehearsed material of their life becomes fodder for the debate they're currently having with the given topic.

A student who feels more confident about working familiar material from his writer's notebook or from previously drafted memoir pieces will be able to move beyond a formulaic response that merely repeats the prompt in the first sentence. Mark's delightful practice response to the prompt "Tell about a time you learned an important lesson" (Figure 9–1) demonstrates how he held the idea of the prompt—learning a lesson—in his mind as he told a suspenseful, engaging story from his past.

He tells about a time when he and his friend, Howard, threw snowballs at a car, and then the angry driver decided to have it out with the boys. Mark pulls readers into the action immediately with the alarming, "I am so dead, I thought. . . . " He proceeds, in that first paragraph, to set up the most tense moment of the whole story, when the driver of the car steps out to confront them. But he freezes that moment in his lead paragraph, then in the second paragraph goes backward in time to describe how this whole fiasco began, "one snowy winter day in January."

Mark's memoir essay is rich with metaphor—the snowball looked like a "cracked open egg against the side of that speeding vehicle"—and voice: "I am so dead"; "if Howard had a few more brain cells," and complex, varied sentences. It is clear that he has written and rewritten this material, finding the perfect tempo, tone, and imagery, and figured out how to structure it so that it truly feels suspenseful. All Mark needed to do to ensure that this response matched the prompt was to reflect, which he had learned how to do from his teacher, Barbara Clements and her super lessons about the elements of memoir, in his final sentence: "Maybe because of that [the experience he just described], I am always more careful and watchful while playing now!"

I demonstrated for my students how I could take one of my well-rehearsed memoir vignettes, perhaps the one about the peacock that landed on my head (page 116), and bend it to fit a number of test prompts. I usually challenged them to trip me up— to think of a question that I wouldn't be able to force my story to illustrate. They tried really hard. Chad said, "Tell about your favorite relative and why."

I cleared my throat as if to give a speech and replied, "I have several relatives whom I enjoy seeing once in a while, or who have been important to my mental or physical

Snowballs

I am so dead, I thought, as the car came speeding in reverse towards my friend, Howard, and me. What is the driver going to do? My only hope of escape was to jump behind a telephone pole to conceal myself. The car stopped in front of us and the door swung open. I am so dead, I repeated. This was quite a predicament we got ourselves into.

One snowy winter day in January, my friend Howard and I were throwing snowballs across a four way intersection. We were seeing who could hit a parking sign across the street first. I wasn't having very much luck, so Howard took a crack at it. He lofted a perfectly round snowball into the air.

Just then a car came zooming out of nowhere, really speeding, and it didn't even stop for the stop sign. The snowball, which was once round, looked like a cracked open egg against the side of that speeding vehicle.

We let out a sigh of relief when the car kept on going and didn't stop. That moment was very short lived because when the car reached the end of the street it started rocketing in reverse towards us and I hid. If Howard had a few more brain cells he would have probably done the same, but he just stood there as still as frozen water in a stream.

A guy stormed out of the car and slammed the door shut with such anger it made me shake. He picked up a handful of snow and threw it at my friend exclaiming, "How do you like snow being thrown at you, huh? Huh? Huh?"

My friend just stood there and pretended he was from another country. "No, no, I can't speak no English" he repeated over and over again. I don't think the guy was buying it, and this "conversation" continued for about another five minutes. I felt guilty, safe behind my little pole, out of harm's way. I thought that I should have been helping him, but Howard was handling it pretty well and it seemed apparent that the guy was going to give up soon, and after a while, he did.

He got into his car with a sour enough look on his face to spoil milk and drove off. I hopped out from behind the telephone pole behind which I was hiding and gave Howard a pat on the back. It was a job well done. When I did this I am not sure if the guy saw me as he was driving away. Hopefully, he didn't see me, but to this day I still think that that car will come shooting out of the intersection and try to track me down. Maybe because of that, I am always more careful and watchful while playing now!

Figure 9–1 *Mark's Essay Response to a Sixth-Grade Prompt: "Tell About a Time You Learned an Important Lesson"*

development. But once I met a person who was like the grandfather I never had. We called him *El Viejo,* and I will never forget him."

Hands shot up, and several students squirmed in their seats, wanting me to call on them. They were positive they could stump me.

"I know, I know!" Teresa called out. "You didn't get any presents in your story! How about this: 'Of all the presents you ever got, what was your favorite?'"

I settled back in my chair, crossed my legs, stroked my chin, as if thinking hard. My kids had smug looks on their faces—she can't answer this one! they thought. I began slowly, softly thinking out loud: "When most people think of the presents they have been given, they remember the best video game or the shiny purple bicycle they got when they were ten. But I think that presents come in all sorts of packages, and sometimes the best gifts are things you can't buy or wrap up with ribbons. The best present I ever got was some kind words spoken by a stranger one time when I was scared and lonely."

"Ah! That's not fair! That doesn't really fit!" Michael yelled out.

"Yes it does!" said wise London. "And Ms. Bomer would probably get a high score because grown-ups really like that kind of story that has a moral at the end."

"Well, now you get to try to stump one another," I told them. In pairs or in their test study groups, I asked them to first invent one or two test prompts and then to take turns asking each other to try to fit their memoir material into the prompts. All this work was done orally at first, and I wanted them to know each other's material so well that they could help their partners if they got stuck.

My students practiced bending their material to fit different prompts by writing just the leads and endings, the framework of their responses. I usually had them wait to write a full response, including the middle portion, until the Monday or two before test week; then they workshopped it (got feedback from writing buddies and revised based on that feedback) for a week. I had them write one or two responses for homework as well.

I brought families in on the fun, too. In fact, a good activity for parents night that would help put parents' minds at ease by showing that their child was prepared for the test would be to do something like the following:

1. Show parents or guardians the test prompts.
2. Have one of their own child's memoir vignettes out, ready for them to work with.

3. Have them try to fit the vignette to the prompt.

4. Invite them to try this at home with their child.

During the week immediately preceding the test, I asked students to respond to a new prompt during our simulated test week (see next section), and we repeated the whole cycle of feedback and revision, paying particular attention to ensure that everyone answered the question posed in his or her beginning and ending paragraphs.

Practicing for Test Conditions

After several weeks of reading sample prompts, and writing and scoring practice essays, I set up a test simulation week the week before the scheduled testing days. We pretended that Monday, Wednesday, and Friday were test days, during which we tried a dry run of each portion of the standardized exam. I asked parents to treat this week as if it were the real thing, making sure kids got plenty of sleep and a good breakfast, whether breakfast happened at home or in school. (I always stocked my classroom with healthy snacks, especially during tests; I fed those children who did not get breakfast elsewhere whole-wheat toast, peanut butter, and fruit. Everyone got bottles of water to drink during the test also.)

We arranged the room to look exactly as it would look on testing day. My usual classroom setup used round tables instead of desks and provided areas with rugs, cushions, even a small couch or two, where children snuggled up to read and write. During test simulation week, however, I asked children to find their special testing spots, where they were most able to shut the world out and focus on the tasks. Obviously, they had to find isolated spots and could no longer sit close to friends or writing partners. I made sure during testing to have an individual desk or table spot available for each child in the event he or she needed one.

However, each year, several kids would prove to me that they focused best in odd spots in the room. One boy was obsessed with a wooden cube I bought at Goodwill, about two feet on each side, which he could move anywhere in the class he needed to. He sat on the floor and wrote on the block. Another boy took tests lying on his belly on the bare linoleum floor. I'm not usually one to announce test scores as proof of anything, but this boy scored in the ninety-ninth percentile on the math and literacy portions both years that I had him as a student. Of course, there were also many students who opted to sit straight up at a desk or table.

So during test simulation week we discovered what conditions were necessary for each student to feel comfortable and perform to his or her best ability on the test. Kids figured out if they needed sweaters, if they preferred supersharp or stubby pencil tips, if they wanted to kick their shoes off. I timed the simulated test practice to last as long as they would be given during the real tests. For the writing test, I gave all students the same prompt, one they had never seen. I read their practice tests afterwards, and on Tuesday and Thursday, we spent the day fine-tuning any issues that came up from the rehearsals. On Friday, I had children practice whatever section I felt they needed a little extra help with.

Although by the spring, my students were quite used to writing for extended periods of time from our thirty to forty minutes of daily writing during writing workshop, they still needed practice sitting and focusing on a task that looked exactly like what they could expect to face on the test. Many students struggle during test situations because they lack the physical and mental stamina it takes to perform those tasks.

Remembering What Writing Is For

Sometimes teachers ask, if states and districts expect students to be able to respond directly to prompt questions, why don't we spend time all year long having them write in response to our prompts? I know that seems to make sense. But I sound the warning bell again: be careful what you devote time to in the classroom, for that becomes what school means to children. Wouldn't it be more meaningful for them to spend longer and longer periods of time (thereby gaining stamina) lost in a book or revising a feature article they are writing? If we spend our days reading, writing, and discussing, those activities alone will result in higher test scores.

We could spend an entire school year perfecting students' responses to test prompts, but at the end of such a year, what will these students know how to do in writing? Will they know how to find their own terrain of topics? Will they have knowledge of a variety of genres and styles? Will they have any chance to develop their unique writing voice, something that can take years to achieve? Will they be able to use writing to solve problems, to help them think through an idea, or to convince someone of their side of an argument? And most importantly, of course, will they love to write? I don't think so. All they will know is how to perform on one type of task for an external evaluator. Most of them will come to hate writing.

All teachers want their students to experience success on the tests that are now a reality in every public school in the country. But we must not let the tests take away what is most important about writing. I want to help my students use writing to think and learn, to remember, to move others. I make sure my students know that writing is an activity for life while tests are temporary hoops to jump through.

Epilogue

Our Nation's Memoir; Why We Write

America is so young. We are writing our nation's memoir, establishing our national identity, and revising it as more painful truths are revealed:

We are largely a nation of immigrants who escaped poverty and persecution in our ancestral lands.

We are a nation of people who continue to need to escape from our native countries, but many of us are often shut out or sent back.

We are recent descendents of slaveholders and of slaves, who are still trying to figure out how to make recompense and how to forgive each other.

We are a nation that up until September 11, 2001, lived in a naïve bubble of security. We believed we were immune to things that other countries have dealt with for centuries.

We are a nation that believes it is number one, and we are a nation that refuses to recognize the patterns of history—no country or empire stays number one for long, not if it isolates itself from the rest of the world and refuses to act for the good of all. As I write this book, it feels as if the crown tilts precariously; tarnish creeps up the sides. Venice, that beautiful city that rises like a dream from the sea, was the wealthiest city in the entire world from 1100 to 1400. Now, you can walk among its gaudy, gorgeous ruins as if it's a movie façade or a Disneyland simulation. Venice looks as if it could topple back into the sea if you gave it a good, strong push.

How will we write our story so that our children and grandchildren, seven generations hence, will be proud of us?

The year I taught fifth grade in Texas was 2001. Maria wrote bravely and honestly in her notebook about what was happening at home with her father—the fighting, the hitting, and the drinking—in powerful, violent images. She did not wish to transform her notebook entries into a published memoir. The truth stayed in her writer's notebook until we studied poetry. During that genre study, she transformed the images of her feelings of fear and helplessness to imagine and empathize with what the victims of September 11, 2001, might have experienced:

Twin Towers

The black
Smoke flooding
Into the
Blue sky
If you
Follow the
Clumps of
Smoke
You will
Find two
Planes crashing
Into two
Buildings
The sound
Of it is
Like a
Wild thunder
Storm
On the ground
Below
You can
Hear people
Screaming and
Yelling because
Of the fear
They have
Inside

Them
The world
Comes crashing down
Tower
By
Tower

Maria's empathy and compassion, her ability to imagine her way into how things are for others, is what will help her create a better world, I believe. This leads me to a last reason to write memoir:

We write memoir to create a better world

In Hebrew there is a phrase that has become a personal mantra since I learned of it: *Tikkun Olam. Tikkun* means to "repair" or "heal." *Olam* means "world." The phrase refers to a way of thinking or a set of actions people can take toward the world. That is, instead of orienting toward greed or just getting by, we might work to make the world better by healing the injustice and misery that plague us. Not only acts of kindness, but jarring, painful, ground-shaking actions, when we step outside of ourselves to care about something and someone unrelated to our own needs.

In "Tikkun's Politics of Meaning," Michael Lerner describes something called "communities of meaning"—collectives that operate around a shared value or ethic. He offers up this challenge: "get together a group of people in your profession and imagine how every detail of your work would be different if you were to allow your changed paradigm (productivity defined in terms of creating loving human beings who are ethically, spiritually, and ecologically sensitive) to govern your work" (1994).

If *Tikkun Olam*—repairing the world—became the standard for our schools, it would be a paradigm shift no less violent to our current sociopolitical world than, dare I say it, a nuclear explosion. This might be a subject for another book, but think for one moment how it relates to schools and teaching children: what would be the first thing children would see as they entered a school building that sought to heal injustice? How would the school day begin? What would the curriculum be? If putting someone else's needs over your own were the standard being assessed, who in our classroom would get exemplary marks, and who would be the low-performing students?

We know there are things that don't make sense. How do we make any sense of people who strap bombs on their chests and walk into a crowded place to blow themselves up? This is senseless. But if we don't look for meaning in tragedy, some think that we will go mad.

We had just moved to Texas when 9/11 happened. My first, gut reaction when I watched the image of the plane flying into the World Trade Center was that I was not where I should be, in the city of my adult life; I was not at home. Maria gave me a one-thousand-piece puzzle of the skyline of New York City that year for Christmas. She asked me several weeks beforehand if it would be too hard to look at a picture of the World Trade Center. My students knew I had lived in New York, and they loved to hear stories about the "big city." Maria had noticed my split second of shock every time I happened upon a picture of the buildings in a book or magazine.

She begged me to open her present in front of the class, wanting my response, I guess, wanting to give me what I loved and to see me moved by it, and I was. The photograph was taken from the harbor, looking toward the southernmost tip of Manhattan, of that instantly identifiable skyline, with the twin towers rising so strikingly higher than anything else around. It was taken at dusk, when the sky turns blue and lavender, when lights in the office buildings come on and reflect in the water. I learned many subtle shades of violet over the next five months as I tried to put the tiny pieces together into a whole. Maria said she picked this puzzle out special—it was more beautiful than the daytime version, and when finished, it could stick together and be hung on the wall forever. "Here in this classroom," she said, looking around, as if she were picturing that the puzzle and I would still be here in the future.

I assumed Maria would want to help me put it together. I set it up in a corner of the carpeted meeting area and invited everyone to work on it during choice time or rainy-day recess. I did not imagine myself working on the puzzle. I've never had patience for puzzles of any kind, much less one with dozens of little blue pieces. But Maria did not want to work on it, and other kids gave up pretty quickly. So one afternoon, after a particularly dicey teaching day, I locked my classroom door and sat before the puzzle. I picked out all the edge and corner pieces, as I had learned to do when I was about Maria's age, and built the frame quickly. My childhood puzzle-solving strategies, few though they were, came flooding back. I thought, "Hey, I could teach problem solving with this tool! We could devise strategies together!" But still, I couldn't get very many students interested in working on the puzzle.

I worked on the puzzle on rare rainy days, when students stayed indoors and had quiet choice times instead of recess, or whenever I had had a difficult day at school, which was often. I found such peace, such release in the process. I became addicted to it, actually, and I knew I had to get the Twin Towers up before school let out for the summer and Maria went away to middle school. Sometimes people would try to find me in my classroom and would never think to look in the corner for a forty-five-year-old woman kneeling over a puzzle. A student said to me one day, "Like I said, Ms. Bomer, you're like a piece of that puzzle, hidden in the corner like that."

It felt like a selfish waste of time, working on this puzzle. I should be working on those lesson plans I'm supposed to turn in, I thought. But I was feeling healed, finally, by putting the pieces of that image back together. I knew it was only a metaphor, even as I proceeded with it. But metaphor has the power to heal.

One day, I waited to see who in my class would notice that I had gotten the Twin Towers up. In the perfect story, it would have been Maria who noticed. And maybe if this ever becomes part of my memoir, I will revise by telling a lie and saying that she had quietly watched and waited for me to build the towers. That *feels* like the truth. But my most troubled, struggling boy noticed it first, and I believed him to be a genius for discovering this. Everyone gathered around after his shouts of "They're up, they're up!" and the children looked at me, with their precious, open, ten-year-old faces, to monitor my response—as if some elf or the Easter bunny had come in and completed this puzzle. My response did not disappoint. Tears rolled down my face just because my students were waiting for them. They will remember my personal stories about New York City. They will remember this moment in front of the finished puzzle as another in the thick ground of stories about September 11, 2001, and its aftermath of wars, which will have to be tilled and revised for centuries before we can lay them to rest.

Writing a life can help change the world. Reading someone else's life can help change the world. We can teach each other that we are all human—flawed, jealous, hurt, kind, wishing to be noticed, wishing to be loved—so how can hatred exist? The ability to compose our lives into texts creates possibility that the present and future can be different than, better than, the past, through the belief that each person matters in the history and evolution of the planet. We can create a better world, I and Thou, together.

Recommended Literature

Out of the two hundred memoirs I have read, I selected the following as representative and useful texts for teaching this genre in your classroom. The categories correspond roughly to age appropriateness, although the lines blur in almost every case. Many that I list for grades six and up actually make fantastic read-aloud selections for younger grades, and vice versa. Some novel-length memoirs I include in the grades eight and up group because they contain references to sexuality, drugs, and other mature issues, or because the content might seem dense or presumably dull for younger kids. Then again, I include some memoirs written for an adult audience under the categories for young people because there is nothing in them that would prohibit a young person from reading them. I advise reading any books from this list first, keeping your age group in mind.

I know I have missed many amazing examples; please accept my imperfect list, and add to it your own loves.

Picture Books

Most of these are not technically memoirs, but they are rich, evocative first-person narratives that help kids think about the mystery and meaning of self, relationships, and memory, or that showcase possible text structures for students' memoirs.

ADA, ALMA FLOR. 2002. *I Love Saturdays y Domingos*. New York: Atheneum.
ALIKI. 1996. *Those Summers*. New York: HarperCollins.
BAHR, MARY. 1995. *The Memory Box*. Morton Grove, IL: Albert Whitman.
BAYLOR, BYRD. 1979. *Your Own Best Secret Place*. New York: Scribner's.
———. 1982. *The Best Town in the World*. New York: Aladdin.
BRADBY, MARIE. 2000. *Momma, Where Are You From?* New York: Orchard.

BRIDGES, RUBY. 1999. *Through My Eyes*. New York: Scholastic.

BRINKLOE, JULIE. 1985. *Fireflies*. New York: Aladdin.

BUNTING, EVE. 1993. *Fly Away Home*. New York: Clarion.

CAINES, JEANNETTE. 1977. *Daddy*. New York: Harper & Row.

———. 1982. *Just Us Women*. New York: HarperTrophy.

CARLSTROM, NANCY WHITE. 1990. *Grandpappy*. Boston: Little, Brown.

CHALL, MARSHA WILSON. 1992. *Up North at the Cabin*. New York: Lothrop, Lee & Shepard.

CISNEROS, SANDRA. 1997. *Hairs/Pelitos*. New York: Dragonfly Books.

COONEY, BARBARA. 1982. *Miss Rumphius*. New York: Puffin.

———. 1991. *Roxaboxen*. New York: Lothrop, Lee & Shepard.

CREWS, DONALD. 1991. *Bigmama's*. New York: Trumpet Club.

———. 1996. *Shortcut*. New York: HarperTrophy.

CURTIN, GAVIN. 1998. *The Bat Boy and His Violin*. New York: Scholastic.

CURTIS, JAMIE LEE. 1996. *Tell Me Again About the Day I Was Born*. New York: Joanna Cotler Books.

DEPAOLA, TOMIE. 1973. *Nana Upstairs & Nana Downstairs*. New York: Puffin.

———. 1981. *Now One Foot, Now the Other*. New York: G. P. Putnam's Sons.

———. 2005. *Stagestruck*. New York: G. P. Putnam's Sons.

DORROS, ARTHUR. 1991. *Abuela*. New York: Trumpet Club.

DRAGONWAGON, CRESCENT. 1984. *Always, Always*. New York: Macmillan.

———. 1987. *Diana, Maybe*. New York: Macmillan.

DRUCKER, MALKA. 1992. *Grandma's Latkes*. New York: Trumpet Club.

FOX, MEM. 1985. *Wilfrid Gordon McDonald Partridge*. La Jolla, CA: Kane/Miller.

FRIEDMAN, INA R. 1984. *How My Parents Learned to Eat*. Boston: Houghton Mifflin.

GARZA, CARMEN LOMAS. 1990. *Family Pictures/Cuadros de familia*. San Francisco: Children's Book Press.

———. 1996. *In My Family/En mi familia*. San Francisco: Children's Book Press.

GRAY, LIBBA MOORE. 1995. *My Mama Had a Dancing Heart*. New York: Orchard.

GREENFIELD, ELOISE. 1974. *She Come Bringing Me That Little Baby Girl*. New York: HarperTrophy.

HENDERSHOT, JUDITH. 1987. *In Coal Country*. New York: Dragonfly.

HERRERA, JUAN FELIPE. 2000. *The Upside Down Boy/El nino de cabeza*. San Francisco: Children's Book Press.

HOESTLANDT, JO. 1993. *Star of Fear, Star of Hope*. New York: Scholastic.

JOHNSON, ANGELA. 1989. *Tell Me a Story Mama*. New York: Orchard.

———. 1997. *The Rolling Store*. New York: Orchard.

KHALSA, DAYAL KAUR. 1989. *How Pizza Came to Queens*. New York: Clarkson N. Potter.

———. 1990. *Cowboy Dreams*. New York: Clarkson N. Potter.

LAKIN, PATRICIA. 1994. *Don't Forget*. New York: Tambourine.

LAMINAK, LESTER. 2004. *Saturdays and Teacakes*. Atlanta: Peachtree.

LEVINE, ELLEN. 1989. *I Hate English!* New York: Scholastic.

LEVINSON, RIKI. 1985. *Watch the Stars Come Out*. New York: Dutton.

LORBIEKI, MARYBETH. 1998. *Sister Anne's Hands*. New York: Puffin.

MACLACHLAN, PATRICIA. 1994. *All the Places to Love*. New York: Scholastic.

———. 1995. *What You Know First*. New York: Joanna Cotler Books.

MARTIN, BILL JR., AND JOHN ARCHAMBAULT. [1966] 1987. *Knots on a Counting Rope*. New York: Trumpet Club.

MASON, CHERIE. 1993. *Wild Fox: A True Story by Cherie Mason*. Camden, ME: Down East Books.

MITCHELL, MARGAREE KING. 1993. *Uncle Jed's Barber Shop*. New York: Simon & Schuster.

NOLEN, JERDINE. 1999. *In My Momma's Kitchen*. New York: Amistad.

ORR, KATHERINE. 1990. *My Grandpa and the Sea*. Minneapolis: Carolrhoda.

PAULSEN, GARY. 1993. *Dogteam*. New York: Bantam Doubleday Dell.

PEREZ, AMANDA IRMA. 2002. *My Diary from Here to There/Mi diario de aqui hasta alla*. San Francisco: Children's Book Press.

POLACCO, PATRICIA. 1987. *Meteor*. New York: Putnam.

———. 1988. *The Keeping Quilt*. New York: Trumpet Club.

———. 1994. *My Rotten Redheaded Older Brother*. New York: Aladdin.

———. 1998. *Thank You, Mr. Falker*. New York: Scholastic.

———. 2002. *Let's Go Home*. New York: Simon & Schuster.

POMERANTZ, CHARLOTTE. 1989. *The Chalk Doll*. New York: HarperCollins.

RECORVITS, HELEN. 2003. *My Name Is Yoon*. New York: Farrar, Straus, Giroux.

RINGGOLD, FAITH. 1991. *Tar Beach*. New York: Scholastic.

RYLANT, CYNTHIA. 1982. *When I Was Young in the Mountains*. New York: Dutton.

———. [1985] 1993. *The Relatives Came*. New York: Aladdin.

SAY, ALLEN. 1993. *Grandfather's Journey*. Boston: Houghton Mifflin.

SMUCKER, ANNA EGAN. 1989. *No Star Nights*. New York: Alfred A. Knopf.

STANEK, MURIEL. 1989. *I Speak English for My Mom*. Niles, IL: Albert Whitman.

STEPTOE, JOHN. 1969. *Stevie*. New York: HarperTrophy.

STEVENSON, JAMES. 1986. *When I Was Nine*. New York: Greenwillow.

TURNER, ANN. 1990. *Through Moon and Stars and Night Skies*. New York: Charlotte Zolotow.

WABER, BERNARD. 1972. *Ira Sleeps Over*. Boston: Houghton Mifflin.

WILLIAMS, VERA B. 1982. *A Chair for My Mother*. New York: Greenwillow.

WOODSON, JACQUELINE. 1997. *We Had a Picnic This Sunday Past*. New York: Scholastic.

———. 2000. *Sweet, Sweet Memory*. New York: Hyperion.

———. 2001. *The Other Side*. New York: Penguin Putnam.

YIN. 2001. *Coolies.* New York: Philomel.

YOLEN, JANE. 1987. *Owl Moon*. New York: Philomel.

———. 1991. *All Those Secrets of the World*. Boston: Little, Brown.

ZOLOTOW, CHARLOTTE. 1973. *Janney*. New York: Harper & Row.

———. 1974. *My Grandson Lew*. New York: Harper & Row.

Grades Four and Up

BITTON-JACKSON, LIVIA. 1997. *I Have Lived a Thousand Years: Growing Up in the Holocaust*. New York: Scholastic.

BULLA, CLYDE ROBERT. 1985. *A Grain of Wheat: A Writer Begins*. Boston: David R. Godine.

CISNEROS, SANDRA. 1989. *The House on Mango Street*. Houston: Arte Publico.

DEPAOLA, TOMIE. *26 Fairmont Avenue* series. New York: Scholastic.

DRUCKER, OLGA LEVY. 1992. *Kindertransport*. New York: Scholastic.

EHRLICH, AMY, ED. 1996. *When I Was Your Age: Original Stories About Growing Up*. Cambridge, MA: Candlewick.

———. 1999. *When I Was Your Age: Original Stories About Growing Up,* Vol. 2. Cambridge, MA: Candlewick.

FLETCHER, RALPH. 2005. *Marshfield Dreams: When I Was a Kid*. New York: Holt.

FRITZ, JEAN. 1982. *Homesick: My Own Story*. New York: Dell.

GREENFIELD, ELOISE, AND LESSIE JONES LITTLE, with material by PATTIE RIDLEY JONES. 1979. *Childtimes: A Three-Generation Memoir*. New York: Thomas Y. Crowell.

HOPKINS, LEE BENNETT. 1995. *Been to Yesterdays*. Honesdale, PA: Wordsong/Boyds Mills.

JIMENEZ, FRANCISCO. 1997. *The Circuit: Stories from the Life of a Migrant Child*. New York: Scholastic.

———. 2001. *Breaking Through*. Boston: Houghton Mifflin.

LITTLE, JEAN. 1986. *Hey World, Here I Am!* New York: HarperTrophy.

LOWRY, LOIS. 1998. *Looking Back: A Book of Memories*. Boston: Houghton Mifflin.

MOHR, NICHOLASA. 1994. *Growing Up Inside the Sanctuary of My Imagination*. Englewood Cliffs, NJ: Julian Messner.

NHUONG, HUYNH QUANG. 1982. *The Land I Lost: Adventures of a Boy in Vietnam*. New York: Lippincott.

PARKS, ROSA, WITH JIM HASKINS. 1994. *Rosa Parks: My Story*. New York: Scholastic.

Grades Six and Up

ALICEA, GIL C., WITH CARMINE DESENA. 1995. *The Air Down Here: True Tales from a South Bronx Boyhood*. San Francisco: Chronicle.

BRUCHAC, JOSEPH. 1997. *Bowman's Store: A Journey to Myself*. New York: Dial.

BYARS, BETSY. 1991. *The Moon and I*. Englewood Cliffs, NJ: Julian Messner.

CARLE, ERIC. 1997. *Flora and Tiger: 19 Very Short Stories from My Life*. New York: Philomel.

CHRISTENSEN, BONNIE. 2003. *In My Grandmother's House*. New York: HarperCollins.

CLEARY, BEVERLY. 1988. *A Girl from Yamhill*. New York: Dell.

DAHL, ROALD. 1984. *Boy*. London: Puffin.

FRITZ, JEAN. 1985. *Homesick*. New York: Dell.

JIANG, JI LI. 1997. *The Red Scarf Girl: A Memoir of the Cultural Revolution*. New York: Scholastic.

LITTLE, JEAN. 1987. *Little by Little*. Ontario, Canada: Viking Kestrel.

LOBEL, ANITA. 1998. *No Pretty Pictures: A Child of War*. New York: Avon.

MELTZER, MILTON. 1988. *Starting from Home: A Writer's Beginnings*. New York: Puffin.

MYERS, WALTER DEAN. 2001. *Bad Boy: A Memoir*. New York: HarperTempest.

NAYLOR, PHYLLIS REYNOLDS. 2001. *How I Came to Be a Writer*. New York: Aladdin.

PEET, BILL. 1994. *Bill Peet: An Autobiography*. New York: Houghton Mifflin.

RYLANT, CYNTHIA. 1989. *But I'll Be Back Again*. New York: Orchard.

SATRUPI, MARJANE. 2003. *Persepolis: The Story of a Childhood*. New York: Pantheon.

SENDAK, PHILIP. 1985. *In Grandpa's House*. New York: Harper & Row.

SPINELLI, JERRY. 1998. *Knots in My Yo-Yo String: The Autobiography of a Kid*. New York: Knopf.

WATKINS, Y. K. 1986. *So Far from the Bamboo Grove*. New York: Lothrop, Lee & Shepard.

YEP, LAURENCE. 1991. *The Lost Garden*. Englewood Cliffs, NJ: Julian Messner.

ZINDEL, PAUL. 1991. *The Pigman & Me*. New York: Charlotte Zolotow.

Grades Eight and Up

ALMOND, DAVID. 2003. *Counting Stars*. New York: Laurel Leaf.

ANGELOU, MAYA. [1970] 1997. *I Know Why the Caged Bird Sings*. New York: Bantam.

APPELT, KATHI. 2004. *My Father's Summers: A Daughter's Memoir*. New York: Holt.

BODE, JANET. 1989. *New Kids in Town: Oral Histories of Immigrant Teens*. New York: Scholastic.

CAMPBELL, BEBE MOORE. 1989. *Sweet Summer: Growing Up with and Without My Dad*. New York: Ballantine.

CHEN, DA. 1999. *Colors of the Mountain*. New York: Random House.

COFER, JUDITH ORTIZ. 1990. *Silent Dancing: A Partial Remembrance of a Puerto Rican Childhood*. Houston: Arte Publico.

CRUTCHER, CHRIS. 2003. *King of the Mild Frontier: An Ill-Advised Autobiography*. New York: Greenwillow.

DUNCAN, LOIS. 1982. *Chapters: My Growth as a Writer*. Boston: Little, Brown.

HURSTON, ZORA NEALE. [1942] 1984. *Dust Tracks on a Road*. Urbana: University of Illinois Press.

KERR, M. E. 1983. *Me, Me, Me, Me, Me: Not a Novel*. New York: Charlotte Zolotow.

KINCAID, JAMAICA. 1985. *Annie John*. New York: Plume.

MOMADAY, N. S. 1969. *The Way to Rainy Mountain*. New York: Ballantine.

PECK, RICHARD. 1991. *Anonymously Yours*. New York: Beech Tree.

SANTIAGO, EMERELDA. 1993. *When I Was Puerto Rican*. New York: Vintage.

SHREVE, SUSAN RICHARDS, ED. 2003. *Dream Me Home Safely: Writers on Growing Up in America*. Boston: Houghton Mifflin. [*Contains some material more suitable for high school students.*]

SOTO, GARY. 1986. *Small Faces*. Houston: Arte Publico.

WELTY, EUDORA. 1984. *One Writer's Beginnings*. Cambridge, MA: Harvard University Press.

WIESEL, ELI. 1982. *Night*. New York: Bantam.

VILLASENOR, VICTOR. 1991. *Rain of Gold*. Houston: Arte Publico.

Anthologies for Grades Eight and Up

AUGENBRAUM, HAROLD, AND ILAN STAVANS, EDS. 1993. *Growing Up Latino: Memoirs and Stories*. Boston: Houghton Mifflin.

CONWAY, JILL, ED. 1992. *Written by Herself: Autobiographies of American Women: An Anthology*. New York: Vintage.

DILLARD, ANNIE, AND CORT CONLEY, EDS. 1995. *Modern American Memoirs*. New York: Harper-Perennial.

ESTEPA, ANDREA, AND PHILIP KAY, EDS. 1997. *Starting with I: Personal Essays by Teenagers*. New York: Persea Books. [*Contains some material that may be more suitable for high school students*]

GATES, HENRY LOUIS JR., ED. 1991. *Bearing Witness: Selections from African-American Autobiography in the Twentieth Century*. New York: Pantheon.

HALPERN, JOEL, AND LUCY NGUYEN-HONG-NHIEM, EDS. 1989. *The Far East Comes Near: Autobiographical Accounts of Southeast Asian Students in America*. Amherst, MA: University of Massachusetts Press.

Works Cited

ADAMS, HENRY. [1918] 1931. *The Education of Henry Adams.* New York: Modern Library.

ADAMS, NOAH. 1996. *Piano Lessons.* New York: Delta.

ALICEA, GIL C., WITH CARMINE DESENA. 1995. *The Air Down Here: True Tales from a South Bronx Boyhood.* San Francisco: Chronicle.

ALLENDE, ISABEL. 2004. *My Invented Country: A Memoir.* New York: Perennial.

ALMOND, DAVID. 2003. *Counting Stars.* New York: Laurel Leaf.

ANDERS, GIGI. 2005. *Jubana! The Awkwardly True and Dazzling Adventures of a Jewish Cuban Goddess.* New York: Rayo.

ANDERSON, CARL. 2000. *How's It Going? A Practical Guide to Conferring with Student Writers.* Portsmouth, NH: Heinemann.

———. 2005. *Assessing Writers.* Portsmouth, NH: Heinemann.

ANGELILLO, JANET. 2002. *A Fresh Approach to Teaching Punctuation.* New York: Scholastic.

———. 2005. *Making Revision Matter.* New York: Scholastic.

ATWELL, NANCIE. 1987. *In the Middle: Writing, Reading, and Learning with Adolescents.* Portsmouth, NH: Boynton/Cook.

AUGUSTINE. [397] 1991. *Confessions,* trans. Henry Chadwick. Oxford: Oxford University Press.

AUSTER, PAUL. 1982. *The Invention of Solitude.* New York: Viking Penguin.

AVI. 1996. "Scout's Honor." In *When I Was Your Age: Original Stories About Growing Up,* ed. Amy Ehrlich. Cambridge, MA: Candlewick.

BAKER, RUSSELL. 1987. "Life with Mother." In *Inventing the Truth: The Art and Craft of Memoir,* ed. William Zinsser. Boston: Houghton Mifflin.

BARNES, KIM. 2000. *Hungry for the World: A Memoir.* New York: Anchor.

BARRINGTON, JUDITH. 2002. *Writing the Memoir: From Truth to Art.* Portland, OR: Eighth Mountain.

BARTON, SHELLE, SHEYENE FOSTER HELLER, AND JENNIFER HENDERSON. 2004. "'We Were Such a Generation'—Memoir, Truthfulness, and History: An Interview with Patricia Hampl." *River Teeth: A Journal of Nonfiction Narrative* 5 (2): 129–42.

BITTON-JACKSON, LIVIA. 1997. *I Have Lived a Thousand Years: Growing Up in the Holocaust.* New York: Scholastic.

BLUME, JUDY. 1984. *The Pain and the Great One.* New York: Atheneum.

BODE, JANET. 1989. *New Kids in Town: Oral Histories of Immigrant Teens.* New York: Scholastic.

BOLLAS, CHRISTOPHER. 1992. *Being a Character: Psychoanalysis and Self Experience.* New York: Hill and Wang.

BOMER, RANDY. 1995. *Time for Meaning: Crafting Literate Lives in Middle and High School.* Portsmouth, NH: Heinemann.

BOMER, RANDY, AND KATHERINE BOMER. 2002. *For a Better World: Reading and Writing for Social Action.* Portsmouth, NH: Heinemann.

BRUCHAC, JOSEPH. 1996. "The Snapping Turtle." In *When I Was Your Age: Original Stories About Growing Up,* Vol. 2, ed. Amy Ehrlich. Cambridge, MA: Candlewick.

BRUNER, JEROME. 1993. "The Autobiographical Process." In *The Culture of Autobiography,* ed. Robert Folkenflik. Stanford, CA: Stanford University Press.

BUBER, MARTIN. 1958. *I and Thou,* trans. Ronald Gregor Smith. New York: Scribner's.

BUCHHOLZ, BRAD. 2001. "A Time for Going," *Austin American-Statesman,* November 21, K1.

BYARS, BETSY. 1991. *The Moon and I.* Englewood Cliffs, NJ: Julian Messner.

CALKINS, LUCY. 1994. *The Art of Teaching Writing,* 2d ed. Portsmouth, NH: Heinemann.

CALKINS, LUCY, AND COLLEAGUES. 2004. *Units of Study for Primary Writing: A Yearlong Curriculum.* Portsmouth, NH: Heinemann/firsthand.

CALKINS, LUCY, KATE MONTGOMERY, AND DONNA SANTMAN. 1998. *A Teacher's Guide to Standardized Reading Tests: Knowledge Is Power.* Portsmouth, NH: Heinemann.

CAMBOURNE, BRIAN. 1988. *The Whole Story: Natural Learning and the Acquisition of Literacy in the Classroom.* Auckland, NZ: Ashton Scholastic.

CARR, MARY. 1995. *The Liar's Club.* New York: Viking Penguin.

CISNEROS, SANDRA. 1989. *The House on Mango Street.* Houston: Arte Publico.

———. 1992. "Eleven." In *Woman Hollering Creek and Other Stories.* New York: Random House.

COFER, JUDITH ORTIZ. 1990. *Silent Dancing: A Partial Remembrance of a Puerto Rican Childhood.* Houston: Arte Publico.

COLES, ROBERT. 1989. *The Call of Stories: Teaching and the Moral Imagination.* Boston: Houghton Mifflin.

CRUTCHER, CHRIS. 2003. *King of the Mild Frontier: An Ill-Advised Autobiography.* New York: Greenwillow.

CRUZ, NICKY. 1971. *Run, Baby, Run.* Plainfield, NJ: Logos International.

Curtis, Jamie Lee. 1996. *Tell Me Again About the Day I Was Born*. New York: Joanna Cotler Books.

Daly, Mary. 1973. *Beyond God the Father: Toward a Philosophy of Women's Liberation*. Boston: Beacon.

Danticat, Edwidge. 1997. "In the Face of Silence." In *Starting with I: Personal Essays by Teenagers*. New York: Persea Books.

de Beauvoir, Simone. [1958] 1974. *Memoirs of a Dutiful Daughter*, trans. James Kirkup. New York: Harper & Row.

DePaola, Tomie. 1989. *The Art Lesson*. New York: Putnam.

Dewey, John. [1916] 1944. *Democracy and Education: An Introduction to the Philosophy of Education*. New York: Macmillan.

Dillard, Annie. 1987a. *An American Childhood*. New York: Harper & Row.

———. 1987b. "To Fashion a Text." In *Inventing the Truth: The Art and Craft of Memoir*, ed. William Zinsser. Boston: Houghton Mifflin.

Dostoevsky, Fyodor. [1880] 1991. *The Brothers Karamazov*. New York: Vintage.

Drucker, Olga Levy. 1992. *Kindertransport*. New York: Scholastic.

Dunn, Samantha. 2002. *Not by Accident: Reconstructing a Careless Life*. New York: Holt.

Edelsky, Carole. 2003. Theory, Politics, Hope, and Action. Keynote address, Urban Sites Conference, National Writing Project, Santa Barbara, CA.

Eggers, Dave. 2000. *A Heartbreaking Work of Staggering Genius: Based on a True Story*. New York: Simon & Schuster.

Ehrlich, Amy, ed. 1996. *When I Was Your Age: Original Stories About Growing Up*. Cambridge, MA: Candlewick.

———. 1999. *When I Was Your Age: Original Stories About Growing Up*, Vol. 2. Cambridge, MA: Candlewick.

Fletcher, Ralph. 1996. *A Writer's Notebook: Unlocking the Writer Within You*. New York: HarperTrophy.

———. 2005. *Marshfield Dreams: When I Was a Kid*. New York: Holt.

Fletcher, Ralph, and JoAnn Portalupi. 1998. *Craft Lessons: Teaching Writing, K–8*. Portland, ME: Stenhouse.

Flynn, Nick, and Shirley McPhillips. 2000. *A Note Slipped Under the Door: Teaching from Poems We Love*. Portland, ME: Stenhouse.

Frankl, Viktor E. [1959] 1992. *Man's Search for Meaning: An Introduction to Logotherapy*, trans. Ilse Lasch. Boston: Beacon.

Fritz, Jean. 1985. *Homesick*. New York: Dell.

Gantos, Jack. 1998. *Joey Pigza Swallowed the Key*. New York: Farrar, Straus & Giroux.

GILBAR, STEVEN. 199. *The Open Door: When Writers First Learned to Read.* Boston: David R. Godine.

GORNICK, VIVIAN. 1987. *Fierce Attachments: A Memoir.* New York: Farrar, Straus & Giroux.

GRAVES, DONALD. 1983. *Writing: Teachers and Children at Work.* Portsmouth, NH: Heinemann.

GRAY, LIBBA MOORE. 1995. *My Mama Had a Dancing Heart.* New York: Orchard.

GREALY, LUCY. 1994. *Autobiography of a Face.* Boston: Houghton Mifflin.

GREENE, MAXINE. 2001. *Variations of a Blue Guitar: The Lincoln Center Institute Lectures on Aesthetic Education.* New York: Teachers College Press.

GREENFIELD, ELOISE, AND LESSIE JONES LITTLE, with material by PATTIE RIDLEY JONES. 1979. *Childtimes: A Three-Generation Memoir.* New York: Thomas Y. Crowell.

GUSDORF, GEORGES. 1980. "Conditions and Limits of Autobiography," trans. James Olney. In *Autobiography: Essays Theoretical and Critical,* ed. James Olney. Princeton, NJ: Princeton University Press.

HAMPL, PATRICIA. 1999. *I Could Tell You Stories: Sojourns in the Land of Memory.* New York: W. W. Norton.

HEARD, GEORGIA. 1995. *Writing Toward Home: Tales and Lessons to Find Your Way.* Portsmouth, NH: Heinemann.

———. 2002. *The Revision Toolbox: Teaching Techniques That Work.* Portsmouth, NH: Heinemann.

HERRERA, HAYDEN. 1983. *Frida: A Biography of Frida Kahlo.* New York: Perennial.

HESSE, KAREN. 1999. "Waiting for Midnight." In *When I Was Your Age: Original Stories About Growing Up,* Vol. 2., ed. Amy Ehrlich. Cambridge, MA: Candlewick.

HINDLEY, JOANNE. 1996. *In the Company of Children.* York, ME: Stenhouse.

HOWE, JAMES. 1996. "Everything Will Be Okay." In *When I Was Your Age: Original Stories About Growing Up,* ed. Amy Ehrlich. Cambridge, MA: Candlewick.

HULL, JOHN N. 1990. *Touching the Rock.* New York. Pantheon.

JANECZKO, PAUL, ED. 1990. *The Place My Words Are Looking For.* New York: Bradbury.

JIANG, JI LI. 1997. *The Red Scarf Girl: A Memoir of the Cultural Revolution.* New York: Scholastic.

JIMENEZ, FRANCISCO. 1997. *The Circuit: Stories from the Life of a Migrant Child.* New York: Scholastic.

———. 2001. *Breaking Through.* Boston: Houghton Mifflin.

JOHNSON, ANGELA. 1997. *The Rolling Store.* New York: Orchard.

JORDAN, JUNE. 2000. *Soldier: A Poet's Childhood.* New York: Basic Civitas Books.

KINGSTON, MAXINE HONG. 1977. *The Woman Warrior: Memoirs of a Girlhood Among Ghosts.* New York: Vintage.

KONIGSBERG, E. L. 1999. "How I Lost My Station in Life." In *When I Was Your Age: Original Stories About Growing Up,* Vol. 2., ed. Amy Ehrlich. Cambridge, MA: Candlewick.

KOOSER, TED. 2005. *The Poetry Home Repair Manual: Practical Advice for Beginning Poets.* Lincoln: University of Nebraska Press.

LAMAR, JAKE. 1991. *Bourgeois Blues.* New York: Plume.

LAMINAK, LESTER. 2004. *Saturdays and Teacakes.* Atlanta: Peachtree.

LEE, LI-YOUNG. 1995. *the winged seed: A Remembrance.* St. Paul: Ruminator Books.

LEJEUNE, PHILIPPE. 1989. "The Autobiographical Pact." In *On Autobiography,* trans. Katherine Leary. Minneapolis: University of Minnesota Press.

LERNER, MICHAEL. 1994. "Tikkun's Politics of Meaning." *Tikkun: A Bimonthly Jewish Critique of Politics, Culture, and Society* (May/June).

LINDBERGH, REEVE. 1996. "Flying." In *When I Was Your Age: Original Stories About Growing Up,* ed. Amy Ehrlich. Cambridge, MA: Candlewick.

LOBEL, ANITA. 1998. *No Pretty Pictures: A Child of War.* New York: Avon.

LOWRY, LOIS. 1998. *Looking Back: A Book of Memories.* Boston: Houghton Mifflin.

MACNEIL, ROBERT. 1989. *Wordstruck: A Memoir.* New York: Viking.

MAYES, FRANCES. 1996. *Under the Tuscan Sun: At Home in Italy.* New York: Broadway Books.

MAYNARD, JOYCE. 1973. *Looking Back: A Chronicle of Growing Up Old in the Sixties.* New York: Doubleday.

MAZER, NORMA FOX. 1999. "In the Blink of an Eye." In *When I Was Your Age: Original Stories About Growing Up,* ed. Amy Ehrlich. Cambridge, MA: Candlewick.

MCCOURT, FRANK. 1996. *Angela's Ashes.* New York: Scribner.

MILOSZ, CZESLAW. [1968] 1981. *Native Realm: A Search for Self-Definition,* trans. Catherine S. Leach. Berkeley: University of California Press.

MOHR, NICHOLASA. 1994. *Growing Up Inside the Sanctuary of My Imagination.* Englewood Cliffs, NJ: Julian Messner.

———. 1996. "Taking a Dare." In *When I Was Your Age: Original Stories About Growing Up,* ed. Amy Ehrlich. Cambridge, MA: Candlewick.

MONTAIGNE, MICHEL. [1595] 1958. *Essays,* trans. J. M. Cohen. Middlesex, England: Penguin.

MORI, KYOKO. 1999. "Learning to Swim." In *When I Was Your Age: Original Stories About Growing Up,* ed. Amy Ehrlich. Cambridge, MA: Candlewick.

MORRIS, JOHN. 1966. *Versions of the Self: Studies in English Autobiography from John Bunyan to John Stuart Mill.* New York: Basic.

MURRAY, DONALD. 1987. *Write to Learn.* New York: Holt, Rinehart and Winston.

Myers, Walter Dean. 1996. "Reverend Abbott and Those Bloodshot Eyes." In *When I Was Your Age: Original Stories About Growing Up,* ed. Amy Ehrlich. Cambridge, MA: Candlewick.

———. 2001. *Bad Boy: A Memoir.* New York: HarperTempest.

Nafisi, Azar. 2003. *Reading Lolita in Tehran: A Memoir in Books.* New York: Random House.

Nhuong, Huynh Quang. 1982. *The Land I Lost: Adventures of a Boy in Vietnam.* New York: Lippincott.

Nia, Isoke. 1999. "Units of Study in the Writing Workshop." *Primary Voices, K–8* 8 (1).

Norman, Howard. 1999. "Bus Problems." In *When I Was Your Age: Original Stories About Growing Up,* Vol. 2, ed. Amy Ehrlich. Cambridge, MA: Candlewick.

Nye, Naomi Shihab. 1999. *What Have You Lost? Poems Selected by Naomi Shihab Nye.* New York: Greenwillow.

———. 2002. *Nineteen Varieties of Gazelle: Poems of the Middle East.* New York: Greenwillow.

Olney, James. 1980. "Autobiography and the Cultural Moment: A Thematic, Historical, and Bibliographical Introduction." In *Autobiography: Essays Theoretical and Critical,* ed. James Olney. Princeton, NJ: Princeton University Press.

Ondaatje, Michael. 1982. *Running in the Family.* New York: Vintage.

Osborne, Mary Pope. 1996. "All-Ball." In *When I Was Your Age: Original Stories About Growing Up,* ed. Amy Ehrlich. Cambridge, MA: Candlewick.

Parks, Rosa, with Jim Haskins. 1994. *Rosa Parks: My Story.* New York: Scholastic.

Patterson, Katherine. 1996. "Why I Never Ran Away from Home." In *When I Was Your Age: Original Stories About Growing Up,* ed. Amy Ehrlich. Cambridge, MA: Candlewick.

Pritchett, V. S. 1977. *Autobiography.* The English Association Presidential Address. London: The English Association.

Ray, Katie Wood. 1999. *Wonderous Words: Writers and Writing in the Elementary Classroom.* Urbana, IL: National Council of Teachers of English.

Ray, Katie Wood, with Lester Laminak. 2001. *Writing Workshop: Working Through the Hard Parts (and They're All Hard Parts).* Urbana, IL: National Council of Teachers of English.

Rivera, Diego. 1992. *My Art, My Life: An Autobiography.* Mineola, NY: Dover.

Rodriquez, Richard. 1982. *Hunger of Memory: The Education of Richard Rodriquez.* New York: Bantam.

Rosen, Michael. 1999. "Pegasus for a Summer." In *When I Was Your Age: Original Stories About Growing Up,* Vol. 2, ed. Amy Ehrlich. Cambridge, MA: Candlewick.

Rylant, Cynthia. 1982. *When I Was Young in the Mountains.* New York: Dutton.

Sacks, Oliver. 2002. *Oaxaca Journal.* Washington, DC: National Geographic Directions.